Structured
Rapid Prototyping

An Evolutionary Approach
to Software Development

Structured
Rapid Prototyping
An Evolutionary Approach
to Software Development

JOHN L. CONNELL

LINDA SHAFER

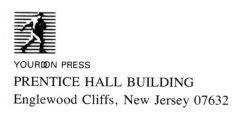

YOURDON PRESS

PRENTICE HALL BUILDING

Englewood Cliffs, New Jersey 07632

Library of Congress Cataloging-in-Publication Data

Connell, John L.   (date)
    Structured rapid prototyping.

    (Yourdon Press computing series)
    Includes index
    1. Computer software–Development. 2. Electronic
data processing–Structured techniques. I. Shafer,
Linda   (date). II. Title. III. Series.
QA76.76.D47C65 1989   005.1   88-33901
ISBN 0-13-853573-6

Editorial/production supervision: Gretchen K. Chenenko
Cover design: Wanda Lubelska Design
Manufacturing buyer: Mary Ann Gloriande

The publisher offers discounts on this book when ordered
in bulk quantities. For more information, write:

> Special Sales/College Marketing
> Prentice Hall
> College Technical and Reference Division
> Englewood Cliffs, New Jersey 07632

 © 1989 by Prentice-Hall, Inc.
A Division of Simon & Schuster
Englewood Cliffs, New Jersey 07632

Printed in the United States of America
10 9 8 7 6 5 4 3 2 1

ISBN 0-13-853573-6

PRENTICE-HALL INTERNATIONAL (UK) LIMITED, *London*
PRENTICE-HALL OF AUSTRALIA PTY. LIMITED. *Sydney*
PRENTICE-HALL CANADA INC., *Toronto*
PRENTICE-HALL HISPANOAMERICANA. S.A., *Mexico*
PRENTICE-HALL OF INDIA PRIVATE LIMITED. *New Delhi*
PRENTICE-HALL OF JAPAN. INC.. *Tokyo*
SIMON & SCHUSTER ASIA PTE. LTD.. *Singapore*
EDITORA PRENTICE-HALL do BRASIL. LTDA.. *Rio de Janeiro*

Contents

Preface

The material in this preface was written just before the book went to press — several months after the first draft of the book was completed. The interim period provided time for reflection as to what the probable worth of this book will be to you, the reader, in the near future. These reflections provide worthy material for a preface.

We assume that you are somehow involved in software development. You are a programmer, an analyst, designer, test engineer, quality controller, software manager, information systems manager, computer systems manager, or perhaps even a user of computer systems. You are interested in finding ways to build better software application systems. You want to participate in building systems that do a better job of meeting users' needs. You feel a desire to build these systems faster and at a lower cost than is possible using conventional approaches. If many of these descriptions fit you, you are reading the right book.

The authors have used the techniques described herein for the successful development of dozens of large, complex software applications. Hundreds of satisfied end users have been favorably impressed by the benefits they derive from the structured rapid prototyping approach. Over the last four years, the approach has been spread through the medium of public seminars sponsored by data processing management associations. Both authors have delivered many seminars every year in all corners of the world. Attendees, convinced of the potential benefits, have reported successful application of this approach to software development.

The bad news is that some organizations have tried what they thought was rapid prototyping with mystifyingly mixed results. Prototyped systems have sometimes proven to be difficult to maintain and may have poor performance characteristics. Amazingly, there is a renegade trend toward thinking that rapid prototyping is nothing more than hacking together some quick and dirty code, neglecting the need to complete rigorous and well-structured requirements and design specifications, then tweak the code until it does acceptable things. It is this dangerous trend that often gives prototyping a bad name.

Fortunately for you, this book has nothing to do with hacking or quick and dirty programming. As the name implies, this book presents a structured methodology for the rapid creation and iterative refinement of dynamic requirements models— models that can evolve into deliverable software systems. It is a methodology that encompasses the entire software life cycle, from preproject planning to postdelivery maintenance. This is not only an approach that can be categorized as acceptable software engineering; it is an approach that epitomizes superbly elegant, state-of-the-art software engineering.

Unlike structured analysis and structured design, *structured rapid prototyping* is very dependent on the availability of particular kinds of software development environments and tools. If this were not true, you would merely be hacking up some code and calling it a prototype, wouldn't you? The technological advances being made in the development and refinement of prototyping tools in recent years have been absolutely astounding. The advances are coming faster than a book such as this one, with lengthy publishing lead times, can track them. Between the first draft and the technical rewrite, new products and old products with new features became available. Changes were made to the manuscript. During copyediting more advances were made. As the book goes to press, the product evaluations contained in Chapter 12 are already beginning to look somewhat dated.

The solution to the prototyping technology dilemma is to perform your own product evaluations, rather than relying on published reviews. The principals and the techniques recommended for rapid prototyping in this book have remained constant through several years of changing prototyping environments. This will continue into the future. Pick prototyping products that have remained robust, frequently adding new features to keep up with the fierce competition. In this way, you will not be left behind in the technology race.

A final word of advice is to approach the following material as if it were a graduate course of study. Structured rapid prototyping is a technique you must take some time to learn. As with structured design or structured analysis, it cannot be described in 25 words or less. Therefore, this preface does not describe very completely what rapid prototyping is. You must read the entire book. By the time you finish, you will be a competent rapid prototyper, building superior software for the good of your organization and the greater enhancement of your career.

We'd like to give special thanks to Nancy, Don, Jason, and Leslie for their support throughout this project.

John L. Connell
Linda Shafer

Structured
Rapid Prototyping

An Evolutionary Approach
to Software Development

1

Introduction

The phrase *rapid prototyping* has become so commonplace in software engineering circles that most software professionals feel they know what it is and how to do it. The truth is that many software developers harbor misconceptions about prototyping. Some think it can be used to solve performance or response time problems. Others think it focuses on compressing the front end of the development life cycle by eliminating what is often referred to as *analysis paralysis*. The most popular misconception focuses on the word *rapid*, as its use makes people assume that rapid prototyping is a panacea that will shrink development costs by an order of magnitude. None of these notions have anything to do with a useful approach to software rapid prototyping.

The purpose of this first chapter is to clear up such misconceptions before we begin to explain the specific concepts of *structured* rapid prototyping contained in the following chapters. In some respects, *rapid prototyping* is an unfortunate choice of words. The word *rapid*, used in connection with software development, would almost seem a contradiction in terms, as it suggests that there is now some magic way to shortcut lengthy development lead times. A survey of published case studies would reveal that application of various approaches to software rapid prototyping yields longer development lead times as often as shorter. The term *prototype* brings with it connotations from other engineering disciplines where it means a one-of-a-kind full-scale model used to test design alternatives. None of the published work on software rapid prototyping advocates the development of full-scale test models. The reader is therefore encouraged to dismiss normal connotations of rapid and prototyping from the subject matter at hand.

A software rapid prototype is a dynamic visual model providing a communication tool for customer and developer that is far more effective than either narrative prose or static visual models for portraying functionality. It has been described as

- Functional after a minimal amount of effort
- A means for providing users of a proposed application with a physical representation of key parts of the system before system implementation
- Flexible—modifications require minimal effort
- Not necessarily representative of a complete system

Some people wonder why a more accurately descriptive term is not used to label this process. The answer is, legacy. The phrase "rapid prototyping," while less than perfectly descriptive, has been accepted by most of the software engineering community and has been used in publications since 1981. Other terms, like "protocycling" have been offered, but "rapid prototyping" seems to have stuck.

RAPID PROTOTYPING—THE CRITICAL QUESTIONS

The ideas presented in this book were distilled from a combination of experiences with prototyping projects and a series of public seminars taught by the authors. The seminars in particular have provided some valuable insights regarding the typical misconceptions people have about rapid prototyping. These misconceptions are often presented as questions by seminar attendees. Frequently, if the questions are not addressed and answered satisfactorily at the very beginning of the seminar, the person concerned will have a difficult time concentrating on and understanding the rest of the presentation. In a book presentation where there is no opportunity for interactive dialog between readers and authors we must assume that readers will have similar types of questions as seminar attendees. Therefore, the rest of this chapter presents some typical questions regarding rapid prototyping concepts and the answers to those questions. It is hoped that this approach will help to clear the initial cobwebs of confusion and pave the way for a smooth exposition of the main topic of this book: structured rapid prototyping—what, why, and how.

What Critical Objectives of Software Development Are Most Effectively Achieved through Rapid Prototyping?

Rapid prototyping is basically an analysis technique. Most of the literature on the subject advocates using rapid prototyping to discover the true and complete set of functional requirements for a proposed software system. Conventional structured analysis paper models, although far superior to narrative prose for specifying functional requirements and dataflow interfaces, still leave room for misunderstandings such as the one portrayed in Figure 1-1.

In the drawing, the automobile is used as an analogy for software systems. Suppose finished automobiles were not available for customers to see at dealerships. Suppose instead that the salesperson interviews the customer about his or her func-

Figure 1-1 Systems analysis communication problems.

tional requirements for an automobile. Without having an opportunity to kick the tires and experiment with various options, the customer might have a difficult time precisely stating requirements. Furthermore, the salesperson might misunderstand what the customer says.

In the scenario depicted in Figure 1-1, the customer says, "I want classy transportation," conceptualizing a mental model resembling something similar to a Porsche. The salesperson misinterprets this statement of requirements as a desire for "classic transportation" and conceptualizes a mental model that resembles a Dusenburg. Whenever there is no physical representation of a proposed product, there will be at least two mental models of the proposed product—the developer's and the customer's. Unfortunately for the paying customer, it will always be the developer's concept that is actually built and delivered.

In the software business the customer will usually not be able to view anything like a physical representation of the final system until the test phase of a development project—many months or even years after the original statement of requirements. At this point it may be discovered that the system under development will do a very poor job of meeting the customer's needs. In projects with very long development lead times—a situation that continues to be the norm—the customer's needs may change significantly between the time of requirements specification and final product test. With evolutionary rapid prototyping, one can respond quickly to the customer's continually changing needs, even after delivery of the final product.

Using a conventional software development approach, the coupling of long development cycles with difficulties in communicating and understanding desired functional requirements, results in a very low probability of delivering an acceptable software system. The typical results are illustrated with the continuation of the automobile analogy, shown in Figure 1-2, where the finished Dusenburg has been consigned to the junk yard. The Dusenburg project turned out to be a very expensive and very slow form of "prototyping." The final product, although elegant and of high quality, was of little use to the customer. This discovery process took too long, cost too much, and doubtless resulted in a very angry customer.

The automobile analogy is similar to scenarios taking place daily in the software world. The fact that software developers have been delivering unacceptable final products for many years has not gone unnoticed. Version 1.0 of most systems will either be scrapped or hastily and extensively modified beginning immediately after delivery. Fred Brooks documented this fact most eloquently in 1975.[1]

Parts replacement, used as a means to convert a Dusenburg into something more like a Porsche, would be unthinkably expensive. Yet, this is the very sort of thing that happens during the "post-implementation tuning" phase or during a "major enhancement" project in the software business. In practice, very few software professionals have taken Brooks seriously because of the large expense involved in building two systems to deliver one correct system. Instead, an illusion of correctness is created during development projects. The slogan is, "Do it right the first time." The customer is asked to sign off on requirements specifications that cannot be fully

Figure 1-2 An expensive prototype.

understood because there are no working examples of functionality. As a result, the customer is forced to accept delivery of a product that does not meet true user requirements. The leverage for this forced acceptance comes when it can be shown that the system meets stated contractual requirements as approved by the customer. From the software developer's point of view, this is a description of a "successful" project. The customer may have a different view of how successful it really was.

Rapid prototyping was formally introduced in the early part of this decade as an alternative to the forced delivery of functionally incorrect software systems. New development tools were suddenly available. These tools made it economically feasible to build two systems—a prototype and a final product—to deliver one correct system. The new tools were powerful enough to allow quick low-cost prototype development to portray the "look and feel" of a proposed system. There was enough flexibility that modifications could be made easily without locking developers into a specific technological solution. The "man-machine interface" could be tested thoroughly. Where certain algorithms or functions were known—for example, the specification of how FICA tables are calculated in a payroll system—these algorithms could be dropped into a friendly environment for a thorough test.

Returning again to the automobile analogy, suppose our salesperson from the previous scenario was able to take a more conservative approach. Fearing the possibility of having misunderstood the customer's needs, he refuses to completely specify the details of the automobile for manufacturing to produce. Instead, a simple chassis with wheels and an engine is ordered as shown in Figure 1-3. After all, the customer has requested an automobile and all automobiles have these parts. This simple, intentionally incomplete, version of the product will be much less expensive and time-consuming for manufacturing to produce. When it is delivered, the salesperson can ask the customer to experiment with it and describe some

Figure 1-3 An intentionally incomplete working model.

additional, but not necessarily all remaining, desired features. The product is then returned to manufacturing to have the additional features added. Such iterations continue until the customer is completely satisfied with the product. As an analogy, this represents the rapid prototyping process fairly well. While it might be more expensive to build an automobile from scratch than to initially produce a Dusenburg from the original statement of customer requirements, it is much less expensive and much more effective than ultimately trying to convert a Dusenburg into a Porsche.

Are Either Special Software or Hardware Tools, or Both, Required to Do Rapid Prototyping?

The answer to this question depends on what you want to do in the way of prototyping. Do you want to develop a rudimentary screens-only prototype or a model with working functions and live data? A screens-only prototype can be developed with something as basic and universally available as a text editor. More advanced software development tools, available only very recently, allow the fast production of the readily modifiable working models described here as rapid prototypes. Hardware is significant in that specific tools will only operate on certain machines and other tools require certain minimal hardware system configurations to operate efficiently.

Specific development tools have always been at the core of the thinking of those who advocate rapid prototyping. It is likely that Bruce Blum had MUMPS™, a fourth-generation nonprocedural language, in mind when he wrote his early articles on rapid prototyping.[2] It is probable that Bernard Boar had IDMS/R™, the quasi-relational database, in mind when he wrote the first book on rapid prototyping.[3] The authors of this book also have a certain *type* of integrated software development environment product in mind. We do not, however, have any *specific* vendor's product in mind. Chapter 3 will give you the criteria with which you can select, from a wide field of current offerings, the product you feel currently offers the most powerful rapid prototyping capabilities. No particular product is endorsed because the technology is moving so rapidly that any such endorsement is bound to become obsolete as soon as proclaimed. For those who would like to see an evaluation of currently available tools, for what such an evaluation is worth, the authors have summarized their experience with prototyping tools in Chapter 12.

At least six different tool-dependent approaches to prototyping in current use can be identified. Figure 1-4 depicts each of these approaches as a "camp" with the tools recommended by that camp inside the teepees. In the artificial intelligence (AI) camp, rapid prototyping involves the use of LISP or PROLOG in an environment consisting of a dedicated machine running compilers, debuggers, and editors for one or both of these languages. This camp's concept of rapid prototyping is writing code for AI applications faster. The mainframe camp assumes that a large mainframe computer will be used because the database management system (DBMS) recommended to prototype with is a network structure database which operates only in that environment. This particular DBMS is advocated because it is believed to have a superior, fully integrated data dictionary. The Not Invented Here (NIH) camp consists of companies that have spent large sums of money developing proprietary

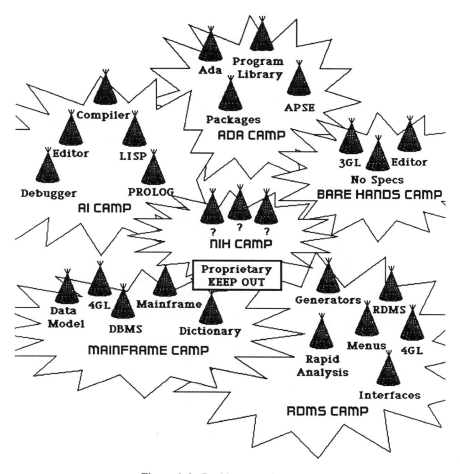

Figure 1-4 Rapid prototyping camps.

rapid prototyping systems that are perhaps relational, artificially intelligent, and require no human interaction. The developers believe that even though their tools are unavailable to the general public, it would be a mistake to attempt serious rapid prototyping without such tools. The Ada camp's notion of rapid prototyping is based on reusable code packages and program libraries used to create "mix and match" working models. The "bare hands" camp concept of rapid prototyping is based on the perceived absence of a requirement to undertake complete, thorough, rigorous analysis and design. Most of these camps have worthwhile approaches—although the bare hands approach can make life more difficult than necessary.

It is probably unwise to try the techniques described in this book without the use of the type of tools recommended. Doing so will result in the type of prototype referred to by the analogy shown in Figure 1-2—very slow to produce and very expensive to modify. Good prototyping tools are not always cheap, thus many managers harbor wishful thoughts about the ability to do rapid prototyping without special tools. It must be pointed out that one development tool will build many systems, people time is the most expensive part of the equation, and trying to build Porches with Swiss Army Knives will be much more expensive in the long run than investing in adequate tools up front.

Can Rapid Prototyping Be Used as an Evolutionary Development Technique to Produce Deliverable Software Systems?

This question is related to the previous one. The answer is, it depends on the tools in use. The question assumes that it is, for some reason, desirable to evolve prototypes into final products, rather than to discard the prototype and then use a different set of tools to develop the final product. This assumption is valid if evolution would be less expensive than a rebuild. Using some prototyping tools, evolution is not always less expensive and it is sometimes not even possible. A target system might conceivably require an environment inhospitable to the best prototyping tools. In such cases, prototyping would continue to serve as a communication vehicle and requirements specification technique but would lose the advantage of being evolvable.

Much of the material in the following chapters will help explain why a certain type of development environment architecture is necessary to accomplish evolutionary rapid prototyping in a cost-effective manner. What is desired is an architecture that allows very easy replacement of functional modules, transparent interfaces to other development environments, ultimate flexibility in creating and modifying data storage structures, and very little operating overhead associated with basic application structures. If any of these characteristics are not present, then the tool is only suitable for producing disposable prototypes.

This book concentrates on the technique of evolutionary rapid prototyping, not because one must always evolve the prototype for prototyping to be useful, but because having the possibility of evolving to a final product makes the cost of all software development less. In addition, the more of the prototype that can survive into the version of the system referred to as the final product, the easier will be requested modification work on that system, using the tools described here. In other words, prototyping presents the opportunity to do software maintenance much earlier in the life cycle, and to do it faster and cheaper. With the right tools and the right approach, rapid prototyping techniques can be applied to make modifications to a system throughout its useful economic life.

What Types of Application Systems Are Best Suited for Rapid Prototyping?

The notion that there are some types of applications suitable for rapid prototyping and others which are not is a commonly held belief. Appearing in the literature and overheard at conventions and seminars are references to the limitations of prototyping—only good for producing toy systems, not good for developing performance-critical or algorithm-intensive applications.

Certainly the rapid prototyping approach will have a higher payoff for some systems than for others. These distinctions are made in Chapter 2. Certainly there are types of applications which will cause difficulties for prototypers due to the nature of the tools used to produce prototypes. How such difficulties can be overcome is explained in Chapter 6 in connection with describing the process of evolving prototypes. Examples of evolutionary strategies are given in the case studies included in Chapter 8.

One must decide if the customer interface to a system is important to its success upon delivery. Any potential new application which one suspects has a risk of building functionality not acceptable to the user, or has a risk of failing to build needed functionality, is a strong candidate for rapid prototyping. Complete honesty would therefore force most software developers to conclude that all proposed applications are not only suitable for rapid prototyping but cry out for its use.

Are Structured Software Specification and Development Techniques Compatible with Rapid Prototyping?

Although changes to the traditional software development life cycle under the umbrella of *Structured Rapid Prototyping* will be discussed, we do not advocate throwing out all previous tools used in analysis, design, coding, and testing and replacing them with quick and dirty prototype development. We propose a methodology for software development that combines the best of the structured analysis, design, and assessment techniques with new prototyping techniques in an approach that alters the life cycle to accommodate the development, demonstration, and refinement of a working model during the analysis phase of a project to help discover the true and complete set of system functional requirements.

In other words, there is no need to throw out that which has been proven effective simply because it has not been proven foolproof. The objective will be to add value, not merely to replace one valuable tool with another. Structured programming, a way of organizing code, was first advocated at a time when the random approach to program development seemed to be causing maintenance problems after software was delivered. Structured design, a way of organizing programs, was later advocated as a means of helping to assure that single programs and groups of programs would be developed in a structured manner. Structured analysis followed as an attempt to avoid building elegant solutions to the wrong problem.

Structured analysis has matured more than the other structured techniques, perhaps because of early frustrations experienced in attempting to completely and accurately prespecify detailed functional requirements with static paper models. Structured analysis approaches undergo frequent enhancements. A recent enhancement has been the introduction of the three-dimensional approach to structured analysis. This approach was first described in *Controlling Software Projects* by Tom DeMarco.[4] Mr. DeMarco uses the analogy of an architect specifying a building in three dimensions: side elevation, front elevation, and floor plan. He advocates that software architects use the same approach by preparing a function interface (dataflow) model, a stored information (entity-relationship) model, and a system event path (state transition) model.

Carrying the architectural analogy a bit further, it would seem that architects must frequently experience the same frustrations with paper models as do software developers. Blueprints, like structured design, are primarily designed to be communication tools for use among building professionals, not as communication tools for use between builders and customers. Why else would architects go to the additional trouble of developing an elaborate scale model for complex projects? The architect's scale model has much in common with the software developer's rapid prototype. Both can be built cheaply and rapidly, in comparison with the final products. Both are a physical representation of what is stated in the paper specifications. Both are often the most effective way of discovering the customer's true needs.

Note that the architect, experiencing difficulties in communicating with customers over details of paper specifications, does not decide to stop preparing blueprints. Blueprints are still needed by building professionals to specify the details of the customer-approved scale model. There must be a tight coupling between paper specifications and physical models. Similarly, in software development, the three types of paper models recommended by DeMarco are still required to build a good system. The recommendation of this book is to simplify the process of initial analysis, to avoid specifying things you are not sure of, and to add a fourth dimension to structured analysis by developing a rapid prototype in addition to paper specifications. An illustration of this four-dimensional approach to structured analysis is shown in Figure 1-5.

How Does Rapid Prototyping Differ from "Top-down" or "Incremental" Implementation?

Top-down implementation involves the development of the first couple of levels of dataflow diagrams which are then used as the basis for the first couple of levels of design which are, in turn, used as the basis for initial coding. This initial coding would include "real" code in COBOL, FORTRAN, C, Pascal, or whatever the final system is intended to be, but only for the high-level or control modules. Details of the system would be left as "stubs" or "dummy" routines until the time comes for that level to be implemented. In this manner, the skeleton of the system can be demonstrated to the user faster than with the traditional systems development approach.

Rapid prototyping *is* top-down implementation. Nothing about the two concepts presents a contradiction. The discernible advantage of the methodology presented here is that no "real code" need be written to develop the initial prototype, because we now have better tools at our disposal. Fourth-generation languages, visual programming, screen generators, function generators, procedure interfaces, and report writers make it possible to present the top level to customers much faster than writing code. Modules created with such tools will be fast and convenient to change during the prototype iteration phase. All interfaces between and among modules will be tested early in the life cycle, without producing code that has been patched to the point that it becomes overly complex. No "harness" or "driver" code need be written to experiment with detail modules during prototyping.

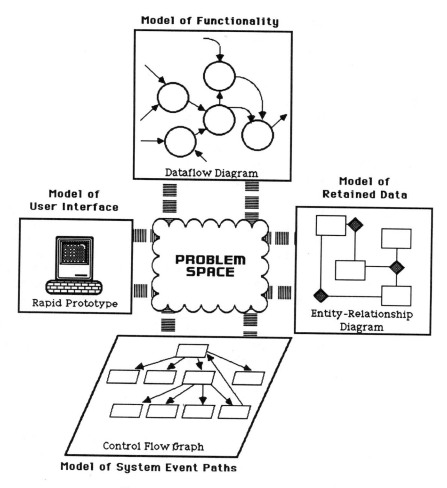

Figure 1-5 Four-dimensional system model.

To What Extent Should End Users Be Involved in Rapid Prototyping?

In a well-planned rapid prototyping project, about 50 percent of the development effort, from iteration to final approval of prototype functionality, is the contribution of involved users. Prototyping teams are typically composed half of users and half of professional software developers. Successful rapid prototyping projects make clear, in a plan prepared at the beginning of the project, what the users' roles are and what their responsibilities will be. This is one way that you can tell whether or not real rapid prototyping is occurring. When more conventional software development techniques are employed, the users are told to go away after approval of specifications, are not involved with the project during the coding phase, and do not interact with the project team again until the last part of the test phase. On a rapid prototyping project, users will always be present, involved in frequent brainstorming sessions with the software developers.

In the early days of rapid prototyping, the user's role was limited primarily to that of reviewer. In many situations this is still the case because, while prototyping tools are much easier to use than conventional tools, many users haven't the time to master them in addition to performing their usual jobs. There are now a couple of new considerations for users. First, modern prototyping tools are very intuitive. Extensive training in the computing field is not a prerequisite to learning the use of these tools. A short, one-week training course can make effective prototypers out of end users. Second, the continued increase of end user computing—coupled with the increasing proliferation of personal computers in the workplace and some very worthwhile prototyping tools that operate on personal computers—has provided the catalyst for an increase in end user rapid prototyping.

The question is, really, is prototyping most appropriately done by users or software professionals? It is most probable that the correct answer is, "Neither—prototyping is most effective when undertaken by teams of professional developers and users." A project that uses evolutionary rapid prototyping to produce a complex application system will always benefit from the contributions of professional software developers and highly trained and experienced prototypers. The challenge in today's software development environment is to redefine the appropriate roles for users and developers with respect to rapid prototyping. A rapid prototype is much more the user's product than the developer's. The professional software developer, on a rapid prototyping project, assumes more of a consultant's role than a supplier's role.

What Are the Cost and Risk Reduction Benefits of Rapid Prototyping?

Fred Brooks advised that it would be wise to plan on throwing away the first version of any newly developed system. Now we have an economical means of doing so. The first demonstration of a rapid prototype will be intentionally imperfect, but it will be very inexpensive to produce and very easy to modify. Therefore, we no longer need to claim that we will "do it right the first time." Instead, we can confess that we will probably get it wrong the first time, but we can also guarantee that the system we will ultimately deliver for production operation will be closer to the right system. Thus, although rapid prototyping will not dramatically shorten development time, the new capabilities offered by this approach are directly translatable into dramatic savings in total life cycle costs.

Rapid prototyping will not shorten development time significantly because developers today do not spend very much time on a project actually developing software. Most of the development portion of an application's life cycle is spent preparing requirements specifications, design documents, test plans, user guides, and other documentation. Rapid prototyping does not provide opportunities to eliminate any of these documentation tasks. In fact, readers are encouraged not to attempt shortcuts in these areas. Rapid prototyping is not a quick and dirty approach—it can be thought of as a *complement* to existing structured development techniques rather than an *alternative* to those techniques.

Within the community of computer professionals, it is a well-known fact that the cost to correct an error in a computer system increases dramatically as the system life cycle progresses. It has been documented by respected authors such as DeMarco,[4] Boehm,[5] and McClure[6] that the cost of correcting an error increases by orders of magnitude as the system moves from the development stages of analysis and design, to become most expensive during the postimplementation or operation phase. Prototyping serves to eliminate many of these errors in the very early stages of a project, before any code has been written. Changing a prototype is quick, easy, and painless—if it is anything else, the wrong tools are being employed. Prototyping is best at catching the most glaring errors and the ones most costly to correct: those involved with delivering the wrong system to the user. Faulty, incorrect, inconsistent, ambiguous, incomplete requirements result in faulty estimates and usually in production systems that are not what the user wanted.

In addition to a realistic expectation of significant savings in total software costs, there are intangible benefits associated with rapid prototyping as well. Some of these intangibles may well represent potential economic gains, but they are difficult to quantify. There is a direct and immediate benefit to delivering the right application system (functionally correct software that meets the user's true requirements) on or about the date specified in the project plan. Strategic plans will have been made to run a portion of the organization's business using the new system. A system that does not provide the useful and required information the user expects, is extremely difficult to use, does not provide information in understandable formats, or provides inaccurate information, will put a definite crimp in such strategic plans. This problem typically exists, but is not planned for, with most newly implemented conventionally developed software. Such problems do not go away until after effort and expense have been expended on the typical six-month "post implementation tuning" phase.

Rapid prototyping implements the right system at delivery time by allowing users to experiment with iterations of incremental versions of a working model of the system. Experimentation takes place at the beginning of a development project and is allowed to continue throughout the life cycle. Changes are encouraged as opposed to the normal approach of prematurely freezing incorrect specifications. By examining options in various versions of the prototype, users are frequently stimulated to discover requirements they would otherwise be unaware of until implementation. An intelligent user might say to the conventional analyst, "How do you expect me to accurately state the detailed functional requirements of the system until I have had an opportunity to experiment with the options?" Unfortunately, the answer, without rapid prototyping, is usually, "If we miss a few things now, we'll pick them up during system tuning—trust me."

What Are the Risks Associated with a Rapid Prototyping Approach and How Can They Be Minimized?

Rapid prototyping is a *risk avoidance* approach rather than a *risky* approach. That is, rapid prototyping does not introduce any new political or economic risks to the software development process, but it does significantly reduce several risk factors associated with software development as just described. Nevertheless, things do go wrong with some rapid prototyping projects and when they do, it is often because of the differences between this approach to software development and the conventional one, combined with an imperfect understanding of these differences.

So, there are some risks attendant to the process. Chapter 8 describes many of these risks based on the authors' experience. Suggestions are offered for minimizing the risks. Basically, rapid prototyping project risks come under these categories:

- Mistaken concepts of rapid prototyping concerning definitions, objectives, and correct application of the technique
- Disagreements with users and customers regarding methodology, standards, tools, and so on
- Out-of-control users who want to iterate and evolve a prototype into a system that does everything for everybody all of the time
- Budget slashes and effort shortcuts—temptations brought about by use of the word "rapid"
- Premature delivery of a prototype instead of a final (thoroughly documented and tuned) product
- Overevolved prototypes—substituting elegance and efficiency for flexibility
- Either unsupportive or untrained maintenance personnel or both

The solutions to these problems on a global basis involve education and training programs. For a particular project, the solutions involve correct management practice and adequate project planning. Attempting a project where the parties involved harbor incorrect conceptions about rapid prototyping will often lead to failure. Make sure before beginning a project that a project plan (written document) exists which contractually defines methods, deviations from standard tools and techniques to be used, time lines, user responsibilities, and deliverables. Use the plan as a proactive tool during the project to prevent difficulties in converging on a solution during prototype iteration and to prevent budget slashing, effort shortcuts, and premature implementation of the prototype. Maintain a prototyping stance and mind set over the entire life cycle to avoid overevolved prototypes and unsupportive maintenance personnel.

What Is the Future of Rapid Prototyping as a Software Development Approach?

Rapid prototyping is not a flash in the pan—it is here to stay. This powerful new approach to software development is only just now beginning to be used in many organizations for the development of many new, large, complex applications. This is perfectly understandable given that the proper application development environment tools to do prototyping have only been introduced in the last few years. Dramatic improvements in the capabilities provided by such tools continue to appear in new releases. The effort that vendors are putting into these new products is a response to the market demand for better prototyping environment development tools. New product development is one way to tell that rapid prototyping is where the action is. How many significant new improvements to COBOL or FORTRAN compilers have been introduced lately?

In a recent speech, Jerry Pournelle, editor at *Byte* magazine, likened COBOL programmers to a bunch of dinosaurs standing around discussing whether or not to grow another horn, thicker armor, another spike, or a longer tail while failing to notice that the mammals were eating their eggs. In the computer field, mammals may take the form of PCs, PC software, prototyping tools, CASE tools, expert systems, or any new thing that beats the socks off doing business the same old way because, "That's the way we've always done it."

Despite much publicity, rapid prototyping—particularly evolutionary rapid prototyping—is still considered a radically new approach to software development. The average software development shop is still using the conventional life cycle approach involving reliance on paper products for analysis and design and writing third-generation language programs and job control procedures to implement the design. There are, however, a significant number of organizations that have had successful experiences with rapid prototyping experiments. These experiments have produced application systems that are an order of magnitude higher than normal in end user utility. Prototype-developed software has exhibited a distinct tendency to better satisfy true user requirements and produce information and functionality that is more complete, more accurate, and more meaningful. Thus, new thinking is emerging regarding the advisability of replacing the traditional waterfall-based life cycle methodologies with the iterative, incremental, and evolutionary rapid prototyping approach. This book presents guidelines for formalizing such thinking in terms of recommended modifications to existing methodologies and standards.

We are confident that, within the next two or three years, evolutionary rapid prototyping will become the normal method for developing new applications—the standard approach to software development. Market economics will cause this to happen as it becomes more and more evident that rapid prototyping produces better systems at a lower cost.

New system hardware architectures—distributed processing, integrated local-area and wide-area networks, powerful personal computers linked together with intelligent file servers—have created problems for those who are still using the conventional approach to software development. Rapid prototyping thrives in these environments. Many rapid prototyping development environment toolkits allow data to be shared and distributed more easily than ever before. Data transfer is accomplished effortlessly between machines and databases made by many different vendors. Newer software products have been developed with the newer hardware architectures in mind, and rapid prototyping environments are designed with flexibility as the ultimate objective. The new hardware-software environments are facilitating the following: end user prototyping, uploading and downloading of prototypes, distributed prototyping, and system conversions. This means that many problems can only be solved by the application of the rapid prototyping approach. These trends are not going away—they are the wave of the future.

REFERENCES

1. F. P. Brooks, Jr., *The Mythical Man Month,* Reading, MA: Addison-Wesley, 1973.

2. Bruce Blum and R. C. Houghton "Rapid Prototyping of Information Management Systems," EDRS, 1982.

3. Bernard Boar, *Application Prototyping: A Requirements Definition Strategy for the 80s,* New York: John Wiley, 1984.

4. T. DeMarco, *Controlling Software Projects,* New York: Yourdon Press, 1982.

5. B. W. Boehm, *Software Engineering Economics,* Englewood Cliffs, NJ: Prentice-Hall, 1982.

6. J. Martin and C. McClure, *Software Maintenance: The Problem and Its Solution,* Englewood Cliffs, NJ: Prentice-Hall, 1983.

2

Critical Issues in Software Rapid Prototyping

Rapid prototyping is no longer considered a revolutionary or even "new" idea. It began creeping into computer system development literature about 1980, although some farsighted individuals were writing about it long before then. It has appeared in serious, academically respected publications as well as in "pop computer" magazines and newsletters. There are several professional seminars taught on the subject, and special classes on prototyping are held at the large computer conferences. Even large hardware vendors' user group meetings have special tracks on prototyping.

Because other authors, software customers, and software professionals are beginning to tout the process, a review of existing literature would be appropriate here. But because the bulk of the literature has occurred in monthly trade journals and in weekly newspapers, a simple summary may suffice. You will find some worthwhile reading in the references at the end of this chapter. Other papers and full-length books will be referenced in later chapters.

A GLOBAL VIEW OF SOFTWARE PROTOTYPING

Software prototyping means many things to many people. Let us begin, therefore, by trying to reach some common agreement on definitions. What is software prototyping? How is it done? Why is it done? When is it done? These are the issues we examine next.

Helping Users Select and Evaluate Software

When we need software, we have two options: We can become experts ourselves by getting degrees in computer science or reading everything we can get our hands on—a voluminous amount of material when one considers the number of new publications on the newsstands and the number of new books in the technical libraries—

or we can trust someone else. If we decide to become experts ourselves, we will probably go to work for a university and teach operating system principles or database design, or we will go to work for a vendor and write operating systems or database systems. In other words, if we are among those who know the most about computers, we will be able to recognize quality software, but we will be among those who program the least. If we are not expert and must then trust someone else *and* our needs are either personal or small, or both, we can talk to a friend who knows what we need. If we don't have such a friend, we can walk into one of the many personal computer stores that have sprung up like Chinese restaurants in shopping centers and bare our souls to someone who talks like a used car salesman and looks surprisingly like our fifteen-year-old son. If our needs are professional and large, we are faced with a similar indignity: We go to the data processing department or the management information system (MIS) department of our company and beg. We beg for a system that is easy to use, will fill our needs, will help us be more professional at our job, and will be delivered during our lifetime. Prototyped computer systems offer software customers a way to deal directly with a computer and be less dependent on the complexities of human communications.

Prototypes and Software History

Prototyping seems like such a simple concept. It has long been recognized in engineering and other disciplines. A model is built, then it is "tested" or "test driven" or whatever term applies to the idea of "trying it out." Why has such a common laboratory procedure not always been part of software development? We really don't know. Maybe because software is so intangible. We can't plug it in and empirically observe the reaction in a physical object. We can't sit in it or drive it. There are no nationally recognized benchmarks of what is good or bad. *Consumer Reports* is unable to tell us if we are getting our money's worth. Ralph Nader can't tell us what is unsafe. There is no way to compare one product to other products that might match our wants and needs. The federal government offers no help either with regard to quality or cost. There are no blue books which quote prices for new or used software. There are really very few market standards.

Maybe we did not prototype in the past because we simply did not have the appropriate tools. Third-generation procedural languages, such as FORTRAN and COBOL, are too cumbersome to perform a task that requires ease of change. We now have what we never had before: screen formatters, program generators, full-screen word processors, report generators, database query languages, and relational databases. Such tools give us the ability to rapidly modify data storage structures interactively; the ability to create, demonstrate, and modify the prototype using menus and screen forms that minimize programming effort; and a resulting prototype that may often evolve into the final production system.

Prototyping Properties

Typically, the first thing appearing in an article about prototyping is a definition. Like many other terms in the computer industry, the concept will be pushed around for a long time before the phrase "rapid prototyping" conjures up similar mental images in a group of computer professionals. Ultimately, a respected standard-setting organization like the American National Standards Institute (ANSI) will offer a definition we can all accept and live with. Even with a simple and often-used term such as "maintenance," the National Bureau of Standards decided to offer three official flavors of it—"corrective," "perfective," and "adaptive"—before software maintenance professionals could communicate without first defining terms. Boeing Aerospace was one of the industry leaders that raised our consciousness about variations in "testing" and provided formal definitions for "verification" as opposed to "validation."

Lacking such a formal definition for the term "rapid prototyping," "applications prototyping," or "software prototyping," early attempts at defining the properties of a software prototype are offered next. You will notice that, while a general notion of prototyping results from combining all these properties, there is quite a bit of philosophical conflict between some pairs of terms. A software prototype has been profiled as

- Functional quickly
- A miniature model of a proposed system
- Easy to modify
- A working model written in a fourth-generation language
- Always rewritten in a procedural language for implementation
- A model used to determine design correctness
- A quick way to approximate a problem solution
- Always discarded
- Something that models human interfaces to computers
- Something that promotes communication between developers and users
- The nucleus of an evolving system
- Not operating at high performance levels
- Not intended to be the final system
- Not having advanced system features
- A display-only mock-up of reports and screens
- A feasibility study
- Always used with "live" data
- A requirements definition strategy

There have been similar attempts to define prescribed methods for doing rapid prototyping. Conflicts are also noticeable between some pairings of these prescriptions. Various writers and speakers have stated that prototyping

- Must be done by experienced prototypers
- Replaces the traditional development life cycle
- Adds phases to the traditional development life cycle
- Always involves the use of fourth-generation languages

- Parallels traditional application development through systems analysis
- Requires active data dictionary and directory systems
- Requires release control mechanisms for administration
- Applies only to mainframe application system development
- Applies only to small uncomplicated systems
- Cannot be used for real-time systems
- Is best accomplished in a data-driven, rather than procedure-driven, mode

ALTERNATIVE APPROACHES TO SOFTWARE PROTOTYPING

Today there are several competing philosophies regarding how one should do rapid prototyping. Some of these philosophies are published while others are simply in widespread use by practitioners. This section describes four of the most common competing philosophies:—throwaway, quick and dirty, design-driven, and mock-up prototyping—and contrasts these approaches with evolutionary prototyping, the approach concentrated on in this book.

Throwaway Prototypes

A throwaway prototype describes a product designed to be used only to help the customer identify requirements for a new system. Developers are sometimes constrained to throwaways by the tools used to prototype with if such tools are not suitable for use in production systems. Products produced with throwaway prototyping tools cannot be implemented or even evolved into a deliverable system. All elements of the working prototype will be discarded, as intended, after system requirements have been identified. Only the derived requirements will be maintained, paving the way for work on the real system. A throwaway prototype can be thought of as nothing more than a dynamic requirements specification.

If the prototyping model presented in this book is used, it is to be considered *evolutionary* not *throwaway*. However, if one wishes to use as much of the evolutionary model as possible in the absence of evolvement-supporting tools, then the products from some of the phases in that model can be salvaged. High-level analysis, for example, will be the nucleus for further analysis and design and will be retained in all instances.

An example of a throwaway prototyping tool is a stand-alone fourth-generation language with poor performance characteristics. Another example is the toolkit that will only operate on a stand-alone personal computer—the resulting prototype cannot be made to operate in a multiuser environment. Some prototyping environments are only intended by their vendors to produce rapid facsimiles or models of an application system. No means is provided with throwaway tools of tweaking a prototype for performance.

Some sources in the literature say that throwaway prototyping tends to add about ten percent to development costs. This figure may be based on the assumption that prototyping will be a task undertaken in addition to all the usual tasks and that the usual tasks will take as long as they always did. Actually, effective throwaway prototyping will significantly reduce revisions of requirements and design documents and will go a long way toward reducing nasty surprises during the test phase. Still, it is certainly cheaper to evolve prototypes into production systems than to throw them away and start all over.

Quick and Dirty Prototypes

Quick and dirty is an old term describing the approach of quickly bringing up a version of a system, then modifying it until the customer can grant minimal approval. In the past, it meant writing programs in standard languages before performing much, if any, analysis or design. The programs were modified based on feedback from users as they saw the output. The resulting software is almost sure to be expensive to maintain because the code has been patched many times, even before it is delivered, and is rarely accompanied by any documentation. Without minimally adequate tools for rapid prototyping, any working model produced as a prototype at the beginning of a development project will, by definition, be quick and dirty.

Paraphrasing Meilir Page-Jones, care must be taken so that something intended to be temporary does not actually become permanent, like many of the "temporary" dwellings built quickly after World War II that are still occupied. Program code is no exception. As soon as it is "running," it may be forgotten by management and developers as they press on to the next more exciting or more demanding problem. It will not be forgotten by the programmers who maintain it in a nightmarish situation in which what was once "quick" suddenly becomes very slow to modify and "dirty" now becomes even dirtier. Throwaway code must be developed only when there is a definite plan for how and when it will be discarded. Even then, it is a risk.

Quick and dirty prototyping is particularly insidious because at first it appears to work beautifully. The usual methods are employed to sell the benefits of prototyping to management and users. The project slogan becomes, "Down with analysis paralysis—up with rapid prototyping." Sure enough, a working version of something becomes rapidly available for demonstrations. Although each prototype iteration mysteriously takes significantly more effort than the last, total development cost is slashed as the milestones whiz by.

Wait a minute—this all sounds a little too familiar!

Quick and dirty prototyping is nothing more than the reincarnation of the methods used to develop software when computers first arrived on the scene. Since coding represents only ten to twenty percent of total development costs today, of course we can slash development costs if we skip doing a thorough job of analysis and design before beginning to write programs. Even using either "blitzing" or "top-down implementation," or both, code is created and that code must be changed as a result of prototype demonstrations. Once code is changed, despite our best and most "structured" intentions and despite when in the life cycle it is done, it is now "patched" and is on the road to becoming more complex and more difficult to modify. Many software contractors today are fond of the quick and dirty prototyping approach when the final system *and its maintenance responsibility* will be turned over to some government agency upon completion. Remember why structured analysis, structured design, and structured programming became so popular in the first place? They were worthwhile attempts to control the maintenance dilemma created by the unstructured development methods used during the 1950s and 60s.

Detail Design-Driven Prototypes

Design-driven approaches to prototyping are derived from engineering disciplines where "prototype" means a preproduction model of a system. The model is complete and as perfect as it can be made to be. It is then "test-driven" to uncover any defects which can be corrected before delivery of the final product. In computer terms, a system is developed using traditional techniques for analysis, design, and coding. Customers see the results of high-level analysis such as dataflow diagrams, but they see nothing else until well after a detailed design has been completed. This sort of prototype is problematic because it is so detailed—analysis and design documents being allegedly complete—that it will be expensive to change all the documentation and the system when prototype demonstrations uncover unexpected or undesirable results. Here, the automobile analogy breaks down. For custom-built software, we don't build one, test and refine it, then build 100,000 more from the model. We simply build one.

High-level managers who are responsible for many types of organizational effort, along with software development, are often the types of persons who harbor misconceptions about prototyping—particularly if they have an engineering background. Engineers are taught that a prototype, or "breadboard model," provides an opportunity to explore various design alternatives, but would not dream of developing a prototype of anything before completing rigorous requirements analysis and detailed preliminary design. To do otherwise would be to violate accepted engineering practices.

The problem with carrying over the design-driven prototype concept into software development is that changes requested and required as a result of demonstrating a prototype software system are typically much greater in number and more complicated to achieve than the changes resulting from the demonstration of a well-designed breadboard model of a hardware device. With the design-driven approach, it does not matter what kind of prototyping tools are used. So you demonstrate a functionally complete model of a completely specified system only to discover that 25 percent of the specified requirements are incorrect and an additional 25 percent must be added—what then? Now the requirements and design specifications and the system itself must be drastically overhauled, accompanied by a monumental configuration management task. This sounds a bit like the test phase of a typical project, doesn't it?

Nonfunctioning Mock-Ups

A mock-up provides the customer with visual examples of inputs to and outputs from system processes. The mock-up is sometimes on paper only although it may be a screens-only prototype created on the computer. The examples are manually prepared by the developers. No data are actually input to a computer, nor are results computed and output, but developers often include sample data to be able to show the format of menus, data entry forms, or reports. A distinction is made here between throwaways and mock-ups based on the presence or absence of real data. Obviously, mock-ups are also thrown away after requirements have been defined.

Mock-ups may be inexpensive and helpful, but are not definitive in identifying functional requirements because they lack the capacity for interactive experimentation. The real value of rapid prototyping comes from the presentation, in prototype demonstrations, of various transformations of data familiar to the user. The user will be able to tell if the information produced is accurate. The user will be able to decide if the information is sufficient, intelligible, and easy to obtain. These user determinations are possible only when the user can get an immediately verifiable answer from the prototype to the question, "What happens when I do this?"

This is not to say that mock-ups are of no value. If you are awaiting delivery of hardware, or have not yet selected final system hardware, then you could still profit from the methodology presented in this book. High-level analysis of a "chunk" of a system, which equates to the size of a prototype, and accompanying screens and menus can be very useful in helping to define preliminary requirements. The power of communication and verification of correctness which result from "live" testing of functionality, and from experimenting with user-familiar data, will, of course, be lost.

A Definition of Evolutionary Rapid Prototyping

A formal sentence describing an evolvable prototype might be the following: an easily modifiable and extensible working model of a proposed system, not necessarily representative of a complete system, which provides users of the application with a physical representation of key parts of the system before implementation. Here is an alternative statement: an easily built, readily modifiable, ultimately extensible, partially specified, working model of the primary aspects of a proposed system.

Bernard Boar has defined prototyping as a specific strategy for performing requirements definition wherein user needs are extracted, presented, and successively refined by building a working model of the ultimate system quickly and in context. Most published experts are in agreement that the primary objective of rapid prototyping is to provide a cost-effective means of discovering the true and complete set of system functional requirements that will optimally satisfy the legitimate business needs of the user, given a level of funding acceptable to the customer and the software developer. Evolutionary prototyping techniques can be applied effectively to all phases of the software development life cycle, and user-approved evolutionary prototypes are always considered good candidates for tuning to produce production systems.

Evolutionary prototyping differs from the throwaway approach in that the goal of the former is always to evolve the prototype into the final system. Special integrated prototyping environment toolkits are advocated for doing so. Since, in the majority of cases, most of the prototype will usually survive as part of the final system, evolutionary prototyping usually results in a shorter development cycle and a lower project cost than either throwaway prototyping or traditional development. There are cases where evolutionary prototyping tools are appropriately used to develop throwaway prototypes. Such cases represent the minority of applications, and, even then, expense is no greater than using throwaway tools.

The structured evolutionary rapid prototyping approach advocated by this book differs from the quick and dirty approach in that detailed analysis and design do take place. Structured specification and development techniques are an integral part of the evolutionary rapid prototyping approach. The techniques of evolutionary prototyping are applied concurrently with structured analysis at the beginning of a project. The same techniques are applied concurrently with structured design and development during the tuning phase. If this sounds confusing, remember that we are talking about an iterative rather than a sequential process. Our goal is to specify only that which we are very sure about, to avoid unnecessary rework, but never to use conventional programming techniques without the benefit of a structured detailed design. This goal also differentiates the evolutionary approach from design-driven prototyping.

Unlike the mock-up, the evolutionary rapid prototype performs transformations on real user-familiar data. A prototype must walk a narrow path to use real data, unlike the mock-up, but yet remain easy to modify, unlike the quick and dirty prototype. Once data have been entered into a system, particularly if the amount of data is large and the data entry process is manual, the structure under which the data have been stored becomes increasingly difficult to modify. Good evolutionary prototyping toolkits provide developers with a means for rapidly modifying storage structures while easily preserving stored data.

A model of the evolutionary rapid prototyping process is depicted in Figure 2-1. At this point we will not discuss the details of this model, but rather use it

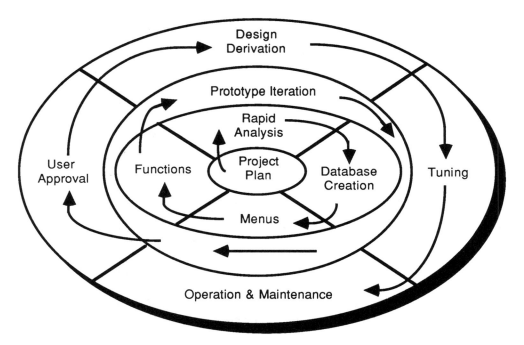

Figure 2-1 The evolutionary rapid prototyping process.

to illustrate that analysis and design are integrated into the process and that the procedure encompasses all development phases from planning to delivery of a new system.

APPLICATIONS BEST SUITED TO RAPID PROTOTYPING

Prototyping will improve the development of any system if one proceeds from the belief that the user interface is the most significant aspect of a system, being basically what the customer pays for, as well as the aspect that is generally the most poorly done. Despite the good press given to the "user friendly" approach over the past few years, conventional software development techniques just do not give the user a chance to see or experiment with the interface to the product until the tail end of a project. Of course, by that time, changes are usually so hard to make that the user accepts the interface that was "developed according to spec," whether it is a good one or not. In a nutshell, what rapid prototyping does best is provide the means for discovering the right user interface. This is the case whether the system is large or small, real-time or not.

For some systems, particularly embedded systems, the user interface may not be the *most* important aspect. The prototyping approach can still be used—there will simply be a change in emphasis. High-level analysis will be performed on the system, and the top or controlling user interface levels will be implemented as drivers or harnesses for the algorithms which are the true subjects of the test.

Small versus Large Application Systems

In the early days of rapid prototyping, the tools used for prototyping had very poor performance characteristics, making them unsuitable as implementation vehicles for systems that featured large numbers of concurrent users or large amounts of stored data. Thus, evolutionary prototyping was only applied to small application systems. With the introduction of prototyping tools with much better performance characteristics, and the addition of features which make possible combinations of prototype modules and modules produced using standard software development techniques within the same system, a prototype of a large system may be evolved into the final deliverable system.

There are those who feel that any system that can be placed directly into production as a result of any form of prototyping is not a "prototyped system" at all, but merely a very "simple system." Most of these critics admit to the advantage of prototyped screens or transactions, test databases and sample reports during the requirements analysis and design phases for very large systems, whether or not the prototypes are candidates for evolution. Our approach will be to consider a user-approved prototype of a complex application to be a simple *version* or *representation* of the final system. As system tuning proceeds to evolve the prototype into the final product, the system will become more complex, more difficult to modify, and will more closely resemble traditionally developed software. When a prototype has been tuned for performance, we do not call it a prototype anymore—we call it an application system.

One of the problems with discussing small versus large application systems concerns how one measures system size. Are we talking about lines of code, amount of machine resources used, amount of data, number of users, number of functions performed, or functional complexity? As a general rule, systems that have evolved from prototypes developed according to the procedures recommended in this book will have fewer lines of code and smaller amounts of stored data than traditionally developed systems. We recommend the use of fourth-generation languages (4GL) and visual programming for prototype development. One line of 4GL may replace 40 or more statements in a third-generation procedural language. A visually programmed module may contain no visible lines of code at all. Evolved prototypes will also be easier for maintenance staff to understand and modify throughout the useful life of the system. Therefore we could agree that prototyped systems tend to be smaller and simpler, even though they often solve large problems.

Real-Time versus Data Processing Systems

The techniques of software rapid prototyping were developed primarily in the commercial MIS environment. It has been only in the last two years that developers of scientific and real-time software have considered investigating a prototyping approach. At first, there was much skepticism of prototyping in the MIS environment, but the prototyping approach has been slowly growing in favor with each new published article and each new successful system implementation.

The literature contains only a few descriptions of successful implementations of real-time or scientific applications from prototypes.[1,2] Therefore, the scientific computing community is at the same level of skepticism regarding prototyping that the MIS community was years ago. The critical issue for real-time applications like flight control systems is often response time—slow calculations simply cannot be tolerated as they can produce disastrous effects. Scientific applications are often algorithm-intensive with lots of number crunching, and little input or output. Prototyping has always concentrated on verifying the correctness of inputs and outputs. We believe that the tools available today are suitable for prototyping such systems and we offer a strategy for evolving prototypes into scientific and real-time systems.

The tools available for prototyping today offer a means for improving the response time of prototype modules to a level equal to that of traditionally developed software. The key word in the previous sentence is *modules*. The modularity of an evolutionary prototype—combined with an integrated environment with interfaces to other types of development environments—is what provides an evolutionary prototype with the ultimate in extensibility. This same modular system concept provides a means for working with algorithm-intensive applications. Complex algorithms can replace simple algorithms during prototype tuning. Various versions of an algorithm can be experimented with easily using a modular prototype as the baseline.

User Interface Intensive Systems versus Embedded Systems

As the MIS community has moved steadily away from batch-oriented systems toward more interactive systems in the last ten years, the importance of the user interface has been acknowledged to be the prominent concern in software development. On the other hand, in the scientific and defense system application environment, many so-called embedded systems are simply failures to realize that the usefulness of computer systems is only as great as the service they provide to the human user. Most systems require input from an operator to function and most provide either information or service, or both, of some sort to a user. These interactions with the user are the characteristics of a system which determine its usability, are most often done poorly, and would benefit most from prototyping.

We have all heard the "does-a-falling-tree-make-a-sound-if-there-is-nobody-to-hear-it" debate. Actually, this philosophical question is similar in nature to asking if there can possibly be a computer system with no human in the loop. Noise can be described as vibrations of the air which, when they cause an eardrum to vibrate, are interpreted by the brain as sound. If no one is in the forest to hear the tree fall, there is only vibrating air, there is no sound. Likewise, computer systems are requested and used by humans who have expectations about such use and the resulting service to be provided. Often software is developed for the purpose of controlling mechanical devices rather than producing reports. During operation, such software receives its inputs from and provides its outputs to devices rather than humans. To determine if a given "embedded" application has a user interface, ask yourself the following questions about the system:

- Are there any human operator controls or override mechanisms?
- Does the system require initialization?
- Do parameters or constraints have to be input before the system is activated?
- Is the observable behavior of the controlled device of interest and in any way variable?
- Does the system provide any information about its status (such as a screen display on a monitor)?

Unless all these questions can be answered negatively, you do not have an embedded system at all but rather one for which the system boundaries have not been correctly defined. If the answers to all the questions are in fact negative, then you probably have been tasked with developing a subsystem; rapid prototyping will still be applicable at a higher level (for the whole system).

Some Dubious Cases

There are some types of software systems that may not be logical candidates for prototyping during development. At least we know of no published record of anyone ever attempting a prototype of such systems. Each presents relatively unique problems to the prototyper. Theoretically, prototypes of these applications could be attempted and, by stretching one's imagination, it is possible to see feasible approaches. The risk of applying a prototyping approach to these applications is that the developers may spend more time trying to devise a workable approach than will be saved by prototyping.

Database management system software would be difficult to prototype because database management systems are used to develop prototypes. The resulting recursiveness is frighteningly confusing. Wouldn't developers be tempted to create a system that looked just like the tool they were using to develop the system? Of course, such meta-models are not out of the question. . . .

The user's view of an operating system such as Unix or VMS would be difficult to prototype because an operating system is nothing but a user interface. This may sound contradictory because we have stated that the user interface is the most important part of any system and also the part that benefits most from prototyping. In most application systems, however, the user interface is only the front door and the entry hall to the house. The real action is going on inside the rooms (the functional modules). Prototyping these applications allows us to experimentally develop the interface which allows the most effective means of accessing modules, entering and capturing required information, and producing correct and necessary output. If the user interface is the whole system, prototyping ceases to have a clearly definable objective and there will be no way to measure success in meeting objectives. How can correctness and completeness be measured, for instance, with no real data to process? Perhaps operating systems could be prototyped in a throwaway mode, but it is doubtful that the prototype could ever be evolved to the final system—*all* operating system modules must be optimized for performance, and the developer must assume that all modules will encounter the problems associated with too much data and too many users.

Many types of commercial software packages for personal computers would be difficult to prototype. These would include graphics packages, word processors, spread sheets, and telecommunications software. The problem with these applications is similar to one of the problems with prototyping operating system software—no real data with which to populate the prototype. In the beginning planning stages of a prototyping project we must assume that we have some combination of automated data files and potential users to provide user-familiar data for use in prototype demonstrations. However, if user's data have been profiled and modeled, then it could be input to the prototype in the absence of the real thing. That is, a meaningful test suite of data could be constructed.

All three of the foregoing examples of difficult applications have one thing in common. They are typically developed as commercial applications rather than as in-house custom-developed applications. They are targeted toward wide markets rather than definable user groups. This leaves developers with a lack of real users and real user-owned data with which to prototype. Real users and real data are the two most indispensable ingredients in a prototyping project.

We have not said these applications are impossible—they are merely difficult. The tools used for evolutionary rapid prototyping are ultimately suitable for developing in-house custom-built software for a clearly defined user group. Database management systems play a central role in most prototyping approaches which means that an assumption has been made about the importance and function of data in the application. The types of applications just listed contain no data at all when delivered to the user.

BENEFITS OF RAPID PROTOTYPING

We have said that emphasizing the word *rapid* in the phrase *rapid prototyping* can lead to dangerous misconceptions about the true benefits of the approach. Following is a list of the realistically achievable benefits to be derived from a structured rapid prototyping approach. These are the merits upon which advocacy of the approach can be appropriately founded.

Quality Assurance and Control

Rapid prototyping could be considered a quality assurance technique, since its primary benefit and ultimate objective is to dramatically raise the level of customer satisfaction with the functionality of delivered software. Software is delivered, using this approach, which contains fewer functional defects. Quality control from the front end is built into a rapid prototyping project since users are involved in early prototype iterations during the analysis phase.

Accommodating New or Unexpected User Requirements

Users are not always certain what they want requested software systems to do. How can users clearly understand and be able to state detailed functional requirements unambiguously before they have an opportunity to experiment interactively with the options? Users are often accused of unfairly changing their minds about desired functionality of a system under development during the test phase of a project. While it is true that users often change their minds late in the life cycle, it is at this point, using traditional development techniques, that they have an opportunity to see the system actually functioning for the first time. Sometimes reality is far different from conceptualizations based on paper specifications. Other times the opportunity to view a function in operation stimulates a perceived need for additional functionality.

Rapid prototyping provides an opportunity to accommodate these changes, which basically represent creative thinking on the part of the user, early in the life cycle and at a very low cost. The result is a dramatic decrease in disruptive and costly change activity during testing and a significant reduction of costly postimplementation perfective maintenance. When users are encouraged to take an active role in the development of a system, that system stands a much better chance to become a source of pride for them. Needless to say, such a psychological phenomenon is positive for system quality and prototyping is valuable in creating the atmosphere to allow it. As the user becomes more active and the system analyst more passive (almost assuming an advisory role at times), the user feels more in control of his or her environment—always a healthy and ethical state of affairs. As the user assumes more control, solutions more readily acceptable become apparent and therefore the organization's needs will probably be better met. When large systems are segmented, sometimes certain segments become candidates for prototyping, even when the entire system does not. For example, perhaps only the data-entry function of a multifunction system will be prototyped, leaving the other functions to more traditional development methods. The segment-prototype technique works especially well with systems undergoing redevelopment, where the redevelopment occurs in phases and redeveloped segments are linked back into an existing system, one by one.

Evaluating Software Enhancement Requests

Most users have requested more of their data processing departments or software vendors than can be delivered. There has been much in the recent literature about the documented application backlog. In reality, that backlog is only the tip of the iceberg. There is an incredibly large and undocumented "invisible application backlog" representing what the user *really* wants if only the current backlog could be eliminated and these true desires could actually be delivered. Prototyping allows the quick assessment of which changes are really needed. By "trying out" changes via prototyping in the enhancement-maintenance phase of the normal system life cycle, the application logjam can be broken, many old requests removed from the books, and only modern and necessary requests for change can be serviced with available resources. A prototype can be used as a feasibility study or a sales kit.

Cost Savings in Development and Maintenance

Just as most life cycle effort is not spent in the coding phase, most of the cost of current software systems is not due to development effort, but rather to maintenance effort. Figure 2-2 illustrates the recent trend for software maintenance to continually consume a larger percentage of the organizational budget in most software departments. For statistics on software maintenance, see references at the end of the Chapter.[3,4,5] Software maintenance is where most of the money is spent today on software applications. The average software department expends about 80 percent of total available resources on maintenance. These figures assume that perfective modifications, sometimes referred to as enhancements or "out of scope" maintenance support, are counted, along with bug-fixing and adaptive or required modifications, as maintenance work. Modifying production code is the same kind of expensive, labor-intensive work no matter how it is classified.

Evolutionary rapid prototyping provides two powerful new ways to help beat down the high costs of software maintenance. The first and most obvious of these is that systems will be produced that will be much easier to modify in place. Chapter 5 shows how structured prototypes are developed in an extremely modular fashion with an absence of hard-to-follow procedural logic. Sometimes, complex procedural logic must be introduced during the tuning phase of a project but, to the extent that original prototype modules survive into the delivered product, they remain as easy to modify as they were during prototype iteration.

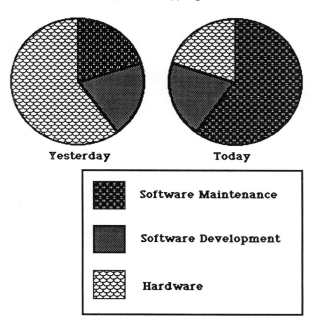

Yesterday   Today

	Software Maintenance
	Software Development
	Hardware

Figure 2-2 Computer operations cost trends.

The second way in which prototyping reduces maintenance costs is by producing systems that need fewer modifications after delivery. It is not widely understood what the primary contributor to maintenance requests is. The authors of this book believe this primary contributor to be the phenomenon illustrated by Figures 1-1 and 1-2—the rather consistent tendency on the part of software producers to deliver the wrong system. Figure 2-3 illustrates one view of the impact of this phenomenon.

As illustrated in Figure 2-3, we know that developers make mistakes during the development phases of analysis, design, and coding. Many of these mistakes will not be discovered until the test phase, when there is an actual working system to evaluate. Some mistakes will not be discovered during testing and will remain latent until some point in the future during operation and maintenance. Figure 2-3 shows that it is believed most test and maintenance effort is devoted to correcting mistakes made during the earlier phases of analysis, design, and coding and that, in fact, most of the total life cycle is devoted to mistake correction and thus represents spoilage. In other words, the conventional approach to software development is to produce a requirements specification that is, at best, probably no more than 50 percent correct. The requirements specification will be imperfectly translated into a design document which will, in turn, be imperfectly translated into software. Only when the coding is complete and testing begins will these errors begin to surface.

Many software engineers, realizing that Figure 2-3 represents an accurate model of the conventional software development environment, have attempted to obtain the high payoffs associated with introducing techniques aimed at discovering errors earlier in the life cycle. Structured walkthrus are an example of one such technique. Others have taken the approach that more time spent at the front end

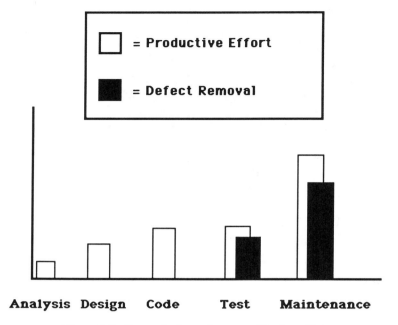

Figure 2-3   Nonproductive software modification effort.

of a project on getting the requirements and design right would result in lower cost during testing and maintenance. Tom DeMarco suggests that inadequate time is often allocated to front end phases due to faulty estimating procedures and techniques. While such assertions and approaches are no doubt valid and useful concepts, it is doubtful that any amount of paper prespecification or static quality assessment will reveal all possible sources of error. Experience shows that the largest number of errors are found when users have the opportunity to experiment with a working system. Rapid prototyping provides this opportunity at the very beginning of the life cycle.

Some data exist which suggest what the nature of early life cycle mistakes might be. As shown in Figure 2-4, 50 percent of the postimplementation requests for changes to existing software occur in the first six months of a system's useful economic life. Could this be, in large part, because it is during these six months that we are scrambling to make the Dusenburg more Porsche-like? We suspect that this is so or the curve would not have the shape it does. At the end of the six-month period, how closely does system functionality resemble that which was originally delivered? For conventionally developed software, this six-month period could be considered an expensive prototype iteration phase. In other words, most early life cycle mistakes consist of failures to incorporate the user's true requirements into the functionality of the software under development. Rapid prototyping provides a means for guaranteeing that the user's true requirements will be incorporated in the functionality of the delivered system.

These intangibles can be converted into tangible economic benefits. As a benchmark, consider a conventionally developed system which cost $1 million to

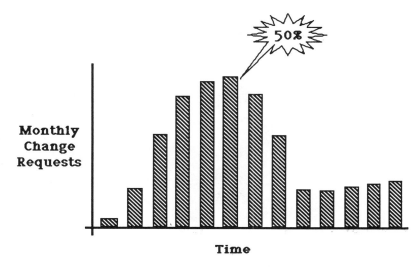

Figure 2-4 Postdelivery changes.

develop and $450,000 to modify during the first six months following its delivery. If most of this postdelivery modification was because it was necessary to incorporate missing required functionality and modify incorrect implementations of specified functionality, then the $450,000 represents a potential savings had rapid prototyping been applied as a development approach. Using rapid prototyping, the changes would have been made to a prototype rather than a delivered system. Using the techniques described in this book, prototypes are no more difficult to modify than paper specifications and prototyping is done during the analysis phase of a project. If the prototype was evolved into the final system, then total development costs would certainly be no more than with conventional methods and the $450,000 saved would represent a net gain.

At this point in the life of the conventionally developed system we can expect to spend another $450,000 on maintenance before the software is retired or rewritten. If an evolved prototype was in place, instead of the conventional system, we could expect additional savings due to increased ease of future changes. We can quantify these savings by inspecting the relationships shown in Figure 2-5.

Very conservative estimates of the increase in the cost of a software change as development proceeds through the life cycle indicate that a change made during analysis would cost at least ten times as much if postponed until after delivery, during the maintenance phase. The cost increases are due to the increasing amount of documentation which must be revised and the increasing level of complexity that must be understood to make the change. Since prototype-developed systems will also require documentation changes and since all prototype modules will not survive evolutionary tuning to become part of the delivered system, we cannot expect a ten to one improvement in required maintenance effort. A two to one improvement would, however, be a very reasonable estimate. Thus, if our benchmark system had been prototyped, we could expect another $225,000 savings in maintenance costs.

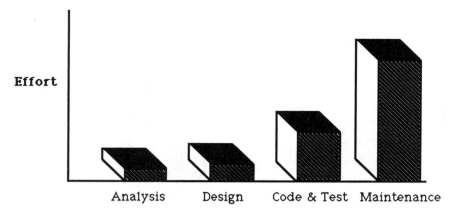

Effort

Analysis   Design   Code & Test   Maintenance

Figure 2-5   Increasing difficulty of system modifications.

Small gains can be made during the development portion of the life cycle, as well, using rapid prototyping. There will be less thrashing during requirements and design specification because detailed specifications can be derived from user-approved versions of the prototype. There will be fewer nasty surprises during the test phase because a fully integrated working system, incorporating the user's actual data, has been undergoing interactive experimental development since the early part of the analysis phase. Finally, there will be significant reduction in time required to develop the actual software. All these development gains, taken together, will probably save no more than 10 percent in total development costs—for our benchmark, $100,000.

A direct comparison of the conventional development approach to rapid prototyping reveals, for our benchmark system, that the former would cost a total of $1.9 million while the latter would cost $1.125 million—approximately 41 percent less. It is interesting to note that the typical misconception of rapid prototyping being primarily a means of reducing coding time would not, even if true, yield an approach that would provide as much in cost savings as the evolutionary rapid prototyping approach. Studies show that coding only consumes 7 to 15 percent of total life cycle effort. Thus, even if coding could be accomplished in 10 percent of the conventionally required time, this would only represent a net savings of 13.5 percent.

Prototypes can often be developed and used to justify and sell a complete system rewrite. This involves the development of a prototype of a present system requiring excessive maintenance effort. The prototype would be presented along with current system maintenance statistics. The potential customers would then be asked to suggest some possible enhancements—the wish list they always wanted but could not have due to the change request backlog. A presentation can be scheduled for a few weeks from the initial presentation when the users will be shown the incarnation of a significant portion of their wish list. The closing argument then is based on demonstrated proof that the excessive maintenance costs of the present system would be drastically reduced once its replacement was in place and the new system would be much more responsive to changing user needs. This particular recommendation of rapid prototyping usage is heresy to those who believe one should never rewrite existing software that works, even when the maintenance effort required to support that system is extremely painful or costly.

User Satisfaction with Software Systems

Even with the use of development techniques such as structured programming, structured design, structured analysis, and information modeling, and with the use of modern software toolkits, systems continue to be problematic. Users continue to complain that systems are late, contain errors, and are often not what they wanted and thought they asked for. With prototyping, a "what you see is what you get" approach eliminates the bulk of the communication problems, allows delivery of systems as least as quickly as ever, and permits the correction of errors due to bad specs in the early, inexpensive phases. When the wrong specifications are designed and implemented (accounting for 60 to 80 percent of errors according to Boar and DeMarco), even the most modern tools and technology cannot salvage the product. It may be slick but totally inappropriate.

When users are allowed the participative approach, they can gain confidence in a system. They "see" first-hand the problems and errors, but they also "see" the mistakes getting resolved quickly before the mistakes haunt the system for life. Such speed is reassuring to a user who can observe the action. That is why "rapid" is such an important part of rapid prototyping—when errors, even philosophy changes, are turned around simply and quickly with amendments to or rebuilding of prototypes, the user is encouraged to believe that the fixes are real and can be exercised. When users "command" the computer directly, there is little chance for communication problems to arise between user and developer; that is, there is a greatly reduced opportunity for incorrect functional specifications.

Productivity Improvements

Generic software packages, communications packages, and all computer hardware have decreased in price over the last few years. Programmers and analysts are drawing ever higher salaries and there is no indication that they will not continue to be paid well for tasks that are increasingly complex, requiring ever more people time. These trends are expected to continue.

It has been said that between 1964 and 1979, the hardware price-performance ratio increased one thousandfold while programming productivity increased only fivefold. Software systems cannot be delivered fast enough to meet user needs and demands, partly because programming productivity is not improving and partly because much of the activity of programming is spent on maintenance of existing systems, which is, in turn, partially due to unsatisfactory systems analysis. It follows that when prototyping improves systems analysis, it improves developer-analyst-designer-programmer productivity in phases following analysis-prototype-design even if these early phases do not shorten development time.

CHANGES IN MANAGEMENT AND METHODOLOGIES

Limitations of and Objections to Rapid Prototyping

As has been often documented, cutting budgets is almost always unwise and is many times the single most obvious reason for the failure of a system under development. How does budget cutting in a prototyping environment differ from budget cutting in the traditional development environment? In several ways. One is that, because visible outputs are quickly available, users and managers are easily seduced into believing that the design-code-test phase as well as the modeling phase can be skimped on. Even mature, experienced managers and analysts must be careful in realizing that menus and screens in a prototype are not backed up with detailed design and that reports may be perfectly formatted using data elements carefully defined, yet still suffer tremendously in the performance area.

There is always the possibility that the rapid prototype will not evolve into the production system. It could be thrown away or replaced several times without producing even a good set of specifications.

A rapid prototype involves the application of fairly radical techniques incorporating fourth-generation language and relational database tools. Yet maintenance personnel may still be thinking third-generation thoughts. Even development personnel may view a change in technique as a criticism of the manner in which they have been trained and in which they take a great deal of pride by following precisely. In a highly technical field, lack of understanding is threatening to one's professional stature; there is a tendency to belittle techniques with which one is not familiar.

The iterative process of prototype demonstration and revision can continue forever without proper project management. As users see success in requirements being met, they may have a tendency to add to the list of items to be prototyped until the scope of the project far exceeds the feasibility study. It is imperative that a project plan be instituted as the first phase of activity, and that the plan be continually refined. If the user desires and the developers have the resources, the plan *can* be infinitely extensible. The power of the plan is in communicating to the customer that as the number of "deliverables" or functions increases or becomes more complex, so does the schedule lengthen, raising the cost.

There is a limited availability of qualified prototypers and even fewer trained maintainers of prototyped systems. Programmers, who are trained to solve information management problems by writing systems composed of program modules, are often uneasy with the transition to rapid prototyping concepts. Unfortunately, there is little training available to help introduce this new way of thinking about system development. The companies that develop the tools for rapid prototyping—that is, relational database management systems—have courseware specific to the use of their tools. Other companies have courseware relating to system development methodologies. What the industry needs is a way to teach rapid prototyping using specific systems and methodologies, such as a specific relational database management system, tailored to each customer's development environment. A hands-on workshop designed to demonstrate the development of a rapid prototype, on-line, works best. The workshop could incorporate a class exercise based on a typical rapid prototyping application.

Performance problems may surface following the implementation of a prototype, particularly if the model is not stress tested and benchmarked. Some functions may simply be too large to be efficiently executed using the prototyping tools, or they may prove impractical for other reasons.

Some people question the future applicability of prototyping. Because much of the argument in favor of prototyping is derived from the premise that the user is never really sure what he or she wants a new system to do, this argument may be diluted if users get "smarter" over time. What if the third, fourth, and all successive software systems present much less uncertainty?

We choose to defer once again to Fred Brooks on this issue. As his 1975 predictions proved to be extremely insightful over time, we believe his recent predictions will prove to be accurate. In his article, "No Silver Bullet—Essence and Accidents of Software Engineering," Brooks says he believes that most software development errors still have to do with getting the system concept wrong, not the syntax or the logic. He believes that software development will always be difficult and that there will never be a magic panacea or "silver bullet." On a positive note Brooks says, ". . . one of the most promising of the current technological efforts, and one which attacks the essence, not the accidents, of the software problem, is the development of approaches and tools for rapid prototyping of systems as part of the iterative specification of requirements."[6]

Issues Dealt with in this Book

The following chapters contain much information about premature implementation—what pressures cause it, and how to avoid it. Training needs for development and maintenance personnel are covered. Techniques are offered for estimating prototyping effort and converging on agreement as to desired functionality, as a result of prototype iteration, within a predefined time limit. Solutions to performance problems are offered as tuning strategies—the feature of this prototyping approach that characterizes it as evolutionary.

REFERENCES

1. M. Alavi, "An Assessment of the Prototyping Approach to Information Systems Development," Communications of the ACM, June 1984.

2. B. Blum and R. C. Houghton, "Rapid Prototyping of Information Management Systems," EDRS, 1982.

3. B. Boar, *Application Prototyping: A Requirements Definition Strategy for the 80s*, New York: John Wiley, 1983.

4. B. Boehm, T. Gray, and T. Seewaldt, "Prototyping Versus Specifying," *IEEE Software*, May 1984.

5. J. Connell and L. Brice, "Rapid Prototyping," *Datamation*, August 15, 1984.

6. F. Brooks, "No Silver Bullet—Essence and Accidents of Software Engineering," *Information Processing 86*, ed. H.J. Kugler, North-Holland: Elsevier Science Publishers, 1986.

3

Tools, Techniques, and Methodologies of Evolutionary Rapid Prototyping

As a development technique, rapid prototyping is unique because it is very dependent on specific kinds of hardware and software. This has always been the case. Before modern tools were available for rapid prototyping, critics of the approach viewed prespecification development of a working model as an invitation to lock developers into a technological solution. With the advent of specific tools for quick model development this problem has ceased to exist—working models can be as easy to modify as paper models. Thus, writers in academic and professional journals and magazines have mostly spoken of rapid prototyping in the context of use of some specific software development tool. Furthermore, such development tools sometimes can only operate on a limited number of makes of computers.

The most common elements of rapid prototyping software environments are a fourth-generation language (4GL) and a database management system (DBMS). The earliest published works on rapid prototyping described how third-generation language programs could be quickly prototyped with a 4GL due to compression of the number of statements required to implement a given amount of functionality and the absence of complex control logic. A DBMS with an integrated 4GL provides the opportunity to quickly generate a working model that faithfully simulates all the information management aspects of a proposed system, incorporating user-familiar data.

Because evolutionary rapid prototyping involves much more than simply developing throwaway models of programs, the required toolkit is much more extensive than merely a 4GL and a DBMS. This chapter profiles the ideal toolkit for evolutionary rapid prototyping. The profile includes recommendations for software, hardware, structured specification techniques, and methodologies. Thus, what is being described is a comprehensive environment for software development, using the evolutionary rapid prototyping approach. Not included in this chapter are descriptions of auxiliary productivity enhancement tools or explanations of how limited rapid prototyping can be accomplished if factors such as organizational politics or budget constraints prevent the acquisition or use of an ideal toolkit. These topics are no doubt of critical interest to many readers, but they are outside the main thesis of this book. Such topics are discussed in Chapter 12.

COMPETING PHILOSOPHIES

Chapter 2 discussed the fact that there are competing philosophies regarding the correct approach to rapid prototyping. There are also competing philosophies regarding the correct set of tools to use for prototyping. Prototypers can be identified as belonging to one of the six "camps" described next, according to their preference in tools. Recall that Figure 1-4 depicted each of these camps as a collection of teepees, with each teepee containing a particular "prototyping" tool. It can be inferred from the following discussions of each camp that the tools used will determine the approach and the quality of the results of prototyping.

The Ada Camp

The Ada programming language environment has been described as a rapid prototyping environment. The obviously positive aspects of Ada as a prototyping language are that, like the UNIX operating system, the language was designed to facilitate the use of callable packages of code and is implemented in a rich support environment to facilitate the writing and management of such packages. The rapid prototyping approach in this camp is based on program libraries containing reusable code in packages. The theory is that, if the library is comprehensive enough, packages can be mixed and matched to rapidly produce any desired functionality.

The problem with this approach is the effort and resulting cost involved in modifying large amounts of Ada code and traditional file structures. If a working model is put into place early in the life cycle to discover system requirements, the Ada code will be expensive to modify if the packages require refinements to accommodate individual user needs. If unstructured patches are made to this code before analysis and design are complete, the packages will become increasingly difficult to maintain. If actual data are used in the model, stored in traditional file structures, file redesign might also become an expensive problem.

Because the U.S. Department of Defense (DoD) is committed to the use of Ada, some positive new developments are beginning to surface. There are links to some of the existing relational database systems for instance. Other developments, such as reusable libraries of Ada modules, to be selected by a front end expert system and coupled with CASE tools, are in the works.

The AI Camp

Vendors of dedicated artificial intelligence hardware have used the term rapid prototyping to describe a development environment containing an AI language compiler, an editor, and a debugger. The philosophy here is that it is not possible to prespecify requirements for AI applications since there is no way of knowing what can be accomplished until something is tried. The objective, therefore, is to write code as fast as possible, try it out, and modify it until it does something "intelligent." Here we have the irony of archaic quick and dirty techniques applied to state-of-the-art software development.

Granted, the typical AI workstation, with high-resolution graphics and pull-down or pop-up menus, is a good piece of hardware to use in working out the details of the user interface. As the existing libraries of AI modules grow and more prototyping can be accomplished using the "building block" approach, the taint of the quick and dirty may disappear.

The NIH Camp

NIH stands for Not Invented Here. The literature contains a few examples of testimonials by persons who claim to have accomplished amazing feats of rapid prototyping with tools developed in their organizations. The tools are usually proprietary, so one cannot get a very clear idea of their nature. When such tools are developed by government contractors or software developers, they are typically not available to anyone outside the organization, as they are being used to gain advantage over the competition. Such tools may be indeed marvelous, but they do not do much toward the cause of advancing software engineering on a global basis.

The Bare Hands Camp

There are those who, for financial reasons or out of an unwillingness to try new tools, do not have adequate tools for rapid prototyping. These are usually the people who state that any sound new development technique, such as rapid prototyping, should not depend on particular hardware or software for its success. Prototypers in this camp have two choices—quick and dirty, and mock-up prototyping. Those who choose the mock-up approach can produce useful display-only prototypes with something as simple as a full-screen text editor. Chapter 13 discusses modifications that need to be done to the evolutionary rapid prototyping approach to accommodate the bare hands approach and accomplish limited prototyping.

The Mainframe Camp

This name is chosen to represent a particular class of rapid prototyping as it is widely practiced in mainframe computing environments. The approach is very similar to the one described in this book, with a few exceptions. The main-frame camp virtually insists on the use of one particular database management system—IDMS/R—as a prototyping tool. IDMS/R is widely recognized as one of the quasi-relational (actually network structured) systems and as such has some inherent schema inflexibility once a database has been defined and populated with data. Anything inflexible is, of course, anathema to evolutionary rapid prototyping. To compensate for this inflexibility, mainframe prototypers place heavy emphasis on detailed prespecification in the form of comprehensive data modeling, while in the same breath denigrating prespecification in the form of functional analysis. The objective is to finalize the database schema by developing a corporate data model that includes every last attribute before beginning to develop a prototype.

Because changes must occur if prototyping is to have any value, the mainframe camp also insists that a good prototyping tool must have a fully integrated and active data dictionary to help manage the changes and predict the expense required to implement them. Since powerful relational databases exist for mainframes, this insistence on the use of an inflexible tool is a bit puzzling. Perhaps it had its beginnings in the days when relational systems had very poor performance characteristics, particularly when applied to large mainframe applications.

The RDMS Camp

RDMS stands for relational database management system. Databases belong to one of three types depending on the model or structure used to store data: hierarchical, network, and relational. A true RDMS allows storage structures to be modified quickly without regard to record management (chains, pointers, keys, and indexes) or database structure (repeating groups and parent-child relationships); there is no danger of losing stored data as a result of schema changes required during prototype iteration. Many commercially available packages offer the necessary flexibility and efficiency to run production systems. Most of these products have a forms interface that allows the applications to be created using visually developed screens and menus rather than written procedures.

Some relational databases the reader may be familiar with are INGRES, ORACLE, and DB2. We review these and other RDMS packages in Chapter 12 with respect to their capabilities as prototyping tools. In Chapter 10 we provide a comprehensive listing of currently available RDMS products, application and report generators, and CASE tools.

By now the reader has probably deduced that the tools in this camp are the ones recommended for use in evolutionary rapid prototyping. Use of these tools provides the heart of prototyping—rapid and effective communication between customer and applications specialist. Forms, screens, reports, and menus can be developed without the use of complex command and control syntax. Rapid turnaround time is possible between critique by the customer and refinement by the developer. Prototypes in this camp always have a possible path for evolution into the production system because the toolkit includes tools for interfacing the prototype modules and database tables with external modules developed in traditional fashion and conventional file structures.

BUILDING EVOLVABLE MODELS

Chapter 6 discusses in detail the techniques that can be used for evolving prototypes into production systems. The critical issue in prototype evolution is always performance—response times of critical modules when executed in an actual production environment. It has been noted that one of the problems with delivering functionally approved prototypes as final products is that prototyping tools, such as 4GLs and DBMS's, do not always provide the necessary performance to adequately accommodate large numbers of users or large volumes of data. This is why early approaches to prototyping were always throwaway.

The solution to performance problems in a prototyping environment requires interfaces to tools outside that environment. Such "seamless" interfaces must be part of the evolutionary prototyping environment. Different vendors have different names for such interfaces, but they all do the same thing—allow a prototype module to call an external module or access an external file. Examples of usage of such an interface would include a menu structure implemented in 4GL which calls a third-generation language program or a 4GL report script which selectively accesses an indexed sequential file based on criteria contained in the RDMS. Using such interface techniques, parts of a functionally approved prototype may be replaced with more efficient parts without throwing the entire prototype away and starting over.

We do not intend to imply that other characteristics of systems contributing to quality such as security, reliability, auditability, or maintainability are unimportant. We simply assume that these characteristics will be addressed in the prototype design derivation phase and are not problems inherent with prototype evolution.

Storing and Manipulating Live Application Data

Users evaluating a model system understandably perform best when they are dealing with familiar data. Test data, especially those concocted by developers, are too foreign to the user to be of value. A good RDMS prototyping environment will allow existing electronic files to be quickly loaded into a rapidly created database structure. During experiments with the working model, users often are asked to use prototype data entry modules to input information. Based on user feedback resulting from such experiments, changes can be made to the schema of a relational database very rapidly, even after live data have been loaded, without fear of losing valuable information.

Required RDMS Features

A complete RDMS-based rapid prototyping toolkit is an integrated development environment which includes a fourth-generation command and query language, a fourth-generation report writer, a menu-structure generator, a screen generator, a function generator, visual programming tools, and the ability to interface and integrate an application prototyped within the domain of the RDMS with procedures (programs and so forth) and data that exist outside the RDMS domain. Figure 3-1 shows an ideal RDMS prototyping environment.

Visual programming techniques may be used to improve the appearance of menus and screens after the customer has seen an initial, crude version. Such cosmetic techniques allow explanatory text to be added to menus, then moved about

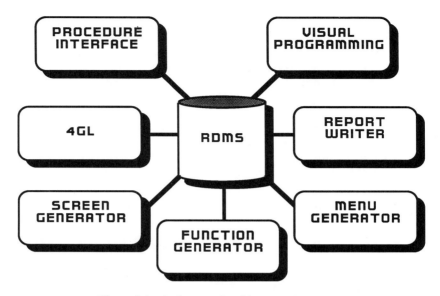

Figure 3-1   An integrated rapid prototyping toolkit.

the screen and edited until a pleasing display is created. The prototyper works in a "what you see is what you get" environment. When the finished screen, created using the visual programming techniques, is to be added to the system, most RDMS products allow the addition of the new function to a menu with a simple command statement. Such a menu takes only minutes to create using tools provided by the RDMS as opposed to days of effort using conventional job control language programming techniques.

Evaluating Available RDMS Packages

Not every RDMS product offers the ideal rapid prototyping toolkit shown in Figure 3-1. There are also many trade-offs between desirable prototyping capabilities and performance, and schema flexibility and hardware considerations. Therefore, no one product can be recommended as best. The best toolkit for you depends on your environment and your needs. Development of modern prototyping tools is very dynamic. New products and significant enhancements to existing products are constantly being introduced. This means that it is impossible to publish a list of recommended prototyping tools. Many of the products on such a list would be obsolete by the time the list was published and the implication that any product not on the list was not recommended would be very misleading. Therefore, only a few specific RDMS products will be discussed at length in Chapter 12. Instead, a means for the reader to evaluate currently available products is offered. This section includes a complete checklist of the characteristics of RDMS products which can be used during official requests for proposals and requests for quotes.

Many organizations have guidelines for evaluating relational database management systems for potential acquisition. The following material, extracted from various requests for quotes at one large organization, is an example of such guidelines.[1]

CHECKLIST FOR EVALUATION OF DATABASE MANAGEMENT SYSTEMS

Query Language   A simple method of accessing the database in an ad hoc fashion

Interactive and Batch Update   A nonprocedural way to add, change, or delete items from the database in either mode

Text Search   An ability to search a text data element for a specified character string, including "wildcards," where only a subset of the string need be given

Mathematics   A capability to provide Counts, Sums, Min, Max, Average, Mode, Median, and so on for a range of data

Select   An ability to select on attributes, including the wildcard function, prearrange attributes for output, and use these Boolean select capabilities: equals, not equal, less than, greater than, less than or equal to, greater than or equal to, "not," "and," and "or"

Boolean Nesting   The provision for Boolean nesting with the operations listed in the Select definition

Record Access, Selection Criteria   The capability to specify selection criteria via the query language, any combination of record types

Concurrent Updating   The ability for multiple users to concurrently update the database at some agreed-upon level of lockout (for example, item, record, file)

File Generation   The ability to create a file, accessible from outside the database, containing the results of a query

Formatting Output   The ability to format a page with control of number of lines per page, page break identification, and headings, at both consoles and printers

Database Access   A method for accessing the entire database for report generation

Conditional Branching   The provision for the user to control conditional branching

Mathematics Availability   The availability of all of the DBMS math capabilities within the report writer

Graphics   The capability to represent data in a graphical format

Export-Import Facility   The capability to interface with other software packages (spreadsheets, word processors, other database products, and so on)

Data Structure Data Definition   The capability for the user to: define data files, accessing capabilities, keys, indices, and relationships; handle input records for fixed, variable, and text format; handle input and manipulation of alphanumeric, integers of varying lengths, and double precision floating point data

Additional Features   Ability to specify read-only access to databases; format optimization for various sizes of databases; ability for users to define edit checks at database generation time; special character checking and verification; statistical information on DBMS system resource usage and remaining resources; optimized access and loading through specifying the storage method (for example, Hash, ISAM)

Data Dictionary   Provision of a data dictionary in which elements are not limited to DBMS-created data sets

Schema   The ability to segregate data elements within the database for specific users

Backup   Normal: A means for backing up and restoring the database. Abnormal: The provision of an activity journal of complete and incomplete updates for use at an abnormal system shutdown, to be used to restore the data to their condition at the beginning of the update procedure prior to abnormal system shutdown

Help   The availability to assist the user through DBMS functions

Maintenance   The provision of utilities to restructure the database without writing application language programs, recover and reload damaged databases from backups, and add or delete keys

The foregoing checklist is offered as an example of some useful and critical criteria often used in selecting an RDMS product. The reader is not encouraged to use this exact list in his or her own product evaluations. Your needs may be better served by a smaller set of criteria and there may be some factors missing from the preceding list. There is a much smaller set of criteria that determines whether a particular product will provide an adequate evolutionary rapid prototyping environment:

- The ability to generate functionality using both 4GL modules and visually programmed modules
- Full support of a truly relational data model
- The ability to generate a flexible application control structure, interfaceable with conventionally developed modules, using either 4GL command language or visual programming, or both

• The ability to operate with adequate efficiency on a hardware configuration available to developers and users

Figure 3-2 gives an example of how four hypothetical systems might be evaluated using such criteria. In the first three categories, a total of five stars are possible, with one star indicating the product is very weak in that respect and five stars indicating maximum strength. The acronyms in the final column stand for mainframe (MF), minicomputer (mC), and personal computer (PC)—indicating acceptable hosts for each product.

	Application Generator	Truly Relational	Visual Programming	Host
PRODUCT A	☆ ☆ ☆ ☆ ☆	☆ ☆ ☆ ☆	☆ ☆ ☆ ☆	mC,PC
PRODUCT B	☆ ☆ ☆ ☆	☆ ☆ ☆ ☆	☆ ☆ ☆	MF,mC,PC
PRODUCT C	☆	☆ ☆ ☆	☆	MF,mC
PRODUCT D	☆ ☆ ☆	☆	☆ ☆ ☆	MF,PC

Figure 3-2 Evaluating prototyping products.

At first glance, the clear winner would seem to be Product A because it is equal or superior to the other three products in all categories. Let us suppose, however, that the organization performing this evaluation must host all production applications on a mainframe. This consideration leaves Product A out of the running. Product B might then be selected, with the realization that prototyping will be a little less rapid, perhaps relying more on 4GL commands than visual programming for application control and function generation.

INCORPORATING STRUCTURED SOFTWARE SPECIFICATION TECHNIQUES

An appropriate set of structured techniques is a critical part of the evolutionary prototyping toolkit. The end product of the application of these modeling tools is the same as for conventional software development—a set of thorough, rigorous, and unambiguous specifications completely describing the functionality, architecture, and design of the system under development. Chapter 4 describes how structured tools are used at unusual times during the rapid prototyping life cycle and discusses the fact that the purpose of applying structured techniques is somewhat different in a rapid prototyping project. The following discussion will focus on what tools will be used for high-level analysis during prototyping. Subsequent chapters will carefully detail when and how they will be used.

The reasons that structured techniques remain valuable in a rapid prototyping environment are as follows:

- They are superior to narrative text or program design tools such as flow charts as a means for augmenting communication between users, analysts, designers, and programmers
- They aid in reducing wasted time by helping to avoid prototyping the wrong thing
- They effectively use partitioning with rigorous balancing to divide complex problems into simple modules

Structured techniques are just as valuable in a conventional development environment. The only difference in a prototyping environment is that developers do not attempt to use structured techniques to completely and accurately prespecify final system requirements and design prior to any development. Instead, the approach is to prespecify an intentionally incomplete working model, prototype partial requirements and design, and evolve both the specifications and the working system concurrently. A system can be viewed as a model of functionality, a model of data, a model of system event paths, and a working prototype model of those three views in combination.

The discussions of dataflow diagrams and entity-relationship diagrams presented next are based on previously published works in the Yourdon series. Happily, these techniques are optimally suited to specification of the prototyping approach detailed in this book. A third structured specification technique, structured design, has been modified somewhat for the evolutionary rapid prototyping approach in that a modeling technique called control flow graphs, similar to structure charts, is presented.

Just as conventional systems analysis produces a requirements definition specifying what the proposed system will do, analysis in a rapid prototyping environment initially produces a specification of what the prototype will do in the form of a preliminary requirements definition. This preliminary specification includes dataflow diagrams (DFDs), entity-relationship diagrams (ERDs), and control flow graphs (CFGs). This is very similar to the three-dimensional system model recommended by DeMarco.[2] DeMarco recommends DFDs for modeling functionality, ERDs for modeling stored information, and state transition diagrams for modeling system states and event paths, an approach to system modeling that has been elegantly refined by Ward and Mellor in *Structured Development of Real-Time Systems*.[3] These are similar to the three dimensions needed to prespecify the architecture of a prototype. When modeling a prototype, DFDs provide a high-level model of the proposed functionality of the prototype—what the system is supposed to do. ERDs provide a blueprint for preliminary database design. CFGs (simplified versions of structure charts) provide a plan for sequence of execution of the system functions. State transition diagrams, an important tool for modeling the required time-dependent behavior regardless of the technology used for implementation, will not be used during this early stage since we will concern ourselves first with basic system functionality. Performance and timing considerations will be addressed later.

Based on preliminary user interviews, an intentionally incomplete paper model is prepared to aid the developer in determining database design and functional modules for the prototype. The following are the critical elements of such a model:

- The system context, showing where the system will obtain data and deliver information (a DFD)
- The essential functions the system must perform to deliver required information using data provided in the system context—capturing incoming data, storing some in the database while passing some to other functions, performing data transformations, and reporting requested information in a user-acceptable format (a DFD)
- The preliminary database design derived from the essential functions diagram (an ERD)
- A preliminary menu and prototype module calling sequence design (a CFG)

It is important to recognize that the foregoing set of diagrams represents only a handful of documents—perhaps two pages of DFDs, one page of ERDs, and one or two pages (levels) of CFGs. The idea is to "think a little, build a little, test a little," then do it again. The models just listed will be expanded and refined during prototype iteration, but will not be fully expanded (taken to "primitive" levels) until the entire system design has been completely derived following prototyping. Using this approach of evolving specifications concurrently with the prototype, it is often quite useful to have a CASE tool for computer-aided drawing and consistency checking.

Dataflow Diagrams

Figure 3-3 shows all of the possible symbols that can be used on a DFD. Circles on a DFD represent data transformation processes wherein incoming information is transformed into outgoing information. The curved vectors are used as connections between DFD objects and represent data flowing from source to destination. Parallel lines represent data stores—data at rest. Rectangles represent sources or destinations for information which exist outside the system under development. All objects

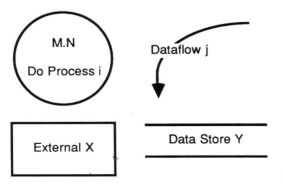

Figure 3-3   DFD objects.

on a DFD have labels. The label for a data transformation process will be used to identify the written policy in the structured requirements specification for how that transformation is to be performed. The labels for dataflows and data stores will be used to identify their definitions in the specification's data dictionary or encyclopedia. There are sets of rigorous and robust rules and guidelines for all of this which were first formalized in DeMarco's 1978 textbook on structured analysis.[4] Since this book is not a structured analysis textbook, the treatment of these techniques here will be more superficial.

Dataflow diagrams, in a structured specification, are partitioned into a leveled set. The complete set will include a context diagram (the system's interfaces to the external environment); an essential functions diagram decomposing the system into approximately seven, plus or minus two, high-level functions; a collection of third-level diagrams decomposing each of the high-level functions into seven plus or minus two lower-level functions; and so forth until DFDs are leveled to the primitive level (tiny enough to be succinctly specified and to represent the smallest meaningful unit of activity).

Figure 3-4 shows a generic example of DFD partitioning. "The System" is decomposed into five processes. Process 2 is decomposed into five primitive level processes: 2.1, 2.2, 2.3, 2.4, and 2.5. A short digression is in order at this point. Prototyping is most effectively undertaken by small teams prototyping a small number of functions for a small number of users. Therefore, one of the values of performing some structured analysis prior to prototyping is that large proposed applications can be first decomposed into easily prototypable components.

In the example shown in Figure 3-4, suppose there were also DFDs decomposing processes 1, 3, 4, and 5 one additional level, and that "The System" was to be large and complex. One of two effective prototyping approaches could be used, based on this analysis. With unconstrained resources or critical time lines, five prototyping teams could be used—one for each high-level process shown on figure zero. With constrained resources, a single prototyping team could develop one process at a time. The team would treat the function being prototyped, together with its interfaces, as the context diagram for the prototype. The guideline for any prototype as to how far to level DFDs before beginning to develop the working model is a context diagram and an essential functions diagram. Of course this means that there will not be data transformation specifications at first, because those are only written for primitive level functions.

A word or two is necessary as to why these limitations are placed on pre-specification. What would it hurt to level DFDs down to the primitive level or to prepare process specifications and a data dictionary before beginning to prototype? One could successfully argue that such exhaustive prespecification would produce a better prototype. While this is true, it will also produce a more expensive prototype and will require much more effort in changing the specification due to discoveries made during prototype demonstrations. The only way to avoid such costly changes is to obtain "user approval" of a "complete" structured specification and then refuse to make changes. But then, what would be the point of prototyping?

Prototypes, produced using tools such as those described earlier, don't have to be correct—they are meant to be modified. A 4GL report writer script or a

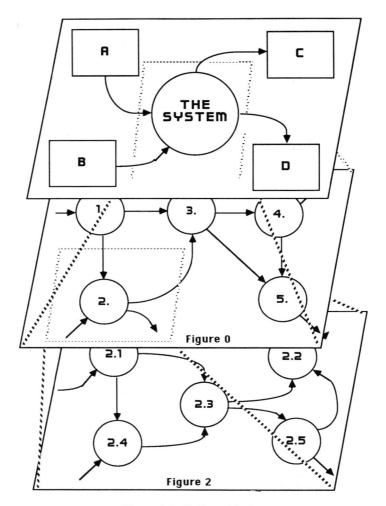

Figure 3-4 DFD partitioning.

visually programmed data entry screen is just as easy to modify and just as easy to understand as a structured English data transformation specification. This means that developers can use prototypes to discover what to specify instead of being forced to make changes to both a working model and a structured specification when users do not completely approve of prototype functionality. Those readers who remain skeptical about this seemingly nonrigorous approach are asked to accept the foregoing premises on faith for the time being and pass final judgment after reading the description of how to develop a prototype in Chapter 4.

The first dataflow diagram produced prior to prototyping is called the context diagram. Figure 3-5 shows a generic example of a prototype context diagram. There is always just one process shown—the system itself. The system is an example of a transformation process because it transforms input data into output data. In

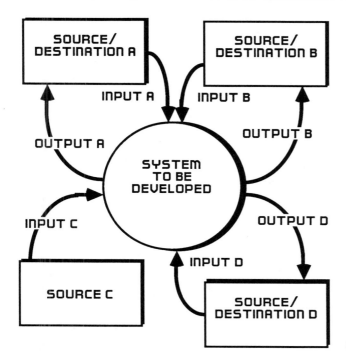

Figure 3-5 Context diagram example.

the system's case these are net inputs and net outputs. Thus the purpose of the context diagram is basically to define the mission of the system to be developed. All computer systems have as their mission the requirement to deliver specified information to specified destinations, using other specified information captured from specified sources. The context diagram is a neat little package, containing on one page a specification of sources, destinations, net inputs, and net outputs.

Sources may be users who input data from workstations using the system's data entry screens. Other examples of sources would include files and databases maintained by other systems. For real-time systems, sources might include electronic sensor devices. Destinations would include users who are to receive specified reports, screen displays, or other system output. Destinations might also include files and databases primarily maintained by other systems but which are to be updated with certain specified information by the system under development. For real-time systems, destinations might include electronic device control mechanisms. This specification of net inputs and outputs gives the context diagram a contractual nature. It defines what the system must produce, who must receive these products, and what resources are necessary to produce the products. Therefore, it provides a useful model for asking the question, "Do you think this would be an interesting prototype?" It also identifies the types of users who will be involved in prototype evaluation.

The second dataflow diagram to be produced is called the essential functions diagram. Figure 3-6 shows a generic example of a prototype essential functions diagram. This diagram shows that the system consists of six primary functions: process B, process L, process J, process M, process X, and process Y. The dataflows

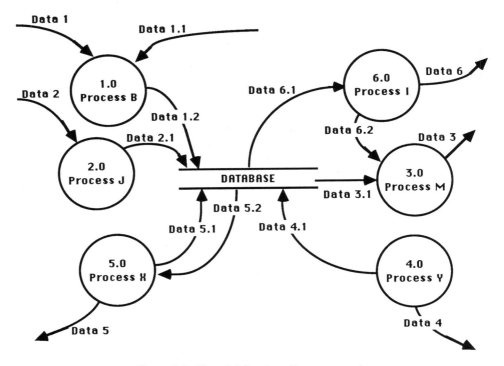

Figure 3-6 Essential functions diagram example.

shown coming to or leaving those processes from off-page are either the same
dataflows shown on the context diagram or parts of a decomposition of a context
dataflow.

There are two things that are a little different between an essential functions
Dataflows make three kinds of connections between objects on a DFD:

- A connection between two processes
- A connection between a process and a data store
- A connection between a process and an external source or destination

External sources and destinations do not have to be shown on any diagram other
than the context to avoid clutter.

There are two things that are a little different between an essential functions
diagram, developed as part of a preliminary requirements definition for a rapid prototyping project, and a figure 0 dataflow diagram developed as part of a conventional
structured specification. First, one and only one data store (representing the RDMS)
must be shown on the prototype essential functions diagram. Second, each process
shown on the prototype essential functions diagram must have a dataflow interface
with this data store. Neither of these constraints is called for by conventional structured analysis.

The reason for both of these constraints is physical. The entire initial prototype—all of the functions and all stored data—will be produced using the RDMS
toolkit referred to earlier in this chapter. For a prototype function to be developed

using one of the RDMS tools, it must use information stored in the RDMS—that's just how these tools work. True, a good toolkit includes interfaces to files and procedures that can exist outside the RDMS environment, but we want to avoid using those interfaces for the first version of the working model to maximize the flexibility of the initial prototype. Conventional structured analysis warns us to avoid getting "physical" in the first version of the specification—the first model should be purely "logical." In prototyping, we must get physical very rapidly because we are about to have a working model in a few weeks. On the other hand, our prototyping tools allow us the luxury, for the first time, of building a physical model that will probably be incorrect, knowing that it will be as easy to modify as the paper models of conventional structured analysis.

The essential functions diagram provides the prototyper with a picture of high-level functionality. It is a mechanism for helping prototypers to collect their thoughts about what the system is supposed to do. It will be used to derive the entity-relationship diagram and control flow graphs that are the other two dimensions of structured paper modeling used prior to prototype development.

To derive an essential functions diagram from the context diagram (sometimes known as the environmental model), the events (or transactions) which occur in the environment and to which the system must respond are identified. This "event-partitioned" approach can be initiated by preparing an event list—a textual listing of those events that will be handled by a process whose job is to produce the required response. McMenamin and Palmer have given us two rules for identifying events, or essential activities:[5]

> To pass the first test, the activity must contain the actions that would be carried out in response to one and only one event if the system were implemented using perfect technology . . .

> The second test is designed to make sure that an essential activity is complete. When all the activities that make up an essential activity have been performed, the system *must become idle* until the event in question occurs again or until a different event occurs.

Another way to get started when decomposing a context level DFD is to look at each point on the context bubble where an arrow touches the circumference. Ask if there is a function (process bubble) that must be performed to receive information from a terminator source or to send information to a terminator destination. Examples of such decomposition techniques are presented in Chapter 5.

Entity-Relationship Diagrams

Recall from the four-dimensional system model presented in Chapter 1 that one view of a system has to do with stored data. An entity-relationship diagram (ERD) is used to model the structure groupings of data to be stored by the system. The following discussion of ERDs is based on published work by Flavin,[6] DeMarco,[2] and Ward and Mellor.[3] Figure 3-7 is an example of the appearance of an ERD—rectangles with connections between them. Rectangles on an ERD represent entities. Entities

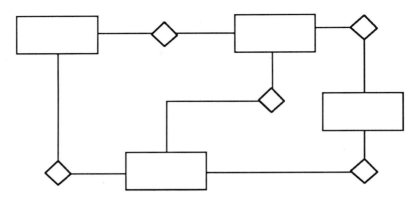

Figure 3-7 Entity-relationship diagram appearance.

are conceptual groupings of data (often called objects) to be stored in the form of physical attributes of application data. Attributes are facts that describe entities. In file design terminology, an entity is the file itself, records represent multiple occurrences of the entity, and fields represent attributes of the entity. In RDMS terminology, entities are database tables, rows in a table represent multiple occurrences of the entity, and columns in the table represent attributes of the entity. The connections between rectangles on an ERD, often shown as horizontal and vertical straight lines with diamonds on them, represent relationships between entities. Entities on an ERD have labels, and relationships are specified on the diagram as to cardinality and relationship type. Cardinality shows the number of pairings (of the mandatory type or the optional type) that one entity has with another. For rapid prototyping, the ERD will be used initially to develop the preliminary schema for the prototype database.

A relationship exists between entities when they share one or more common attributes or are associated for some reason. For example, in a Personnel application, two of the entities might be "Employee" and "Department." The employee entity might have attributes such as "Name," "Employee__ID," "Social__Security__Number," "Department__Number," and "Job__Class." The department entity might have attributes such as "Department__ID," "Department__ Name," "Supervisor," and "Staffing__Level." The logical relationship between employees and departments is that employees work in departments or departments employ employees. This relationship can be supported in the application's data storage structure by having "Department__Number" in the employee data group be the same value as "Department__ID" in the department data group in all cases where the employees are assigned to the departments.

Cardinality is the specification of which entity's point of view is taken by the application. To continue the preceding example, if an employee is always assigned to one and only one department, and the application takes the department's point of view, then this is a 1 to N relationship—for each department there are many employees. If the application took the employee's point of view, there would be a 1 to 1 relationship—for each employee there is one department. Such a relationship is stated: A department employs many employees; an employee is assigned to one department.

There are three types of relationships possible between entities: 1 to N, 1 to 1, and M to N. The letters M and N in this notation both signify "many." Therefore, M to N means many to many. The fact that two letters are used to signify "many" may be a bit confusing at first. The M indicates cardinality in an M to N relationship just as the 1 indicates cardinality in a 1 to N relationship. Figure 3-8 shows an example of each of the three types of relationships.

To understand the examples shown in Figure 3-8, some background is necessary. Suppose that a company is in the business of managing harbors. The company rents slips to ships in the harbors and hires guards to patrol the harbors. The company wishes to have a new automated harbor information management system. ERDs will be used to help design the harbor information database.

Obviously, four of the entities in the database will be harbor, ship, slip, and guard. If we take the harbor's point of view, each harbor contains many ships. Thus the harbor-ship relationship is 1 to N. The one is circled to indicate we are taking the harbor's point of view. If we had taken the ship's point of view, the relationship would be 1 to 1 if each ship has a berth at one and only one harbor. Taking the slip's point of view, each slip is rented to one and only one ship at any given point

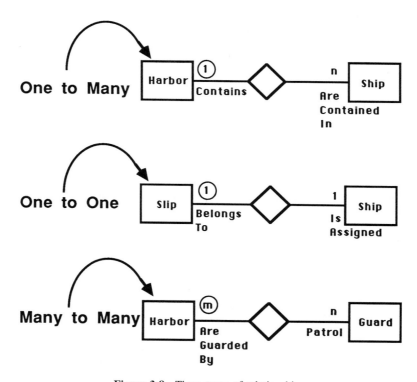

Figure 3-8   Three types of relationships.

in time. The 1 next to the slip entity is circled to indicate this cardinality in the slip-ship relationship.

The guard-harbor relationship is more complex than the other two examples. Each guard has a current assignment consisting of the harbors he or she will patrol. Corporate management has decided that security will be maximized if the same guards do not always patrol the same harbors. This policy pertains even to a single shift, so a guard will make one round of several harbors rather than several rounds of one harbor. From the harbor's point of view, several guards are always on duty at that harbor since, at any point in time, several guards will be making their rounds at any given harbor. Thus, it does not matter whether we take the harbor's or the guard's point of view—this is a many to many or M to N relationship.

ERDs aid in relational database design because they identify the critical attributes that must be present to support indicated relationships, identify problematic M to N relationships, and provide an easily understandable graphic picture of the proposed database schema. Figure 3-9 shows how the graphic representation of the harbor-ship relationship reveals the critical attributes that must be present in each of these database tables. The harbor entity must have a harbor identification—some way of uniquely identifying each harbor. Likewise, the ship entity must have a unique ship identification attribute. Moreover, if the harbor-ship relationship is to be supported, the two entities must have a common attribute. The likely candidate for a common attribute is Harbor_ID since there are fewer harbors than ships and each ship is berthed at one and only one harbor.

Many to many relationships represent a dilemma for relational database design. The RDMS does not support M to N relationships well. Take the guard-harbor relationship for instance. What critical attributes would these entities have to possess? Obviously, the guard table would have a Guard_ID attribute and the harbor table would have a Harbor_ID attribute. We could try to include either a Harbor_ID attribute in the guard table or a Guard_ID attribute in the harbor table, or both, but this would not be sufficient to support the many to many relationship. Alternatively, we could determine the maximum number of harbors a guard may be assigned to and, if that number is four, have Harbor_ID1, Harbor_ID2, Harbor_ID3, and Harbor_ID4 as attributes of the guard table.

There are problems with having multiple harbor IDs in the guard table—or, for that matter, multiple guard IDs in the harbor table. Suppose harbors come in

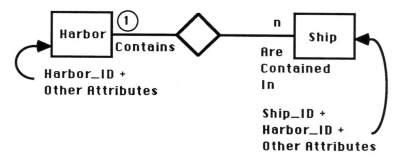

Figure 3-9   Identifying critical attributes.

different sizes. Then some guards might be assigned to two harbors, some to three, and some to four. Guards assigned to fewer than four harbors would have empty attributes in the database schema just suggested. Furthermore, management might at any time change policy and decide that five harbors is the maximum number for any guard, requiring schema revision. Multiple occurrences of a field within a data group are a structure that most hierarchical databases support well, but relational models don't. The structure is referred to as a repeating group.

Fortunately, an ERD not only identifies M to N problems—it provides a means for modeling the solution as well. The solution always involves the creation of a third "joining" entity as depicted in Figure 3-10. In Figure 3-10, the joining entity is "Assignment." Each guard has many assignments and each harbor is covered by many assignments. Two 1 to N relationships take the place of the M to N relationship.

The critical attributes of the assignment entity would be Guard__ID and Harbor__ID. For a given guard, there would be as many rows in the assignment table as the number of harbors that person was assigned to patrol. For a given harbor, there would be as many rows in the table as that harbor had guards assigned to it. In a relational database, using this schema, there would be no need to have guard IDs in the harbor table or harbor IDs in the guard table because of the capability for retrieving information based on joining multiple tables on common attributes. In developing the harbor information management system, two types of reports would be possible by joining information from the harbor, guard, and assignment tables—a report for guards on which harbors they are currently assigned to and a report for harbors on which guards are currently patrolling them. The joining entity is often referred to as an *associative* entity type.

Putting together all of the preceding information modeling analysis for the hypothetical harbor information management system, we can develop a preliminary ERD to model the harbor information database, as shown in Figure 3-11. A couple of observations about this suggested schema are that it is probably wrong, in that it will not accurately describe the schema of the final database design, and it is probably adequate for development of the initial database structure for a rapid prototype. This is why we are using an RDMS—so tables and attributes of tables can be easily added, deleted, and modified during prototype iterations.

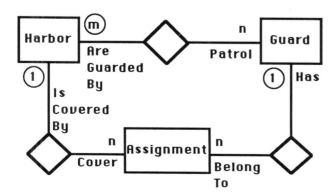

Figure 3-10 The many to many solution.

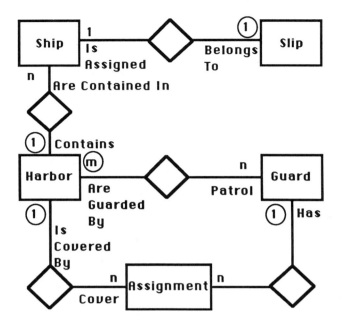

Figure 3-11 A harbor information database.

A data dictionary should be initiated at this point, even if it is manual. Information about ordinality and cardinality can be stored there rather than presented on the ERD if it becomes confusing. A data dictionary is also a good way to double check that each data store on a DFD corresponds to an object on an ERD. Some CASE tools help to automate such record-keeping. If the CASE tool contains encyclopedia capabilities, labels for processes, external objects, data stores, and data flows from the DFDs can now be captured as well as entities, relationships, and attributes from the ERDs.

Control Flow Graphs

The reader may have never heard of control flow graphs (CFGs) until now. They are not mentioned in any of the previous textbooks on structured techniques. The CFG is introduced here as useful for modeling system event paths for the initial prototype. If you are familiar with the structure charts used in structured design (see references 7 and 8), you will notice a suspicious similarity. Structure charts are a design modeling tool rather than an analysis technique. Control flow graphs could likewise be considered a design modeling tool. For that matter, so could the entity-relationship diagrams and state transition diagrams called for by Ward and Mellor as part of real-time structured analysis.[3] All of these models describe how the system is to be constructed (design) rather than what the system does (analysis). The new term, control flow graph, is introduced, not to be confusing, but to liberate the analyst-prototyper from some of the restrictions of a structure chart which are not critical to the early stages of prototyping. At this stage, we needn't bother with coupling, cohesion, or control parameter passing. Our prototyping toolkit will handle these elements for us automatically, and they can be specified later, as part of an "as-prototyped" design. During analysis, we want to get an external view of how the system will operate, not an internal view.

There are many semantic arguments among software engineers about what constitutes analysis—what the system is to do—and what constitutes design—how the system is to perform its functions. We do not wish to complicate these arguments any further, so we'll simply categorize our point of view with regard to the tools being discussed. ERDs are basically data store design tools. CFGs are basically system control structure design tools. Nevertheless, both of these models will be used as part of the rapid prototyping process referred to as "rapid analysis" because they provide two of the three dimensions of the problem space necessary before beginning to develop the prototype—an information model and a system event path model. Now, if you want to say that in prototyping we do some design before attempting any development, so be it. In evolutionary rapid prototyping, analysis, design, and development are concurrent tasks.

For a rapid prototype to be developed using the RDMS tools described recently, the CFG is used to model the menu structure of the initial prototype. Figure 3-12 shows all the possible symbols that can be used on a CFG. Boxes on a CFG represent events that will occur during execution of the system. Vectors are used as connections between CFG objects and represent control flow. A rectangle with rounded corners represents a null module event—specifically, in this scheme of things, a menu choice present only as a means for returning to a previous menu level. An oval represents a unique null module—the menu choice that will be present on only one screen and used to exit and terminate the application. All objects on a CFG, except for the vectors, have labels. The label for a system event will be used to identify either a menu or a functional module. The labels for boxes with rounded corners and ovals will be "return" and "stop," respectively.

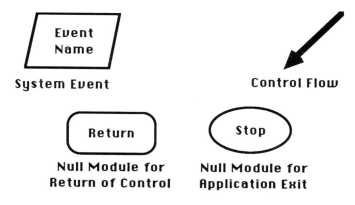

Figure 3-12 Control flow graph objects.

Since there are no previously published sets of rules and guidelines for CFGs, we will offer some at this point. First, let us consider the "magic number guideline"—7 ± 2. A minimum of five things and a maximum of nine things turn out to be a good guideline for limiting complexity in many areas of subject matter. It is a good number of data transformation processes to show on a single dataflow diagram. It is probably a good number of workers for a single supervisor to manage and a good number of assignments for an individual worker. Whenever the objective is to level things in a hierarchical fashion, violation of the 7 ± 2 guideline on the high end will create too much complexity on the level where the violation occurs—violation on the low end will create too much complexity in terms of the number of levels. CFGs are used to model a hierarchical menu structure. Therefore, a sensible guideline for limiting CFG complexity is 7 ± 2 menu choices per CFG. This guideline will have the advantage of also limiting the complexity of the application itself. The initial prototype will have neither too many menu choices on an individual menu (confusing to the user) nor too many menu levels (frustrating to the user).

A useful convention is for every CFG to depict two common types of events—a "help" function and a null control module. The help function, present at every menu level, will describe the events that will occur as the result of choices made from the current menu. This description will appear as a result of the user selecting "Help" from available menu choices. In our RDMS prototyping environment, these help screens will be created by prototypers using visual programming tools. Such screens will provide an up-front, multilevel, interactive electronic user guide. The null control modules, also present at every menu level, will be "Stop" for the highest menu level, and "Return" for all lower-level menus. Figures 3-13 and 3-14 illustrate the two possible types of CFGs.

CFGs share several conventions with structure charts. Control is always presumed to proceed in a top-down fashion, never bottom-up or sideways. Apparently dead-end modules—boxes with arriving control flows but no departing control flows—are presumed to return control to the menu they were invoked from. Each CFG must show all possible exit destinations. For the prototype, these destinations will be either a lower-level menu, a higher-level menu, or "Stop." Modules may,

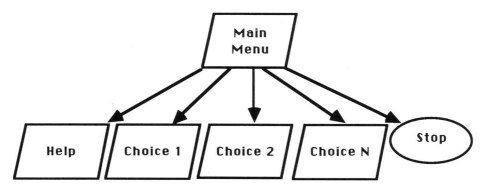

Figure 3-13   Top-level control flow graph.

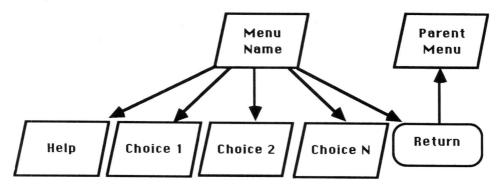

Figure 3-14 Lower-level control flow graph.

of course, be invoked by other modules rather than by menu choices—for example, the "Reports Menu" invokes a 4GL routine to perform database retrievals and calculations followed by a report writer script which reports the results.

If you are familiar with structure charts, you may be wondering how control flow graphs are different. There is much similarity. Basically, CFGs are a simplification of structure charts—a relaxation of the rules for structured design—physically oriented toward the use of RDMS tools recommended for prototyping. For example, the control flow connections on a structure chart are required to be labeled with a specification of coupling between the modules. There are two kinds of couples—data and switches. An example of a data couple is a record created by a managing module and then passed to a managed module. An example of a switch would be an end-of-file encountered by a managed module which would cause return of control to the managing module. There is no such coupling in a prototype created using the RDMS toolkit—or at least coupling would be very difficult, and very unnecessary, to specify.

Retrievals from an RDMS do not encounter an end-of-file. System event paths during prototype execution are under complete control of the user. Control always returns from a managed prototype module to a managing prototype module when the user selects a screen command indicating that he or she is finished using the managed module. In the initial prototype, modules will not create internal records to be passed to other modules—all data will be placed in and retrieved from a common database. For a final product created using evolutionary rapid prototyping techniques, these system characteristics may cease to be pervasive. Some conventional files and programs may exist after the tuning phase. Before this is allowed to happen, control flow graphs must evolve into structure charts. Such an evolution is easy to accomplish by simply adding specifications of couplings to existing control flow graphs.

Again, CFGs are introduced as a structured prototyping tool so we will not be bound by some of the more complicated rules of structure charts—not to add a new notation when we already have plenty of "standard" ones. The purpose is to portray menu choices for the user interface to a proposed prototype—a graphic picture that greatly aids the prototyper in figuring out how and when the system choices will be displayed.

In summary, CFGs provide a preliminary visual model of the proposed sequence of execution of prototype functions. Typically, a menu-driven structure is specified with a main system menu which calls subsidiary menus which, in turn, call input, data transformation, and output functions. There will always be a main menu allowing users to branch to other menus such as data entry, analysis, reports, and graphs. The submenu, reports, will then list a choice of reports the user can produce. The calling sequence of these menu screens will be hierarchical, with control always returning to the previously called menu. The appropriate level of menu nesting depends on the size and complexity of the application. There are, of course, practical limits to nesting. These limits will be discovered during rapid prototyping when the user becomes impatient with having to step through too many menus. When this happens, there is an indication that the application to be prototyped was incorrectly scoped and perhaps should be split into two or more applications.

Quality Assessment and Review Techniques

There are also structured techniques for quality assessment of the models produced using structured analysis, design, and development techniques. These techniques are just as useful and powerful in a rapid prototyping environment as they are in a conventional development setting. The following material is drawn from an existing body of literature on quality assurance, including a plan presented by the authors.[9] It covers the concept of walkthrus in depth. The walkthru discussion begins with a review of Ed Yourdon's work,[10] and then is expanded to include specific walkthru environments for the prototype project team.

Fundamentally, walkthrus are the best method yet discovered for preventing the insertion of defects in software products. Fagan reported in 1976 that, of total defects discovered during the development of a large system, 83 percent were discovered in static testing or walkthru while only 17 percent were discovered by dynamic machine testing.[11] DeMarco, on the other hand, reported that the 1978 to 1980 Yourdon Project Survey indicated that the more effort put into machine testing, the poorer the quality of the resulting product, thus deducing that machine testing is too late an effort to correct problems created earlier in the life cycle.[2] Walkthrus provide a means for detecting and removing defects from day one.

A major difference between rapid prototyping walkthru teams and conventional walkthru teams is that the former are very small. This is because effective rapid prototyping teams are very small. Figure 3-15 illustrates a typical rapid prototyping walkthru team. Only the key roles of presenter, reviewer, and coordinator need be represented. The presenter presents the product, the reviewers review the product, and the coordinator enforces walkthru guidelines. In a quality assurance program implemented at Los Alamos National Laboratory, it was found that the most critical role in a walkthru was that of coordinator. Walkthrus can be an enormous waste of time if not conducted properly. An effective coordinator prevents this from hap-

Coordinator

Reviewers   Presenter

Figure 3-15 The structured walkthru.

pening by enforcing sensible guidelines for walkthru productivity. These guidelines
are what provide structure to a structured walkthru. The following are some critical
guidelines for walkthrus:

- The presenter, coordinator, and reviewers must all be peers
- The product must be small enough to be completely reviewed in one hour oɪ
  less
- The product must be available for study by the reviewers at least 24 hours
  before the walkthru
- No item is to be discussed for more than a few minutes
- Discussion items are to be recorded and distributed to the team after the
  walkthru
- A consensus is to be reached by the team during the walkthru as to the intended
  disposition of discussion items

The authors have seen all of these guidelines flagrantly violated during events
erroneously referred to as structured walkthrus. Picture a large conference room
containing 50 people, one of whom is the presenter, with most of the rest consisting
of management on the development and customer staff. No one but the presenter has
seen anything of the product prior to this review. No rules of conduct are enforced.
The presenter gives a viewgraph presentation with 40 transparencies which continues
from 8:00 A.M. to 6:00 P.M. with a 30-minute break for lunch. The reason for this
extended schedule is that the 49 reviewers all have very sharp questions to ask on
each viewgraph. The presenter feels the need to provide an elaborate oral defense in
response to each question because there are so many managers in the room. No one

is formally recording discussion items or their intended dispositions, so the results of the day are inconclusive. This scenario is hardly exaggerated beyond what is often the common practice. What did this review accomplish other than to spend 500 person-hours of effort? One actual walkthru for a new hospital system was an all-day session where 90 on-line screens were reviewed and approved. Could any of the screens have received proper attention? Was the nintieth one reviewed as carefully as the first?

If anyone in a walkthru has any input to the performance evaluation of the presenter, the walkthru turns from a technical review to a management review. Management reviews are useful for reporting progress, but not for finding defects. Who wants to have their defects aired in front of their management? If the presenter has any input into the performance evaluation of anyone else in the walkthru, that person's opinions may be buried by bullying and intimidation.

The way to make walkthrus an effective means of discovering defects rather than an agonizing and frustrating waste of time is to have a mindless set of rules that can be effortlessly enforced by the coordinator. This is not precognizant behavior, but rather a common knowledge of some general facts. The purpose of a walkthru is to find defects, not to devise solutions or to debate whether or not something is a defect. The presenter and reviewers will either agree or disagree as to whether an item under discussion is a defect. It is certainly possible to ascertain in a few minutes what the issue is and whether or not there is unanimous agreement.

Figure 3-16 suggests that all walkthru discussion items can be classified as one of four things. If the discussion of an item continues for more that three or four minutes, the coordinator should ask a reviewer if the item is a defect. This reviewer may state at that time that a suggestion is being offered but there is no intent to identify a defect. If on the other hand the reviewer classifies the item as a defect, the coordinator will ask the presenter and the other reviewers to agree or

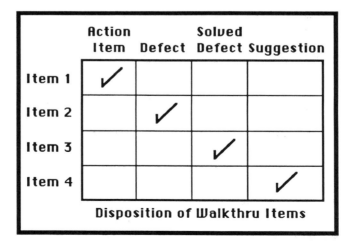

Figure 3-16 How to handle walkthru action items.

disagree. If there is agreement, the coordinator will record the item as a defect—unless the item is trivial enough that the presenter can suggest an easy fix to which the reviewers are agreeable. If there is not agreement, the item will be recorded as an action item.

An action item requires another walkthru. The parties at issue will be asked to research the issue before the next walkthru, at which time they will be expected to present evidence supporting their point of view. Such evidence could include extracts from the literature on structured techniques clarifying certain guidelines which pertain to the issue, a statement from management, or a statement from the user. Since such research represents extra work, the tendency, after a little experience, will be for only very serious issues to become action items. At any rate, extended arguments will not occur during the one-hour walkthru.

Defects without solutions (it is proper not to attempt devising solutions to complex problems during the one-hour walkthru) require another walkthru to review the changes. Since defects with solutions must include unanimously agreed-upon changes, they do not require another walkthru. Suggestions also do not require an additional walkthru—they only require polite consideration on the part of the developers. When a reviewer senses that the presenter is not in agreement with a criticism and also feels that the issue is really not all that critical, the tendency will be to back off from a possible action item by answering the coordinator's question, "Is that a defect?" with, "No, it's only a suggestion that I would have done this differently." Walkthrus are an iterative process that continues until it fails. The last walkthru on a product will find no defects or action items.

The guidelines just presented are critical for a rapid prototyping environment. Turnaround times during the very short phases of rapid analysis and prototype development are so tight that any walkthrus must be timesaving rather than time-consuming. Walkthrus can help prevent developers from prototyping the wrong things or from presenting prototype demonstrations containing obvious defects. They must not be allowed to degenerate into formal management reviews, ego-involved debates, or bull sessions.

The most difficult thing about incorporating walkthrus into a quality assurance program is to determine a sensible policy for what types of products require a walkthru. Do you require a walkthru for a prototype? What would you be reviewing in the case of modules generated with visual programming? If prototypes are to be reviewed by walkthru teams, what about prototype revisions? Then there is the question of intentionally incomplete rapid analysis specifications. The easy way out of all these thorny questions is to require that all projects produce a project plan before anything else, then require that all project plans specify a list of deliverables together with a specification of which products will require walkthru team approval. The advantage of this approach is that it allows quality assurance policy to be tailored for individual projects. Most software organizations have such a diverse range of types of projects that rigid policies are typically doomed to failure.

Walkthrus must not be allowed to drain the "rapid" from prototyping. Walkthrus can speed up rather than slow down the development process. They must last no more than one hour apiece, and occur frequently—at least once a week.

INCORPORATING FORMAL SPECIFICATION METHODOLOGIES

For years, methodologies have traditionally been forced into some sort of step-by-step process, and many attempts have been made to graph the process elements. There have been a few that have lived long lives. Initially, the process was viewed as being in lockstep, where one phase drew to completion before the next phase began. The process assumed the structure of a flow chart as shown in Figure 3-17.

At some point, most developers realized that iterations in the form of validation and feedback between steps would be wise. The authors W. W. Royce in 1970 and Barry Boehm in 1976 presented a model, similar to Figure 3-18 that was found useful by the community.[12]

The model just referred to subsequently lasted at least ten years as a paradigm for development. It need not be belabored here, since some form of the conventional waterfall software development life cycle model appears in most software engineering, analysis, and programming textbooks. The reason its history is so important is twofold: It served as the best paradigm, given the tools available for development, and many of today's professionals grew up with it. This mental model is deeply ingrained in our culture and we must acknowledge the mind-set we are breaking away from. There are useful concepts in the model which will and should remain

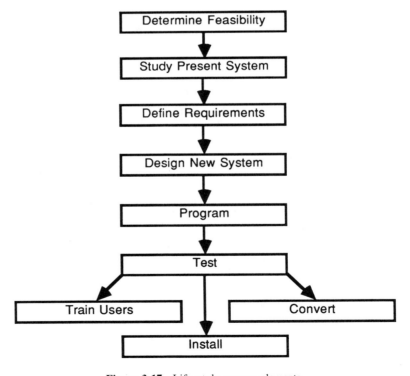

Figure 3-17 Life cycle process elements.

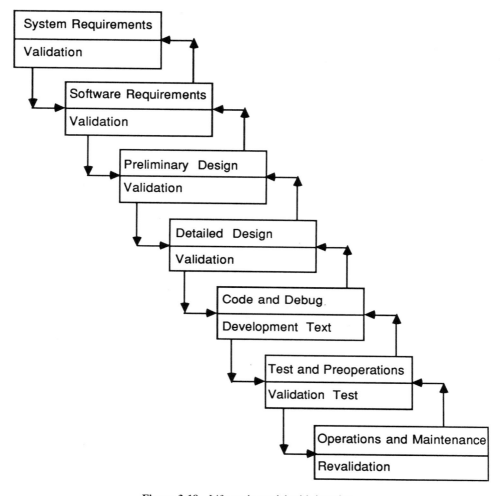

Figure 3-18   Life cycle model with iteration.

as integral elements of future models. Indeed, the popular software folklorist, Bob Glass, pointed out that the argument over whether or not the prototyping activity will replace the conventional development cycle ("prototyping versus specifying") appears more of a pleasant academic debate than a serious problem.[13] The old and the new can be complementary. As discussed in Chapter 4, there are some new activities and some of the timings will be altered, but the basic goals and objectives of system development are not changing. More activities taking place concurrently and the flexibility of system exercise allowed with modern software tools constitutes the bulk of the new twist.

In 1983, Dearnley and Mayhew proposed an alternative to the linear approach, not as a radically different one, but as an addition or graphical "bump-out" to the systems life cycle with which we have become comfortable. Figures 3-19 and 3-20

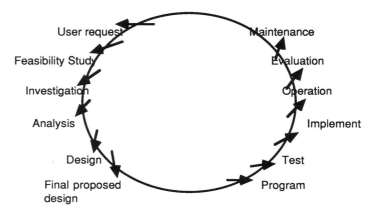

Figure 3-19   Old model (Dearnley/Mayhew).

are adaptations of their comparison of the new with the old. Figure 3-20 is yet another version of the traditional model. Figure 3-20 suggests that, following investigation, one consider prototyping as an alternative to systems development. If one decides it has a worthwhile cost-benefit ratio then, when the prototyping cycle is entered, it may be repeated one or many times. The authors of this approach offer the following explanation, paraphrased: Prototyping is followed by analysis if the prototype is of communications rather than technical value (user requirements are discovered and clarified but more analysis is needed); prototyping is followed by design if it incorporates most of the user requirements; prototyping is followed by the final proposed design if it is highly refined and both internal and external design are acceptable.[14]

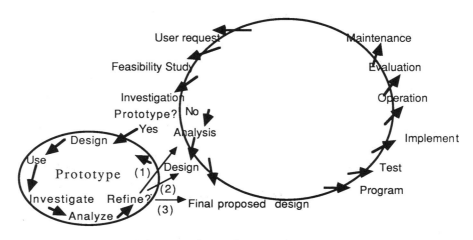

Figure 3-20   New model (Dearnley/Mayhew).

According to Kenneth Lantz in his book, *The Prototyping Methodology*, the following are the basic steps:[15]

- *The establishment of a development project*
- *The study of the present system*
- *The definition of the prototype*
- *The building of the prototype*
- *The exercise of the prototype*
- *The implementation of the prototype which becomes the system*

In this model, the first two phases mirror those of traditional methodologies. *The establishment of the project*, be it on-line or batch, a new development or one based on a software package, begins with a feasibility determination. The cost-benefit analysis used to determine feasibility is initiated with a service request from a user to the software developing organization. Service request forms are a typical vehicle used within organizations to communicate user's needs.[16] Such forms identify the user-requester and describe what is required and why the request is being made. They provide the opportunity for the software organization (or Information Systems Department) to respond with a priority and a time and cost estimate. There is nothing about service request initiation, review, or response during prototyping that diverges from those activities within any other methodology. Pick a service request type of procedure out of your favorite methodology and do not worry about its effect on the prototype. Once the service request has been approved and its feasibility established, a project plan should be drawn up. Details of such a plan are discussed in Chapter 5 where a typical service request is presented.

Certainly, the study of the present system, automated or manual, is basically to learn what functions the system performs, what information it maintains, and how it communicates with other systems. Schematic diagrams, depicting information flow, volumes, and time in chart form, or the document description worksheets, containing detailed information on the distribution, filing, processing, and purpose of every document pertaining to the present system, are certainly helpful in developing the initial prototype. Caution should be used, however, in spending too much time gathering such information. The project may suffer "analysis paralysis," which is most certainly anathema to any prototyping effort.

The Yourdon methodology, which has long advocated fully detailed DFDs on the current physical and current logical system before beginning work on the future logical and physical models, has been updated to reduce the attention to the current models. Creating the current physical model is now viewed as an activity that takes too long, thereby frustrating users, and produces too little useful information, thereby frustrating developers.

REFERENCES

1. Derived from several requests for quotations sent to vendors from Los Alamos National Laboratory, Donald F. Shafer, primary author.

2. Tom DeMarco, *Controlling Software Projects*, New York: Yourdon Press, 1982.

3. Paul Ward and Steve Mellor, *Structured Development of Real-Time Systems*, New York: Yourdon Press, 1985.

4. Tom DeMarco, *Structured Analysis and System Specification*, New York: Yourdon Press, 1978.

5. Stephen M. McMenamin and John F. Palmer, *Essential Systems Analysis*, New York: Yourdon Press, 1984.

6. M. Flavin, *Fundamental Concepts of Information Modeling*, New York: Yourdon Press, 1981.

7. Edward Yourdon, and Larry L. Constantine, *Structured Design: Fundamentals of a Discipline of Computer Program and Systems Design*, New York: Yourdon Press, 1979.

8. Meilir Page-Jones, *The Practical Guide to Structured Systems Design*, New York: Yourdon Press, 1980.

9. John Connell, and Linda Brice, "Practical Quality Assurance," *Datamation*, 31(5), 1985, 106–114.

10. Edward Yourdon, *Structured Walkthroughs*, New York: Yourdon Press, 1978.

11. M. Fagan, "Design and Code Inspections to Reduce Errors in Program Development," *IBM Systems Journal* 15, no. 3, 1976, 182–207.

12. B. W. Boehm, "Software Engineering," *IEEE Transactions on Computers*, C-25(12), 1976, 1226–1241.

13. Robert L. Glass, "Some Thoughts on Prototyping," *System Development*, 5(8), 1985, 7–8.

14. P. A. Dearnley, and P. J. Mayhew, "In Favour of System Prototypes and their Integration into the Systems Development Cycle," *The Computer Journal*, 26(1), 1983, 36–42.

15. Kenneth S. Lantz, *The Prototyping Methodology*, Englewood Cliffs, NJ: Prentice Hall, 1986.

16. John Connell and Linda Shafer, *The Professional User's Guide to Acquiring Software*, New York: Van Nostrand Reinhold, 1987.

4

Evolutionary Rapid Prototyping versus the Traditional Software Development Life Cycle

As pointed out in Chapter 3, rapid prototyping is not antithetical to the traditional life cycle approach. The traditional approach is sequential with occasional feedback loops, while the evolutionary rapid prototyping approach is essentially iterative. The life cycle approach defines sharply separate development phases, while prototyping mixes analysis, design, development, and testing in a much more concurrent fashion. It would be very unfortunate if rapid prototyping were totally incompatible with the traditional life cycle approach. Customers, managers, auditors, methodologies, and internal standards often demand the application of a classical life cycle model to all new software development projects. Such applications of a standard life cycle model are valuable in establishing familiar milestones and deliverables for all project schedules and, of course, managing familiar phenomena involves less risk than managing new approaches.

Fortunately, rapid prototyping is not incompatible with the traditional life cycle. This chapter describes how rapid prototyping augments rather than replaces it. To understand how this can be, you must ask yourself what is good and what is bad, what is essential and what is superficial about the old life cycle model. Familiar milestones and deliverables are essential and often contractually required. On the other hand, sharply defined sequential development phases are superficial—they are based on an assumption of implementation in a third-generation programming language where preparation of complete detailed analysis and design specifications was necessary before beginning to write programs. Now, with the ability to use modern prototyping tools such as those described in Chapter 3, we can develop working models that are at least as flexible as paper analysis and design specifications. Thus we have the possibility of a new approach that is more concurrent and iterative than sequential. A high-level, intentionally incomplete job of analysis and design can be performed as the basis upon which to quickly build a working model for interactive experimentation and testing. As discoveries are made from the experiments, the specifications and the working model are evolved and upgraded together. This approach produces systems more functionally acceptable to the user and specifications more accurate than the traditional approach.

All this can be accomplished without ignoring or intentionally deleting the milestones and deliverables typically mandated by a methodology or life cycle model. Rapid prototyping produces more milestones and deliverables, not fewer. Deliverable specifications and software will be more correct. Several of the traditional milestone dates will be less threatening. To clearly explain how this is so, an understanding must be reached with the reader of what those "traditional" milestones and deliverables are. This is not easy, as different methodologies (for example, MIL-STD versus SDM-Structured™) and environments (for example, government contracting versus banking) use different sets of terminology to describe the same things. Thus, semantics may get in the way of a complete understanding.

To avoid confusion, let us begin by defining a very simple and very general traditional life cycle model based on those presented in Chapter 3 and add some equally common milestones. The hope is that, while this model will not conform specifically to anyone's methodology, it will be familiar and understandable no matter whose methodology you are accustomed to using. Figure 4-1 depicts a generic life cycle model where sharply defined development phases are shown as paths the project must follow. The gates shown represent points in time when the project team must be able to prove they are done with the current phase and are ready to move on to the next.

The gates in Figure 4-1 may be formal reviews or may simply represent the acquisition of a key user's signature on a document. The passing of the requirements gate, for instance, may be heralded by a "system requirements review" or may be achieved by obtaining the chief user's signature testifying approval of a "system requirements definition." In either case, the project team is claiming that they know all the user's requirements and necessary derived requirements and that they have demonstrated such understanding to the complete satisfaction of the user.

Once a project team has "proved" they are done analyzing system requirements, they may begin to develop a detailed system design. The accomplishment of this task is demonstrated by the existence of a preliminary design concept—a "build-to" specification of the system architecture. Once the "build-to" design gate is passed, the project team may begin to write code to the detailed specifications. Coding typically involves discoveries that parts of the original design will not work and that certain alterations result in a better design. The design may, in fact, go through several revisions. When a final, or "as-built," design is ready for publication, it can only be because members of the project team believe they are finished writing all code and are ready to begin testing. During the test phase, programs are tested against a test plan. When all programs pass the specified tests, the test acceptance gate can be passed by a presentation of test results. The integration phase in-

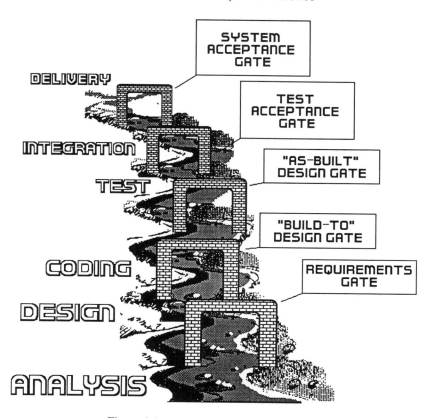

Figure 4-1   Traditional life cycle milestones.

volves placement of the new system into the environment in which it is intended to operate and testing it for operational correctness. Delivery occurs when the customer accepts all the operational characteristics of the new system—the project is finished.

MODIFICATIONS REQUIRED TO TRADITIONAL LIFE CYCLE MILESTONES

Managers and users are so accustomed to thinking of software development in terms of some variation of the model presented in Figure 4-1 that it may be difficult for them to accept any drastic alterations to this model. Fortunately, this will not be necessary. Even though the evolutionary rapid prototyping process is iterative and tasks are not sharply separable, milestone events will still occur at specific points in time. The important questions then are, "Do rapid prototyping milestones occur in a different sequence?" and "Do rapid prototyping milestones signify different types of events?'' Surprisingly, a project plan can and should be prepared showing that the rapid prototyping project will have almost the same milestones, occurring in the same sequence, as the traditional project.

There are only a few required modifications. Rapid prototyping milestones will occur at relatively different points in time. For instance, there may still be an analysis phase and a design phase but, since these phases will encompass different types of activities, they may consume a different amount of time compared to a traditional approach. The following are some suggested milestones for a rapid prototyping project with a description of what each signifies.

The Preliminary Requirements Gate

The first suggested gate associated with rapid prototyping milestones is one that does not exist in a traditional project. Actually, either a preliminary requirements review or document, or both, is not a necessity but rather a compensation. The final requirements gate on a rapid prototyping project will occur after the user has approved the current functionality of the working prototype model, and detailed requirements specifications are complete. This means that the project team must develop and refine the functions of a working model in addition to performing the usual tasks of defining requirements and providing documentation. In most cases the result will be that the final requirements milestone will be arrived at somewhat later than on a traditional project. Since delayed milestones make most managers nervous, the solution is to insert a new and very early milestone into the life cycle. The two phases of rapid analysis and prototyping replace the former one phase of analysis.

Reflecting the new phase in a new milestone is called the *preliminary requirements gate*. It provides an opportunity to establish an understanding between users and developers as to just what appropriate life cycle milestones and deliverable products will be for this project. A project plan and a preliminary requirements document are approved for passage through the gate. At this point, the project plan can serve as an educational tool to explain the new and different aspects of rapid prototyping milestones and deliverables to managers and users unfamiliar with the concepts. Rapid analysis documents are not required to represent system completeness but rather an adequate blueprint for prototyping. In reviewing rapid analysis documents the question is not, ''Do you agree that these are the true and complete system requirements?'' but rather, ''Do you feel it would be useful to experiment with a prototype based on these preliminary specifications?''

Detailed descriptions of the contents of a rapid prototyping project plan and rapid analysis documents are deferred to Chapter 5. For now, assume that the preparation of these deliverables is not an arduous task. For medium-sized projects, an adequate plan and preliminary analysis can be prepared with about 80 hours of effort. For no project should these tasks require more than 200 hours. You may spend more time here if you wish, but the returns may not be worth it. These documents are appropriately brief, incomplete, modifiable, and extensible—similar to the initial prototype.

The Final Requirements Gate

It may be difficult for the uninitiated to understand why the final requirements gate will occur somewhat later on a rapid prototyping project. After all, with evolutionary rapid prototyping, detailed functional requirements are derived from the user-approved prototype. This would seem to imply much less revisionary thrashing during the analysis phase. The slogan of evolutionary prototyping is, "Don't specify detailed functional requirements until you're sure what they are!" The development and refinement of a working model, while it may be rapid, is never free. Revisionary thrashing is, in a sense, simply diverted from paper models to working models. Users will still change their minds about what they want and analyst-prototypers will still make mistakes that require corrections.

The benefit of prototyping to the analysis phase is the development of requirements specifications that are more meaningful to users and will serve as a more accurate baseline for the following development phases. When we come to the final requirements gate at the end of the prototyping phase, two requirements specifications will exist: a dynamic model approved by the user following interactive exercising; and the static paper documentation of the architecture and functionality of the dynamic model. Figure 4-2 illustrates how these two specifications may evolve together during prototype iteration to form the final requirements spec-

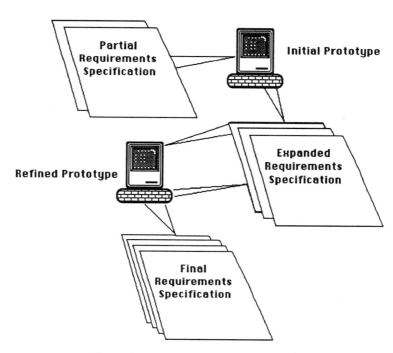

Figure 4-2 Concurrent specification evolution.

ification. Partial requirements specifications are the basis for development of the initial prototype. Demonstrations of the initial prototype to users will result in discovery of inadequacies in both the prototype and the specifications. Expanded requirements specifications can then be prepared as the basis for modifying and refining the original prototype. Demonstrations of the refined prototype will result in discovery of still more inadequacies. The iterative cycle of refining both the paper specifications and the dynamic working model ends when the user approves the functionality of the current version of the refined prototype. At this point, the paper requirements specifications will be accurate and can be published.

A final requirements gate for a rapid prototyping project will occur after user approval of the functionality of a prototype version. The detailed system requirements specifications, based on the working prototype, become baseline documentation which will be used in remaining development phases to evolve the prototype into a deliverable product. Similar to the traditional approach, the final requirements gate establishes only that the user is satisfied with proposed functionality as demonstrated by the prototype—satisfaction with system performance is not required at this point.

The "As-Prototyped" Design Gate

A different name has been applied to this milestone, but it is not really a new gate. It has the same significance as the "build-to" design gate on a traditional project—a detailed design concept exists to serve as the basis for coding. The name "as-prototyped design" has been used to emphasize that the detailed design at this point is documentation of an existing working model rather than a complete blueprint for all new development. Because the design can be derived from the user-approved prototype rather than formulated from scratch using baseline requirements specifications, this phase of a rapid prototyping project will take much less time than the design phase of a traditional project. The prototype serves as the classically missing bridge between analysis and design.

It must not be inferred that detailed design documentation is an unimportant activity on a rapid prototyping project. All such a project has at the end of the prototyping phase is a functionally approved model of the system to be delivered—not a deliverable product. To evolve the prototype into a deliverable product will usually require many traditional development activities requiring a detailed structured design as a baseline blueprint. An appropriate review occurring at the as-prototyped design gate would establish that the user-approved version of the prototype has been thoroughly documented and might identify functions that will probably require performance tuning during the following development phase.

The "As-Tuned" Design Gate

When and only when a prototype has been stress tested and performance tuned to satisfy user response time requirements, a version of the system exists that can be considered suitable for delivery as a final product. "Performance tuning" replaces the extended coding phase to which we are accustomed. The elapsed time between the as-prototyped design gate and the as-tuned design gate will be less than traditional coding time by the extent to which original functionally approved prototype modules can be incorporated into the final product. Evolutionary prototyping sometimes involves throwing away a few of the prototype modules and replacing them with conventionally developed programs, or even changing the database management system from the relational prototype to one better suited for the application (for example, to a text management system if the product is for litigation support). It is during the tuning phase that this activity occurs if stress testing the prototype reveals performance deficiencies that cannot be overcome some other way. Rarely will the entire prototype have to be replaced with other than fourth-generation language programs. Thus, the tuning phase of a rapid prototyping project is usually shorter than the coding phase of a traditional project.

Just as the traditional coding phase will reveal required changes to the original "build-to" design, resulting in an "as-built" design, the tuning phase of a rapid prototyping project will reveal required changes to the as-prototyped design, resulting in an as-tuned design. This design concept represents the final, detailed, internal system design. Its specification becomes the documentation which will be used to maintain the software after it is delivered and placed into operation. A final design review may be held at the as-tuned design gate, demonstrating that system stress testing and tuning have been completed, and seeking approval of the final system design documentation. The as-tuned design milestone occurs after the user has approved the current performance characteristics of the prototype. Only those functions which have been modified during tuning will require changes to system design documents. This gate establishes that the finished product has been thoroughly documented for system maintenance purposes, and that system performance requirements have been satisfied.

The Test Acceptance Gate

Traditionally, testing occurs when a fully designed and coded system is functioning (compiles with zero errors). A test plan is prepared which attempts to devise a set of exercises for the system to perform to verify that the functionality provided satisfies user requirements accurately, consistently, and efficiently. Typically, this is not entirely the case and inadequate time has been allotted to testing due to faulty estimating methods, so the project now enters a "panic-and-rework" mode. As was pointed out in Chapter 2, most of the effort consumed in the traditional testing phase consists of the removal of errors inserted during the analysis, design, and coding phases.

In addition to error removal, the testing phase often presents the first opportunity in the conventional life cycle for users to view a functioning system. If users are unhappily surprised by the functionality of the existing system (the usual case), and are politically successful in arguing for changes to basic system functionality (as they often are), there will be even more panic-and-rework activity. If developers are stronger politically, they may be successful in arguing that users have signed off on requirements specifications and must now accept existing system functionality until after delivery, at which time functional modifications can be made as a perfective maintenance activity. In either case it's pay now or pay later—the functionality is wrong and the system will have to be modified to be useful.

With rapid prototyping, all of this is taken care of much earlier in the life cycle. Users see a functioning model of the system at the very beginning of the project. The level of confidence in system functional correctness is very high after user approval of the refined working model at the end of the prototyping phase. A "test bed" of user-familiar data has been used and experimented with interactively throughout the project. The test phase of a rapid prototyping project involves little more than putting the system through a final set of exercises, usually with volumes of data large enough to represent the flow of the actual system. At this point, developers are confident that the tests will stand a very good chance of completing satisfactorily. A test results review then becomes little more than a formality, necessary only to establish either management or auditor acceptance, or both, of the about-to-be-delivered final product.

The System Acceptance Gate

In the classical life cycle, system integration consists of combining individually tested modules into one whole system and then integrating that system into the target production environment. In the rapid prototyping life cycle, all modules have been part of the total system and demonstrated as such from the time they were first created. Thus this gate will not represent as much of a problem as it does in a conventional project. The importance of this gate to evolutionary rapid prototyping is that it is the last chance to assure that the project plan was followed and that the product delivered is a quality production system, not a prototype.

A Rapid Prototyping Life Cycle Model

Since the same milestone events occur on a rapid prototyping project as on a traditional project and since they will occur at specific points in time, a sequential life cycle model can be derived for evolutionary rapid prototyping. Figure 4-3 depicts such a model. The significant differences between the model shown in Figure 4-3 and the traditional model shown in Figure 4-1 are as follows:

- The path from beginning to end is shorter
- The spaces between gates are smaller
- The rapid analysis and prototyping phases replace the analysis phase
- There is one additional milestone—the preliminary requirements gate

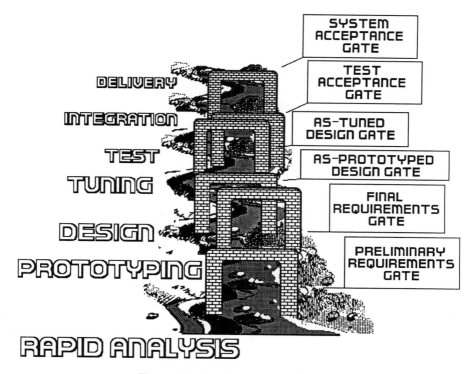

DELIVERY

INTEGRATION

TEST

TUNING

DESIGN

PROTOTYPING

SYSTEM ACCEPTANCE GATE

TEST ACCEPTANCE GATE

AS-TUNED DESIGN GATE

AS-PROTOTYPED DESIGN GATE

FINAL REQUIREMENTS GATE

PRELIMINARY REQUIREMENTS GATE

RAPID ANALYSIS

Figure 4-3   Rapid prototyping milestones.

- Detailed functional requirements are not finalized until they have been validated by a user-approved working model
- A tuning phase replaces the traditional coding phase

MODIFICATIONS REQUIRED TO LIFE CYCLE PRODUCTS

Deliverable life cycle products are those items produced as a result of a contract, formal or informal, between users and developers. There are always two types of products: the software itself and the documentation describing the software. Controlling the content and quality of software documentation is very important to both developers and users because, for most projects, the production of such documents comprises the majority of development effort and expense. As with milestones, the numbers, names, and contents of deliverable documents will vary according to the methodology used and the operating environment. Therefore we have again attempted to reach with readers a common understanding of terms by offering a generic model of traditional life cycle products in Figure 4-4. Not every conventional project produces all of the documents shown; this figure describes a rather comprehensive set. The

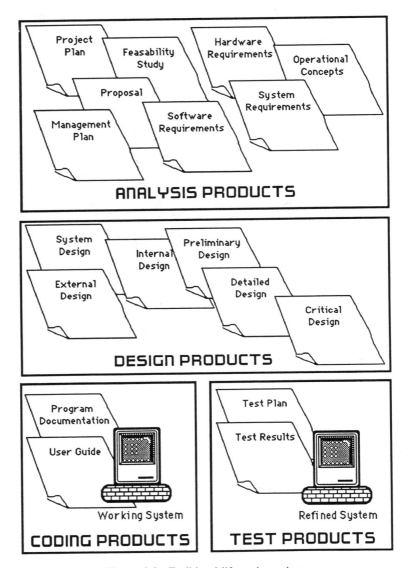

Figure 4-4 Traditional life cycle products.

deliverables in Figure 4-4 are categorized as being a result of either analysis, design, coding, or test activities. Another way to classify deliverables would be as planning documents, requirements documents, design documents, technical documentation, user documentation, test documents, and actual software. Rapid prototyping will produce all these classes of products as well as some possible additions as illustrated in Figure 4-5.

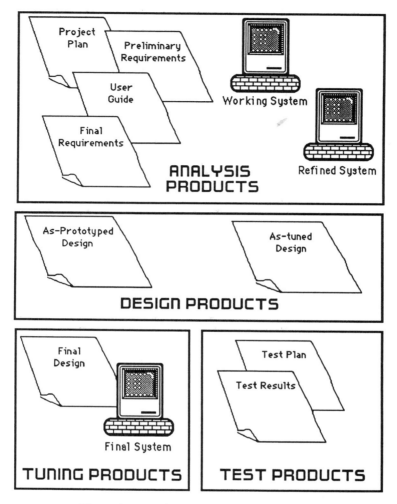

Figure 4-5 Rapid prototyping life cycle products.

Proposals and Feasibility Studies

Often a preliminary system justification or contract proposal must be prepared and accepted before a new development project will be approved. Such documents represent an excellent opportunity to sell the economic and quality improvement benefits of rapid prototyping. As the approach gains more widespread acceptance, prototyping requirements are now included in the requests for proposals issued by many government agencies. The proposal then becomes an opportunity to explain in detail the evolutionary rapid prototyping approach. Given an early draft of customer requirements, it is often possible to prepare a preliminary prototype demonstration as a preproposal activity in order to dynamically demonstrate the advantages of prototyping. In environments where MIS software is developed and maintained in-house, a pilot prototype may be developed to advocate the development of unrequested systems or system rewrites.

The Project Plan

A project plan is an agreement between users and developers which states how, when, and by whom each step of the development process will be conducted. All project deliverables are itemized. For some traditional projects, a plan is prepared; for others, it is not. Some formal development methodologies require the preparation of a project plan; others do not. Because what, how, when, and by whom will all be different from normal for a rapid prototyping project, a written customer-approved plan is essential to the success of this approach.

The problem with formal development methodologies is that they tend to get out of date and preclude the use of new technology and better approaches. Some methodologies in current use pay lip service to prototyping, but few describe an approach that is recognizable as evolutionary rapid prototyping. Prototyping or not, a project plan provides a mechanism for tailoring methodologies to specific projects, and for allowing the use of new approaches. If such a document is subjected to an effective technical peer review (a structured walkthru), some assurance can be had that tools and techniques planned for development use are appropriate to the job at hand.

The plan, the very first product of a new project, need not be verbose—one to four pages are usually sufficient to specify which standards apply to which phases. Specific elements of a project plan include project justification, goals, scope of work, development tools, user responsibilities, deliverables, and a tentative schedule of activities with associated costs. Chapter 5 describes each of these elements in detail. The project plan must be a living document that will evolve along with the actual system, requiring thorough effective review with a strong management commitment in order to succeed.

The Preliminary Requirements Document

A preliminary requirements document specifies the functionality, stored information, and control flow of the initial prototype. Useful tools for specifying these aspects are dataflow diagrams, entity-relationship diagrams, and control flow graphs as described in Chapter 3. What a preliminary requirements document does not do is attempt to specify ultimate system requirements in any great detail. This is where traditional analysts are often separated from experienced prototypers. The traditional analyst may agonize forever over a futile attempt to get the paper models right before proceeding to the next task. The ace prototyper realizes that paper specifications can never be as conclusive as a working model and quickly publishes a preliminary requirements document to be used solely as a blueprint from which to create the initial prototype. Both the document and the working model are intentionally incomplete in the first version.

The goal is to get something in front of the user for interactive experimentation as soon as possible after initial user interviews. The initial prototype must provide an interesting and thought-provoking basis for experimentation rather than a good target for possible delivery as a final product. A worthwhile initial prototype for most applications can be completely demonstrated and exercised in about one hour. The models necessary for a developer to organize his or her thoughts about how to create such a prototype can be effectively presented in a document of only five or six pages.

The Initial Prototype

Although it is necessary to make a firm distinction between a prototype and a final software product, the initial prototype can and should be considered a project deliverable. It represents the creation of a software laboratory into which users will be invited to partake in experiments. As such it represents the second of additional products that are not delivered using a traditional development approach. It is useful to specify in the project plan that such a deliverable will be forthcoming, along with the point in time when it will be delivered, as this clarifies the distinction between a prototype and the final product. Based on the preliminary requirements document, the initial prototype will have the functionality specified by the dataflow diagrams, the database structure specified by the entity-relationship diagrams, and the system event paths specified by the control flow graphs.

Requirements Specifications

Rapid prototyping can be used to develop requirements specifications of a format identical to that produced by a traditional approach. It does not matter whose methodology or which analysis techniques are being used. Chapter 3 recommended use of Yourdon-DeMarco structured analysis and design tools because they seem compatible with the evolutionary rapid prototyping approach. In prototyping, however, the critical requirements specification is the working model, not the paper specification. Final requirements specifications must accurately document the user-approved prototype. Since paper specifications are fundamentally prototype documentation at the final requirements gate, the format used to produce them becomes unimportant. If your favorite techniques are other than DFD's, ERD's, and CFG's, don't worry. Warnier–Orr charts, process hierarchy diagrams, logical data structures, and associative data models, to name a few, can also easily accommodate the rapid analysis stage of prototyping. And if you have a CASE tool that aids graphical design, by all means, use it. The issue of effectively communicating the concepts portrayed by paper models to users for acceptance of proposed detailed functional requirements is no longer critical.

The fact that customer acceptance of paper requirements specifications is no longer critical is a very positive development. Prototyping removes the "mail order catalog" aspect from software acquisition and provides users with a dynamic, "What you see is what you are going to get" requirements specification. Paper requirements specifications have traditionally been about 50 percent correct. Often when software is delivered, there are significant differences between the system documentation and the actual software. If evolutionary prototyping is used as opposed to throwaway prototyping, there is some guarantee that the delivered software will be functionally identical to the user-approved dynamic requirements specification represented by the prototype.

Despite the superiority of dynamic requirements specifications, planning to skimp on the development and publication of detailed paper requirements specifications would be a mistake. Structured analysis techniques still have much value as developers' tools. Dataflow diagrams, entity-relationship diagrams, and control flow graphs help prototypers to collect their thoughts about what the current version of the prototype does and where and how needed changes should be made. If these documents or similar documents are kept faithfully current with the prototype, they will assist prototypers in understanding the detailed internals of elaborate, refined working models by using partitioning as a device to manage complexity. Such models help to control thrashing during prototype iteration by providing baseline documentation of previous versions. That is, it is much less expensive to retain 13 versions of the paper models than 13 copies of a machine-executable prototype.

There are many automated aids for creating and maintaining DFDs, CFGs, and ERDs. The large prototyping project would do well to investigate the purchase of these aids as part of contract negotiation. Chapter 10 lists some CASE tools such as Information Engineering Workbench™, Excelerator™, and Teamwork™ which help with productivity in these areas. Newer CASE tools known as Integrated Project Support Environments (IPSE) are beginning to include all software development activities, from project planning through implementation. Information Engineering Facility™ (IEF™) from Texas Instruments is a tool that almost completely supports the Information Engineering Methodology (IEM) from James Martin Associates. IEF also supports prototyping although it does not use the same set of analysis techniques and tools as presented here.

When paper requirements specifications are published at the final requirements gate, they must detail the functional requirements of the system to be delivered. Such requirements are derived from demonstrations of an evolving prototype. But, of course, users discover additionally required functionality and developers discover mistaken assumptions made about desirable functionality. The best way for prototypers to deal with such discoveries is to immediately return to current versions of the paper specifications to see where changes will have to be made to the prototype and then make those changes, first to the paper models, then to the dynamic model, keeping the two specifications in sync. Final requirements specification publication occurs when the prototype is functionally approved and, therefore, requirements can be finalized.

The "As-Prototyped" Design Document

Design in this life cycle is a documentation task rather than a blueprint for system development. That is, the first published design document on a rapid prototyping project will have been derived from the architecture of the user-approved prototype. This is where the first big problem occurs with old-line software management and some users. Some of these people will point out that "accepted software engineering practice" calls for the creation of a detailed design before the development of any actual software. Deriving a detailed design from a working model violates the specific guidelines of some methodologies and may therefore cause auditors to raise their eyebrows.

It is probably clear by now why detailed design must be derived from the prototype rather than the other way around. Detailed design cannot be undertaken until detailed functional requirements have been finalized. Prototyping is used as a means of discovering detailed functional requirements. To insist that detailed design precede prototyping is to trap developers in a "Catch-22." The solution to this dilemma lies in the project plan, called for as the first project deliverable. It is here that we reveal our approach and seek approval from management and customers for necessary deviations from existing standards and methodology guidelines.

The reason that detailed design, as a necessary prelude to coding, is called for by methodologies is that it provides a means for giving better structure to programs and systems so the final product will be easier to maintain. To write programs without the benefit of a structured design is to return to the quick and dirty prototyping mode of the 1950s and 60s. Many quick patches will be made by developers, probably using the GO TO statement, to correct problems. Variables will not be defined in a data dictionary. Control flow of the system will not be specified. The resulting psychological complexity of delivered software created in this fashion will in turn create a maintenance nightmare.

The evidence of such problems calls for development of a detailed design in the rapid prototyping life cycle immediately after the final requirements gate. During the prototyping phase, no traditional software development is undertaken and no psychological complexity is introduced. The next phase of the project—system tuning—will, in most cases, involve some traditional software development activities such as writing programs in a third-generation language, possibly switching database management systems, and allowing for final I/O devices. These activities must be based on a sound structured design to produce a quality final product. An "as-prototyped" design specification then becomes a "tune-to" rather than a "build-to" document.

The "As-Tuned" Design Document

In the traditional life cycle, the "as-built" design specification often has the same, or very similar, format as the "build-to" design specification. File formats specified in the preliminary design may be modified and new files may be added in the final design. Structure charts may be modified to show different calling sequences than those originally specified, and new modules may be added. File format and control flow specifications will still appear in both documents, however.

Since the tuning phase of a rapid prototyping project will involve some of the same types of activities as the coding phase of a traditional project, the "as-tuned" design document will have the same relationship to the "as-prototyped" design as traditional final design has to preliminary design. Changes will be made only where tuning requires changes to the system architecture. The purpose is the same—to provide a set of documentation that accurately reflects the "as-built" final product and will be effective as a guide during future maintenance tasks.

The Test Plan and Results

If a formal test phase is required by your methodology, the contents of this document need not be any different from the usual. A test plan usually specifies that when certain operator or user actions take place, known system responses are expected and that, when certain data are input, known information is expected as output. On a traditional project, these factors are unknown until test time because it is not until then that actual data are fed to the system, nor do users have a chance to perform any actions on the system until this time. Rapid prototyping makes use of actual data and actual user actions from the time of the very first prototype demonstration through the time the final tuning refinements have been made. Therefore, one must think of a rapid prototype as undergoing system testing throughout the life cycle as the user is continually exposed to the behavior of the system. There is no longer a clearly defined test phase. The contents of a final and formal test plan will not change with prototyping. As succinctly stated by Lantz, test data sets will be voluminous (often a production copy of the system), selected to cover a wide range of data boundaries and conditions, and constructed to test particularly important features.[1] The control of the final test will also not vary from that of a traditionally developed product.

It has already been pointed out that rapid prototyping is extremely useful in helping users and developers discover what data should be input, what information the system should produce, and what user actions should be accommodated. Rapid prototypers do not make guesses about these things in the development of a traditional test plan—they allow such requirements to be revealed during prototype iteration. When the normal time arrives to create a test plan, it can be derived from a synthesis of successful prototype demonstration scripts. On a rapid prototyping project, the test phase is often nothing more than a formality, necessary only if required by methodologies, internal standards, or auditors. There should be no last minute panic here.

The User Guide

Some software engineers have recently been advocating the creation of a user guide as one of the first development activities during the analysis phase, citing the fact that users relate to such documents better than to formal requirements specifications. Such an approach is a good idea for traditionally developed software, providing a "paper prototype" of proposed system functionality. It is still a bit like mail order catalog shopping in that what-if questions can only be answered hypothetically without the existence of a working model. Without the existence of actual ouput from a prototype it will also be difficult for developers to ascertain what data to capture and store. In other words, front end user guides offer no better solutions to classical requirements analysis problems than do structured analysis techniques.

The following approach works well on a rapid prototyping project. Create an on-line version of the user guide. Embed the electronic user guide in the initial version of the prototype as help screens. Allow the users to learn how to use the prototype in a hands-on mode by browsing at their own pace through help screens. Electronic user guides allow developers to provide help to users when and where it is needed. Indeed, in the case of rapid prototyping, such a guide is literally written by the user as he or she suggests improvements during the iterations of the functioning model. Educational information can be tightly coupled to the functional modules referenced. If a paper version of the user guide is a contractually required deliverable, simply wait until the user has approved prototype functionality and then print out the help screens. This is still front end user guide development, isn't it? We just don't commit to paper until we are sure what final system functionality will be. We also develop the user guide concurrently with the prototype instead of as a prelude to software development.

Front end user guide creation during prototype development and iteration allows users to provide early feedback about the quality of the guide as well as the actual system. This solves yet another classical life cycle problem in that user guides produced as the last breathless effort of a traditionally late development schedule are typically incomplete, inaccurate, and unprofessional. Users frequently complain that software manuals have only marginal utility and that it is more effective to learn from experimentation with the system than from reading the manual. Report and output screens which appear in the manual may need to be annotated with controls, edits, and validations that occur during the automated process. For example, it may be obvious from the picture of a screen appearing in the manual that a two-digit code must be entered in response to a prompt. It may not be so obvious that the code must be in the range of 01–50. Those kinds of controls are best spelled out right on the page where the user will see the screen replica. Definition of specific functions should be available to the user by virtue of being embedded in help screens, yet a broad overview of how those functions tie together as an integrated whole may be portrayed via control flow graphs or data flow diagrams included in the manual. Such inclusions are highly user-dependent. Some users can relate to the graphic representation; some users do not want to be bothered. If accepted, such documents are also useful in providing intrasystem maps for communication with other systems. Production of other system-related documentation such as operations guides will not differ from traditional development documentation. Typically, prototyped products are not batch systems; but if they are, then operations guides are obviously as necessary as ever.

The Final Product

When the actual software is finally delivered, it has been ascertained to be functionally correct during prototype iteration. It has been stress tested and performance tuned to meet user response time requirements. It has been thoroughly documented for future maintenance purposes. If all this is true, the software is ready for delivery to the customer. The fact that an evolved prototype rather than traditionally developed software has been delivered will not be transparent to the user other than the fact that system functionality will be far superior to that typically developed. A summary of rapid prototyping life cycle products is presented in Figure 4-5.

MODIFICATIONS REQUIRED TO LIFE CYCLE ACTIVITIES

Although the differences between the traditional life cycle and the rapid prototyping approach are not exactly revolutionary in terms of milestones and deliverable products, the differences in activities performed by developers and users are quite drastic. It is the activities suggested by existing methodologies that will have to be modified by project planning to make the rapid prototyping approach feasible. The traditional activities of modeling system requirements, performing detailed design, developing software modules, and testing may often have the appearance, and sometimes also the reality, of occurring at unconventional times in unexpected phases. This book presents a formalized description of the rapid prototyping process so you will have a clear idea of how the process activities differ from the traditional approach. Such a concept will prove useful in tailoring existing methodologies to accommodate this new approach to software development.

Establishing a New Life Cycle Approach

A new life cycle approach includes project planning as the first activity of the rapid analysis phase, producing a document outlining rough schedules and deliverables. The second activity is rapid analysis itself, during which preliminary user interviews are used to develop an intentionally incomplete, high-level paper model of the system. A document containing the partial requirements specification is output from this task and used to build the initial prototype which is created in the next three phases. Creation of the database is the first of these phases (activity three). Once the initial database is set up, the fourth activity, menu development, may begin, followed by (fifth activity) function development, both using fourth-generation techniques to produce a working model. The model is then demonstrated to the user. User suggestions for improvements are incorporated into successive iterations (activity six) until the working model provides satisfaction. Activity seven involves formal user approval of the prototype's functionality. A preliminary system design document may then be produced (activity eight). The prototype iteration phase is really the heart of rapid prototyping. Through the scenarios provided by the working model, the user may role play and request successive refinements to the model until all functional requirements are met. Stress testing, benchmarking, and tuning follow (phase nine), and the last phase (ten) are very much similar to the same phase found in traditional development—operation-maintenance. Figure 4-6 reintroduces the graphic representation of the rapid prototyping process shown in Figure 2-1 with the task numbers just identified included.

While it may be comforting to think of a process as being essentially sequential, as suggested by the task numbers shown in Figure 4-6, the rapid prototyping process is anything but sequential. Analysis is not over at the end of rapid analysis, task two, but continues through the end of task six, prototype iteration. Anything discovered during prototype iteration will require modifications to the working model created as a result of activities three, four, and five, and expansions of the specifications created in task two. Physical design actually begins with task two when entity-relationship diagrams are used to create the initial database structure in task three. Design

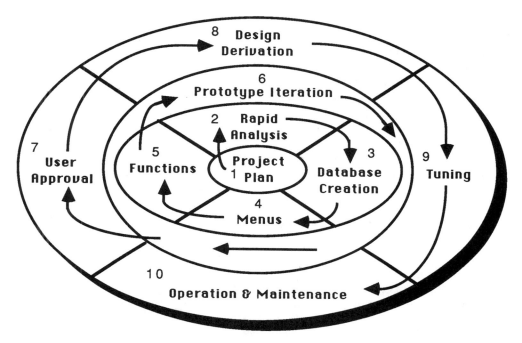

Figure 4-6   The evolutionary rapid prototyping process.

activities continue through the end of task nine, tuning, when detailed specifications published at the end of task eight are modified to incorporate changes resulting from tuning activities. Maintenance, which can be defined as the modification of existing systems, can be said to begin during prototype iteration. This iterative and concurrent nature is one reason why the process model is represented as a set of concentric circles. The model shown in Figure 4-6 can be thought of as consisting of thin semipermeable membranes where information can easily pass in both directions.

Shifting Effort to the Requirements Analysis Phase

A problematic issue in adapting to this new life cycle is that the analysis phase of a rapid prototyping life cycle will probably not be reduced in scope or time. In fact, the rapid prototyping analysis phase will probably take somewhat longer than a traditional project because all traditional analysis activities will be performed in addition to prototype development and modifications during prototype iteration. Compensations come later in the life cycle when design becomes a straightforward exercise in documentation, coding (as a separate phase) is eliminated, and testing becomes a trivial formality rather than a panic and debug activity. The greatest benefits occur after delivery of the product when it becomes clear that the system truly does meet the user's functional requirements and that an expensive postdelivery "system tuning" phase is not necessary.

   There are some schools of thought that give hope to a new kind of "reusable" model developed by prototyping. Such models would be "heavily parameterized" so they can be specialized into specific prototypes with the addition of appropriate tables or callable packages. One example, cited by Taylor and Standish, describes a computer graphics system modeling a radar air traffic control system that was reworked with a minimal amount of effort to produce a live demonstration of a system for controlling ship traffic on the St. Lawrence Seaway.[2] Maps of the airspace were replaced with maps of the seaway, symbols for aircraft were replaced with symbols for ships, and equations for air motion were replaced with equations for ship motion. A trivial example of a general prototype that could easily be respecialized is that of making the classic, straightforward add-change-delete-retrieve to a database. The high-level menu shells are stable enough that only the pointers to a particular database and customized retrievals are necessary to produce an initial prototype to get users or developers started toward a feasibility study.

Using Rapid Prototyping Techniques throughout the Life Cycle

All of the rapid modification techniques used to develop and refine the prototype can also be applied to system modifications made during prototype iteration, system tuning, and even postimplementation maintenance—if the delivered software contains modules created using the rapid prototyping toolkit. The advantages of doing so will be that such changes will be made faster and cheaper and the system will retain maximum flexibility—it will stay easy to modify. It is a statistically measurable and well-documented fact [3,4,5] that traditional techniques applied to software modification often introduce unacceptably high levels of psychological complexity, leading to the premature retirement of expensive systems.

This means that a primary goal of the prototype tuning task should be to minimize the amount of traditional coding activity undertaken. Faster is nice, but not always in the long run when efficiency comes at the expense of modifiability. Users must always be quizzed rigorously about the legitimate business reasons for performance requirements. The long-term costs of response time improvements must always be considered as offsetting possible immediate productivity improvements. Alternatives to coding must also be considered. Chapter 5 will describe in detail some techniques that can be used to improve response time without sacrificing modifiability.

REFERENCES

1. Kenneth E. Lantz, *The Prototyping Methodology* (Englewood Cliffs, NJ: Prentice Hall, 1986).

2. Tamara Taylor and Thomas A. Standish, "Initial Thoughts on Rapid Prototyping Techniques," *New Paradigms for Software Development*, William W. Agresti, ed., IEEE Computer Society Press, 1986, pp. 38–47.

3. John Connell and Linda Shafer, *The Professional User's Guide to Acquiring Software* (New York: Van Nostrand Reinhold, 1987).

4. Linda Brice and John Connell, "Deriving Metrics for Relating Complexity Measures to Software Maintenance Costs," Computer Measurement Group Conference *Proceedings*, 1982, pp. 134–41.

5. John Connell and Linda Brice, "Complexity Measures Applied to an Applications Case Study," Fourth International Conference on Computer Capacity Management *Proceedings*, Institute for Software Engineering, 1982, pp. 121–28.

5

Developing an Initial Rapid Prototype

The intent of this chapter is to give readers a feel for what it is like to develop a rapid prototype. As Chapter 4 indicated, the tasks involved in a prototyping project are somewhat different and are performed in a different sequence than the tasks on a conventional software development project. This chapter describes in detail the activities one would perform to accomplish those tasks on an actual prototyping project. The tasks are discussed in sequential order, beginning with project planning and continuing through to the development of the initial working model to be presented to users for review and feedback. Once prototyping actually begins, many tasks take place concurrently, so the following sequential description of these tasks is not meant to imply an analogy to the lockstep process of the waterfall life cycle model. The descriptions of how activities are performed should give you a feel for why development of the initial prototype, using tools such as those described in Chapter 3, can be described as rapid.

Chapter 3 indicated that the tools used for prototype development are quite different from conventional software development tools and are applied differently. This book does not concentrate on the use of any particular prototyping toolkit software product, but instead discusses the use of a particular class of RDMS-related prototyping tools, the features of which were discussed in Chapter 3. Therefore, keep in mind as you read the following material that the discussions of how to accomplish various prototype development tasks are generic. In other words, the specifics of how to build a working model will vary greatly between various vendors' products. Despite these differences, there are many similarities in the way RDMS prototyping toolkits are applied to the development of working models. These areas of conceptual sameness will be the areas of primary concentration.

This generic approach will admittedly leave readers without the specific knowledge needed to build a prototype using a particular development environment. If, however, you are familiar with the use of a particular RDMS-based development toolkit, then it will be easy to see how the following discussions relate to that environment. Readers who are not familiar with such a toolkit will at least get a feel for the advantages of using such products compared with their current development environments. With the acquisition of an appropriate prototyping toolkit, neophytes will be able to secure training in specific development skills from the vendor.

Another point to keep in mind while reading the following material is that it only covers prototyping up to the development of the initial model of the key aspects of proposed system functionality. This is quite different from the development of a complete, deliverable software system. The tasks involved in evolving such a model to become the final software product are described in Chapter 6. For the time being, remember that the result of prototype development—the topic of this chapter—is only an experimental model. Such a model is *intentionally* incompletely specified and only partially developed. The implicit prototyping strategy is based on the assumption that adding on and modifying functions is more efficient than wholesale replacement of functions. Therefore, in developing the initial prototype and in evolving the prototype, we will only specify and only develop functionality of which we are fairly certain. By adding on functionality in small increments, we will minimize costly errors due to the classic misunderstandings arising from communication problems between developers and users as described in Chapter 2.

PLANNING A PROTOTYPING PROJECT

The first step in prototype development does not involve development at all, despite the fact that prototypers are in a hurry to get a working model in front of users. The first step is project planning. Because the evolutionary rapid prototyping approach is a comprehensive software development strategy, project planning before development is but a brief preliminary delay. Evolutionary rapid prototyping is *how* the software will be developed, not a task within a larger development framework. That means it is necessary to first define, for each project, the differences between this approach and a more conventional life cycle development approach.

The material in this section does not address project management issues in any great detail. Projects are managed so the right mix of talent has access to the necessary tools to deliver the requested quality product. There are some excellent books on project politics[1] and project management.[2,3] Here only project planning is touched upon, and then only as it applies to prototyping. One of the benefits of project planning is that the admission is allowed at the start that this project is unique—there is no standard mold into which it may be expected to fit perfectly. Uniqueness is actually a critical attribute of all software projects. A modifiable toolkit approach is the right approach in an industry where technology changes rapidly. Users and developers should choose newly available tools instead of imposing generic standards that may be obsolete before they are published and almost certainly will be obsolete shortly after publication. Where prototyping is concerned, project plans are particularly useful in that they give some order to what might otherwise be considered chaos, without artificially restricting methods, techniques, or tools.

While flexible development strategies are stressed in this book, one should not assume that prototyping is a free-for-all where all of the accepted rules are tossed aside. Without a project plan, the parties involved in system development will be just as vulnerable to mismanagement as they would with a traditional development approach. There must be a well-understood agreement between the customer and the developer so both parties know and agree upon products, timelines, and responsibilities.

A project plan, like a prototype, will evolve as described soon. One does not know at this early stage whether the prototype will be evolvable into the final product. Therefore it might be appropriate for the preliminary project plan to represent the goals, scope, tools, responsibilities, and deliverables for the prototype only. The schedule will reflect time and effort for prototyping activities only. Upon completion of the prototype, this contract will have been fulfilled and another one will be written and signed for the remainder of the project.

The project plan, a statement of understanding, is the first delivered product of any new prototyping project. When prototyping is used as a feasibility study, there may be one project plan for the prototype, then another for the remainder of the development project, if the project is deemed feasible by the customer. When prototyping is not used as a feasibility study but as a requirements specification and development approach, the project plan should spell out how to get started, what prototyping is all about, who will assume what responsibilities, what tools will be used, and what the deliverables will be. A project plan will lay out seven basic project elements:

- Approach justification
- Goals
- Scope of effort
- Development tools
- User responsibilities
- Deliverables
- Preliminary schedule

The project plan becomes a contractual understanding between developer and user communities—value to be given for value to be received. It is important to avoid preparing a long, poorly understood narrative prose document and then forcing the customer to sign before beginning work. At the same time, it is important to obtain some agreement on critical project elements.

All items but the preliminary schedule may be identified in the original project plan as a complete statement of intent. The schedule, in particular, will continually mature as each phase of the project is completed. The approach justification and goals are unlikely to change much over the life of a project. On the other hand, the remaining elements of the plan are unlikely to remain static. It is, therefore, wise to redefine those last five elements as additional information becomes available during the project. A project plan might define scope of effort, development tools, user responsibilities, deliverables, and schedule in detail for the prototyping phase. It then might contain a section for each of the known remaining phases like design, testing, and implementation where those phases are merely sketched in, to be filled out later in the game. Project plan elements will be in gradually decreasing detail as the phases stretch out from project beginnings, yet the plan will provide an overall cost and timeframe that has been negotiated until both developer and customer are comfortable. The first version of the plan will hold true throughout the life of the project because it is written in general terms. Yet it is to be expected that there will be several versions of the plan, none negating its predecessor, but instead adding and expanding information. Figure 5-1 is an example of a first version project plan. Each part of the plan has particular importance to a rapid prototyping project.

Approach justification is intended to answer such questions as, Why is this project necessary? What benefit is to be gained by performing the project? What problems can project completion be expected to solve? Why is rapid prototyping to be used? Why deviate from the traditional approach?

Goals describe desired outcomes or what is expected to be accomplished. For example, a goal for a relatively minor system might be "Place all inventory transactions on-line," or "Capture all photographic images on the selected topic in file cabinet A and index them for retrieval." The goal for a relatively major system might be to perform a large segment of the Strategic Defense Initiative.

Scope of effort describes all activities expected to be performed during the project and how much effort those activities will require. It explains how the developer expects to go about getting the job done. No anticipated activity should be overlooked, because there is always a great deal more to project development than prototyping and programming. Activities such as writing progress reports, reviews, demonstrations, system exercises, and management strategy sessions are part of all but the smallest projects, and all consume time. One activity frequently unbudgeted is that of walkthrus. How to conduct walkthrus is covered in other textbooks[4] and in other parts of this book; it will suffice here to remind the reader that they are valuable tools for the discovery and removal of defects.[5] The project planner is urged to both perform and plan for walkthrus.

The scope of effort also states the boundaries of the work. Boundaries can describe what is in bounds, such as inclusion of other systems, as well as what is out of bounds. Boundaries distinguish between that which is subject to change as a result of automation and that which must be accepted as a given and left

Project Plan

Revision Date_____   Revision Number_____

Project Justification: The Study Group is in need of an internal tracking system so that better use can be made of available resources and so that customers may receive the highest quality product in the most timely fashion.

Goal: Provide an on-line management tool for rapid retrieval of the status of all on-going products.

Scope of Work: Two development analysts, one manager from the study group and one staff member, half-time, from the study group will comprise the team. The system will be delivered within six months from the start date. The word-processing needs of the study group are not addressed in this system.

The tools used to prototype the system will be Data Flow Diagrams, Control Flow Graphs, Entity-Relationship Diagrams, a relational database and a personal computer.

User Responsibilities: The user will participate in the development of the DFD's, CFG's, E-R's, will walkthru the prototyped version, will attend project reviews, will provide test data and will give final approval to a completed product.

Deliverable Product: The system will provide a menu-driven interactive project tracking system for the study group. It will use the xxx programming language, the yyy relational database management system and a zzz personal computer. A prototype version will be delivered for user approval. The final version will provide data entry screens and information retrieval on the status of all internal projects and staff assignments. A user's guide will be provided.

Figure 5-1 Sample project plan.

alone. Figure 5-2 shows an example of bounded scope of effort. Obviously, what is outside the bounds is the rest of the world. The intent is not to list everything in the universe which is not in the system but to clarify to the user which tasks are the developer's responsibility. Those outside the scope of the project may be the user's responsibility or someone else's, but they are elements associated with the system that do not belong to the project team.

Additionally the scope of effort identifies all tools, automated or not, that have anticipated use. Analysis and design tools, programming languages, and database systems are specified in the project plan.

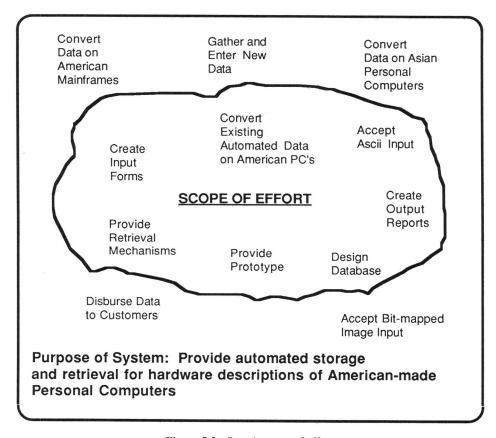

Figure 5-2 Sample scope of effort.

User responsibilities briefly describes the activities and information for which the user is responsible so the goal and schedule can be met.

Deliverables requires a specific description of the deliverable products. A prototype is a deliverable, as are a hardware configuration, a systems requirement document, a systems design document, and a user guide.

Schedules (not shown on Figure 5-1) are anticipated dates for completion of specific milestone events. A hard schedule for design and coding should not be attempted until the prototyping phase has been completed. Amounts and dates of anticipated expenditures other than labor should also appear on the schedule. Schedules can easily take the form of a modified Gantt chart. Start date, target date, and personnel for each milestone can be graphically represented. Figure 5-3 is an example of the well-accepted Gantt chart schedule. Because project plans can and should evolve, a revision number and a revision date are highly recommended.

A survey conducted in 1988 identified at least 135 automated project planning tools on the market. The use of such tools to (at a minimum) track revisions and

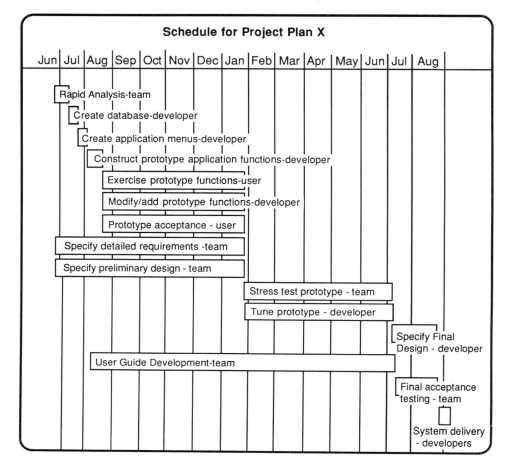

Figure 5-3　Sample schedule.

create Gantt chart graphics is highly recommended. Some CASE tools that are sophisticated enough to qualify as an Integrated Project Support Environment (IPSE) claim to link elements of the project plan to other documents of the project.

In addition to team exercising of prototypes and walkthrus of all deliverables, the entire status of a project should be reviewed periodically, no less often than at the end of a major phase. At that review between users and developers, the project plan should be the document under examination. The accomplishments since the beginning of the project or since the last project review meeting should be noted. The current tasks should be reviewed and modified if inappropriate. Problems in meeting the schedule or any other problems should be aired so decisions can be made to resolve them. Any assumptions which must be true to accomplish successful phase completion must be listed.

RAPID ANALYSIS—AN INITIAL MODEL FOR PROTOTYPING

After users and developers have completed the project plan, the next task is to firm up what will be prototyped. As intent as all parties may be on shortening the development process, there is just no magic way to walk directly to a workstation and start pulling down menus and bringing up screens with a total absence of specifications. Some preliminary analysis work must be done.

Rapid analysis is the first active phase of an evolutionary prototyping project. Brief preliminary user interviews are conducted to gain an idea (acceptably incomplete and probably incorrect) about the basic system functionality desired. The purpose of rapid analysis is to produce an intentionally incomplete model from which a prototype may be developed. The model includes a high-level view of prototype functionality in the form of dataflow diagrams, a preliminary suggestion for a database schema in the form of an entity-relationship diagram, and a preliminary architecture for the prototype control structure in the form of control flow graphs.

In reviewing this preliminary model, an appropriate question for users would be: Does this model adequately suggest an experiment that would interest you? An inappropriate question for users would be: Does this model accurately specify your detailed system requirements? In developer walkthrus of rapid analysis models, appropriate questions include: Does the model provide an adequate description of what is to be prototyped? and Are there any obvious defects? Inappropriate walkthru discussion items at this point are those dealing with completeness of detail. The product of rapid analysis is not a requirements specification but rather a prototyping concept. One of the primary purposes of prototyping is to produce a requirements specification.

A Preliminary Model of Functionality

There are professionals who will vehemently disagree with the idea of users and developers collaborating to produce a context level dataflow diagram. In fact, there are those who contend that arrows, boxes, and circles have always been and will always be anathema to users who should never be confronted with them under any circumstances. Other means of initial communication have been proposed, including filling out preprinted forms, storyboarding, interviews, and writing narrative prose. Many of these tools are useful. Preprinted forms containing some essential questions such as the ones in Figure 5-4 are very helpful, but they should not be handed to the user to be returned filled out and then used by the developer as the factual document from which the system prototype is begun. They are far more helpful as catalysts for conversation in user interviews.

When a doctor diagnoses a patient, he or she rarely begins with, "Tell me everything there is to know about your problem." Rather, the patient is led through a series of questions where the next question is predicated upon the response of the last until, in some fashion of "walking the tree," the problem is defined. "What are your symptoms?" is certainly a good start but rarely good enough to elicit an immediate diagnosis. When preprinted forms are used by the interviewer in a verbal

---

USER QUESTIONNAIRE

Name of organization : _____

Replacement for existing automated system? _____

Planned implementation date: _____

Application description: _____

Number of documents involved : _____

Number of anticipated users of the system: _____

Number of users expected to be on-line at once: _____

Rate at which information flows into the system:_____

Rate at which information is purged from the system: _____

Number of expected retrievals per day: _____

Desired response time : _____

How is information currently entered into the system? _____

How is information distributed from the system? _____

If currently automated, describe equipment: _____

May all new equipment be purchased? _____

Attach an organizational chart .

Attach a floorplan of your facility.

Describe problems with the current process : _____

Attach all written procedures pertaining to the preparation and flow of data.

Figure 5-4 Sample user questionnaire.

question-and-answer scenario, they must be subject to change—rephrasing, adding, and deleting items as appropriate to the particular system need. Still, these collected facts are not the best document from which an on-line prototype may be born. Storyboarding is also a useful technique, but it always gets summarized or collected into written documents which, while often entertaining to read, do not provide the concise information necessary to bring up the very first prototyped menu. One of the most useful techniques for getting started with rapid analysis is to borrow concepts from joint application design (JAD) as proposed by IBM and modified by others. Public seminars on JAD are available and hundreds of JAD leaders are already trained.

The day may come in the not too distant future when expert systems will be used as analysts. There will be a set of rules to help diagnose computer users' problems and suggest solutions in much the same way that medical expert systems operate now. There may even be expert prototyping systems containing rules formalized from the knowledge captured from those recognized as experts in the field. But, for now, dataflow diagrams, while not touted as a panacea, are still a very good way to get more precise dialogue between user and developer started.

The project team has been defined in the project plan. Presumably, some subset of that team or the whole team (no more than about seven) of users and developers will meet in a facility with a chalkboard (or some kind of easily visible, erasable device). It is then the developer's responsibility to go to the board and dive right in to the process. Starting with a big center circle that represents the system—it can initially be labeled "System"—the suppliers and receivers of information can be defined. The result will probably look something like Figure 5-5. It is a phenome-

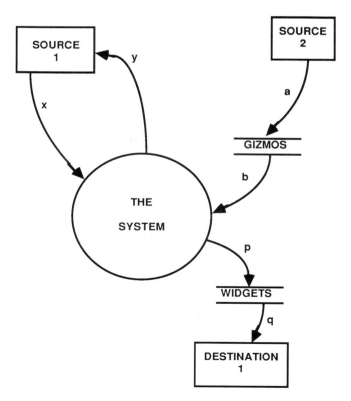

Figure 5-5 Context level DFD format.

nally simple concept, yet it will probably take a little longer than a few seconds. Anyone who has been involved in defining the mission of their organization knows that it is easier said than done. One straightforward sentence describing the special task or purpose for which the organization exists can often be derived only after several hours of creative discussion among top-level management. The context-level DFD may prove to be the same way for some customers. It may appear too simpleminded to require any thought at all, yet the terminal boxes which represent the suppliers of input and receivers of output from the system may be difficult to label when care is taken that all who interact with the system and *only* those who interact with the system are included. All persons, organizations, computer systems, physical devices, and so on that can be either sources transmitting data or destinations receiving data for the initial prototype need to be identified.

Figure 5-6 takes the generic dataflow diagram format as shown in Figures 3-5, 3-6, and 5-5 and ties it to a specific example related to a specific application. This example will be used throughout the remainder of this chapter to develop an imaginary prototype. We appeal to the reader to please understand that this example in no way represents the wide range of uses for DFDs, nor is it meant to imply that prototyping should only be used for small systems such as the one described here. It is indeed trivial, for the practicality provided by an example,

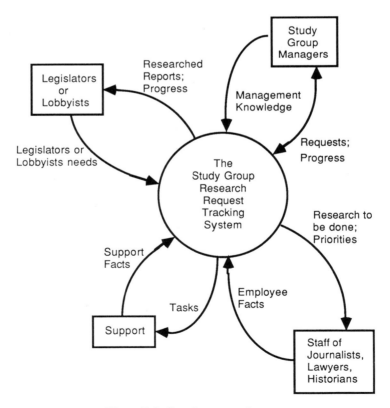

Figure 5-6 Sample context diagram.

yet it does represent one glimpse of a real system and works well for presenting the purpose of a context-level diagram. One major vendor of a quality relational database management system consistently uses the concept of employee records in almost all literature, including informal self-help guides and more formal training seminars. That vendor certainly does not mean to imply that a personnel employee database comes anywhere close to using the full power of their product, but that it provides a vehicle for a common language threaded throughout examples and references. The recharge system example that follows is intended to be thought of in the same light.

Let the recharge system be requested by some organization to the house of representatives for a state to provide project information to outside customers and internal management. Let it be a tiny version of an automated project management system where requests for service can be logged and scheduled and where all costs, be they labor, materials, or machine time, are tracked. Further assume that the user or organization needing this system has contacted a software development group to create it. When the user and developer project team meet to create the context diagram for such a system, and a center circle representing the system is drawn, probably the next most obvious thing to do is to draw a terminal box representing the customer. Presumably, one of the major functions of the system will be to get requests for service from the customers into the system and to get information about the progress and costs of that service out of the system and back to the customer.

Other people who might come to mind as interacting with the system are the managers in the service organization. They might want to review the requests for service, and place schedule and cost estimates on them. They will almost certainly desire summary reports of resources committed, sorted in all kinds of ways—by date due, by type of service to be performed, by remaining cost, by customer, and so on. Who else could supply information to the system and benefit by retrievals from the system? For one, the employees who will actually be performing the services for the customer clearly need to contribute to the system. Only they know how to report how much of their time was spent on a specific request. What might they get out of the system? Very possibly there is a lot of useful information, including whether or not they are ahead of or behind schedule, whether or not they are within budget, and which requests for service have the highest priorities and should be worked on next and more. Another source-destination of information for such a system might be a support group for the staff. The support group could be a secretarial pool or a graphics department doing work for the staff, or internal customer, who does work for the external customer. Almost everyone is familiar with project management, so the point of the context diagram example need not be belabored. Only a few ways this example might work in the real world will be presented for clarity.

Suppose that the user is an organization that writes position papers on state legislation and is called the study group. Suppose the typical customer is an elected state legislator who does not have time to prepare in-depth research on each bill before the legislature. Desiring to place a responsible and well-educated vote for every bill, the legislator subscribes to the service of our user. Sometimes, he or she buys information automatically published by a study group, and sometimes he or she requests that special research be conducted to support or shed light on a theory. Of course, lobbyists may also buy the services of a study group.

The legislators or lobbyists are the customers. The press occasionally uses the services of the study group but, since the press interaction is sporadic and they receive no additional information over that received by the legislators and lobbyists, their needs will not be considered. Customers of the study group submit requests for the service of supplying research papers. They receive the research papers using a desired medium (magnetic tape, microfiche, floppy disk, or hard copy) and they also receive a bill for the service. For requests that cover several subjects or require a great deal of historical delving into archives, they may not receive a final product for several months, receiving progress reports in the interim. Such reports might describe what percentage of the task is complete, how much it has cost to date, and what researchers are assigned to the task.

The managers in this case are the managers of the study groups. They place schedules and costs into the system. They track who's doing what so that when a legislator makes a new request, it will be clear which researcher has the expertise and the time to do the job. They track the progress so that when a special session of the legislature has been called and they know which legislators must have information on certain bills to study immediately, they can reinforce the researchers on those projects with staff from other, less demanding projects.

In this case the researchers themselves are the staff. They are the historians, journalists, and lawyers who combine their skills to provide the legislators with the most complete and fair views of the pros and cons of each bill before the legislature. They report their effort to the system so the customer will be charged the proper amount. They may be asked by management to supply estimates to the system for future work, in which case they will probably consult the system to find out how long a similar job took in the past. For large projects, they may ask the system how much money is left according to the quote they made to the customer—if the job is more expensive than originally thought, management and customer will want to decide whether to stop the effort when the money is used up or whether to pump more money into the research until the effort is complete.

Support in this case may be some high school students who work after school and copy selected press releases. Or support might be a word processing service that attractively formats the research in a final report. Support could include some graphic artists who incorporate charts and graphs into the final report, or it might be an editor who pieces together the research atoms collected by the journalists. They could use the system in exactly the same way as the staff, or they could be viewed as an overhead service and be spread equally across all projects simply as a burden on each staff member.

The idea is that when the users (study group members) sit down with the developers, they will develop a first cut at who gives and takes what information to and from the system. There will be cases in other types of applications where all terminator boxes will not be persons but might instead be an organization, a computer system, a physical device, or something else.

Figure 5-6 provides the highest level map into a system. Now it has been defined who will interact with the system. It is a good start but not quite good enough to begin a prototype. One more level of detail is required as described in Chapter 3 and illustrated in Figure 3-7. The context level DFD must now be broken down into the essential functions DFD, where the major functions are identified. The terminators (sources-destinations) from the context level DFD will be dropped, the information flowing into and out of the system (dataflow) will be retained, and the one major process circle will be expanded to become several more refined process circles. At the time the context level DFD is drawn, an event list is usually prepared. The event list serves to define the processes (one for each event) for a crude first-cut essential functions DFD. Figure 5-7 is an essential functions model for Figure 5-6.

Another method, usable in conjunction with the event list approach, for deriving an essential functions diagram is to begin at the edges by showing all of the dataflows coming into or going out of the system. As this is done, a dataflow may be decomposed into constituent parts so dataflow A on the context diagram may be represented by dataflows i, j, and k on the essential functions diagram. When this occurs during rapid analysis, it is time to begin the preliminary data dictionary for the system. The dictionary might specify, for the preceding example of dataflow decomposition, that dataflow A consists of either dataflow i, dataflow j, or dataflow k. The following is the notational convention for such a specification: $A = [i] j [k]$. After bringing all the context dataflows down to the essential functions diagram, it is then necessary to specify the essential functions—those that either capture incoming data or produce outgoing data, or both. Simply draw several circles (between five and nine is a good number) that connect to the dataflows shown at the edges of the essential functions diagram. Then label the circles according to the primary function they perform—for example, "Capture A" or "Produce X."

Next, for physical reasons due to the prototyping environment being used and because this is not to be a model of the final system architecture but rather a model of the prototype, draw a data store in the middle of the diagram. Show each of the essential functions storing or retrieving data from this store. The data store then represents the RDMS that will be used to develop the initial prototype. Tables from the physical database will provide default table and view screens from which input and output functions can be generated using techniques such as visual programming, query by example, and report by example. In the initial prototype, functions will share common data only through the common database, not by passing files as traditional programs would do. This aspect of the initial prototype may well change during the tuning phase of the project, but for now no direct interfaces between essential functions need be shown. After completion of the preliminary entity-relationship diagram, the essential functions diagram might be revisited with an eye to breaking the single database into more meaningful data stores.

A Preliminary Model of Stored Information

The essential functions DFD shows a data store (study group research database) with an interface to every process shown on the diagram. Requests for research, budgets, and schedules are input to the data store and internal-external states of affairs are output from the data store. An entity-relationship diagram may now be

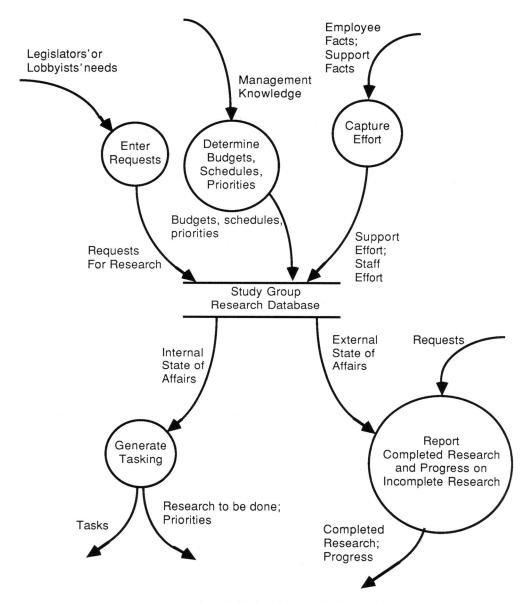

Figure 5-7   Sample essential functions diagram.

derived by inspecting the data store interfaces on the DFD. The ERD will reflect the data we now know will be stored in the prototype RDMS. In this example of a very small system, we know from the essential functions DFD that a study group manages multiple projects and employs multiple staff members; that each project may consist of multiple research tasks and may have multiple staff members assigned to complete it; and that staff members budgeted to assist in the completion of a project charge their time to specific research tasks into which the project is broken. This information gives us a clue about how to arrange the prototype database. A suggested arrangement for stored application data is shown in Figure 5-8.

Keep in mind that the prototype database may evolve into the production database, but it rarely represents the actual production database at this early stage of rapid analysis. The prototype database is simply a way to store user-familiar information so the functionality of the system can be tested and will most likely have to be refined many times before all the user's needs can be met. Nonetheless, it provides an excellent beginning when each entity on the ERD becomes a table in a relational database.

Notice that the ERD becomes another way of describing what the application is all about—another dimension of the problem space. Figure 5-8 can be read as

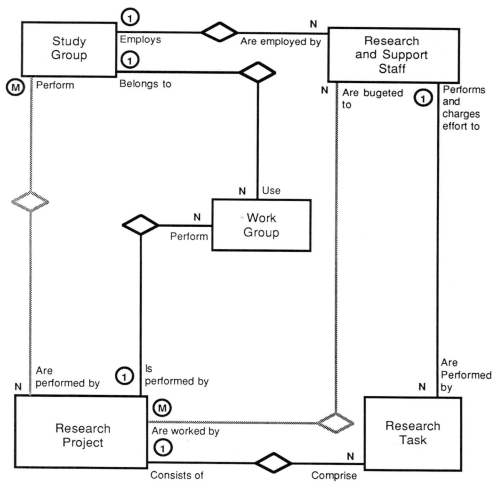

Figure 5-8 Sample entity relationship diagram.

a nonambiguous specification of user data requirements—a rigorous description of how information is managed by the user organization. What this specific ERD tells us is

- Many study groups perform many research projects (a particular study group may perform many research projects and a particular research project may require the efforts of many study groups)
- Each research and support staff member is employed by a specific study group (from the study group's point of view, it employs a specific set of workers)
- A research project consists of a specific set of research tasks
- Many research projects are performed by many staff members (a specific staff member may be assigned many research projects and a specific project may require the efforts of many staff members)

Pausing to reflect on the model as specified thus far, we note that there are two problematic many to many relationships—one between study groups and projects and the other between staff and projects. These relationships are indicated by gray lines on the ERD. If one were to attempt supporting these specified relationships in an actual database schema, problems would be encountered in determining what the critical attributes should be for the tables affected. Should there be multiple project identifier attributes in the study group table or multiple study group identifiers in the project table? Should there be multiple project identifiers in the staff table or multiple employee identifiers in the project table? A workable implementation is to resolve these many to many relationships by placing the multiple identifiers together in a separate relation that sits between and pins the other two.

In developing the initial prototype database schema, the ERD provides assistance by

- Specifying the tables that must be created (one for each entity shown on the ERD)
- Indicating where tables must contain critical attributes (to support the specified relationships)
- Helping to identify and provide solutions to many to many problems as just described

An example of a straightforward indication of critical attributes is the support of the relationship between study groups and staff members. Each entity must first have a means for uniquely identifying every occurrence of that entity. This means that each study group must have as an attribute a study group identifier. Each staff member must have a unique staff member identifier. These identifiers alone, however, will not support the indicated relationship between study groups and staff members. The ERD tells us the user organizational policy is that a staff member is assigned to one and only one "home shop" study group. It also tells us that information is managed, regarding the relationship between study groups and staff members, by taking the study group's point of view—if the staff member's point of view were taken, a one to one relationship would exist since each staff member belongs to one study group. Therefore, the database developer is directed to include a study group identifier in the staff member table. The inclusion of this critical attribute in the staff table will fully support the indicated relationship. Retrievals from the database will be able to include information combined from both the study group and the staff member tables by joining individual occurrences of these entities where the value of the study group identifier is equal.

Rather than creating multiple occurrences of critical attributes in a table definition to support many to many relationships, a better solution is to create a third, "joining" table with simpler relationships to each of the entities in the many to many relationship. It has already been specified that a research project consists of many research tasks. If it is further specified that a staff member performs many research tasks, but a task is too small a work unit to require the effort of many staff members, then the many to many relationship between staff members and research projects need not be directly supported. Instead, the task table would contain a project identifier attribute and a staff identifier attribute. One could query the database about which workers were assigned to a project by simply asking for the occurrences in the task table of workers with a specified project identifier. Likewise, one could find out what projects a specific worker was assigned to by finding the occurrences in the task table of a specified worker identification.

The many to many problem between study groups and research projects is resolved in a similar fashion. A work group entity is created with connections to both the study group and the research project table. The work group table would require as critical attributes a study group identifier and a research project identifier. In this way information can be retrieved relating study groups to research projects by specifying equality to values contained in the work group table.

The information model does not so far contain a detailed list of the attributes (information to be captured and stored) for each entity. This is because one of the points of prototyping is to discover, rather than prespecify, data requirements—just as functional requirements are prototyped rather than prespecified. This is why it is important to use a relational database for prototyping. Only the relational model allows the developer the flexibility to rapidly add, delete, and modify data attributes during prototype iterations. Detailed information modeling, prior to prototyping, becomes unnecessary for the same reason that detailed functional decomposition is unnecessary—the working model is just as easy to modify as the paper models and provides a better mechanism for user verification of correctness. The best way to discover what the user's data requirements are is to provide an intentionally incomplete data set in the prototype and let the user experiment with output based on that set. The user will then provide feedback about what additional information is required and the developer will easily and rapidly be able to include the additional data in the next version of the prototype. With the creation of the actual database, there will be three elements that may be cross-checked (manually, or automatically with a CASE tool) for consistency: Each table in the database will reflect one entity on an ERD; each attribute in the database will match one attribute on the ERD attribute list; each table in the database or entity on the ERD will match a data store on a DFD.

A Preliminary Model of System Event Paths

Before developing the first working model of the system, it is useful to create a paper map of what the system events and control flow paths will look like. Many readers will be familiar with the structure chart notation as software designers have been using this useful tool for years to map out their systems. A popular use is to graphically show how procedural components (subroutines) within a program, or program modules within a system, relate. Structure charts show either data or control information, or both, passing between process blocks. In addition to showing just how a system is partitioned into modules, a structure chart defines their hierarchy, organization, and communication.[6,7,8] We would like to introduce a new notation here, not to be confusing, but to separate in the developer's mind the difference between the user's view and the programmers' view of the system. A control flow graph (CFG) is the road map into the system as the user will see it from his or her workstation. It may not reflect a one for one relationship with software modules in the final system.

The CFG is a way to specify sequences of events that are desirable from the user's point of view. A user requirement might be, "I want the system always to ask me what retrievals I want to do before it asks me about anything else," or "From the main menu, I know I will be performing one of several kinds of data entry," or "I will almost always be doing one of a known number of retrievals." The developer may certainly offer guidance, or, in the absence of a user opinion, offer a suggestion for the whole CFG. Figure 5-9 gives an example of a leveled set of CFGs which adequately describes the study group research request tracking system initial prototype architecture.

What does a model such as the one shown in Figure 5-9 tell the developer? For one thing, it helps to scope the prototyping effort. In the case of this example, 18 screens and functions will be created for the prototype—five menu screens, five help screens, three output functions, and five input functions. Each CFG specifies the choices to be available on one of the five prototype menus. The method for invoking each prototype function is specified. The level of menu nesting is known (three levels). Of course, with pull-down menus, there is less menu-leveling necessary, but it is still wise to lay it out before programming it. One can see at a glance how many user actions will be necessary to get from any one place to any other place within the system.

Control flow graphs, unlike structure charts, assume that the sequence of execution of system functions will always be completely under user control. The reason for this somewhat artificial assumption is again related to physical considerations—this is how the initial prototype will be constructed. All control will be in the user's hands. Complete user control is artificial because, in the case of certain types of applications, such as real-time embedded software or output-intensive transaction processing systems, there will be very little in the way of user interaction with the system. In fact, in most applications there will be modules that are not under direct control of the user.

So why do we prototype applications so the initial working model is under complete control of the user? The objective of rapid prototyping is to discover what the user wants the system to do—not simply to build software faster. The surest path

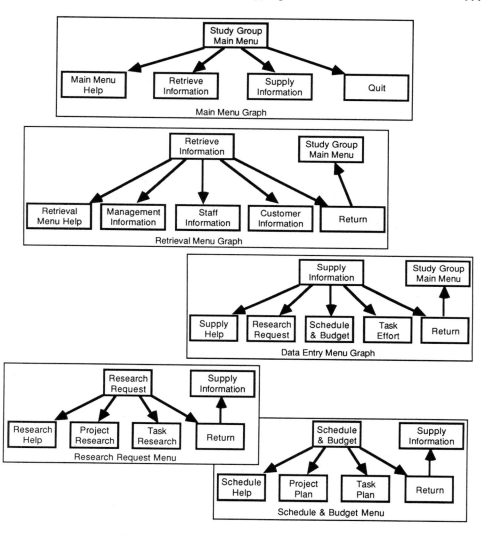

Figure 5-9 A leveled set of control flow graphs.

to such discovery is to get the user intimately involved in experimenting with the prototype. Such intimate involvement can be forced upon the user by putting them in complete control over the invocation and operation of each and every prototype function. As the prototype evolves into the final product, such artificial control can easily be replaced with more realistic control mechanisms—after functional requirements have been discovered.

Some database management systems provide application generators which make the production of the CFGs automated. Using such a tool, a graph is created as prototype screens and functions are developed. Such tools are very handy, particularly during the refinement and evolution of the prototype as new screens and functions are continually being added. Even with automated aids for documentation, however, it is helpful to create a preliminary architecture model before beginning to develop the initial prototype—then use the automated tool to provide configuration management documentation. Such a preliminary paper model will prove useful in structured walkthrus and user reviews in helping to avoid the development of a cute or clever prototype that contains obvious defects or is of little interest to the user as an experimental model (the "so what" effect).

The initial set of CFGs is almost trivially easy to create. Begin with generic templates for the main menu and subsidiary menus. The main menu template specifies calls to a main menu help screen, a data entry menu, a reports menu, a command to exit the application ("Quit," "Stop," or "Exit"), and space for additional choices. A subsidiary menu template specifies calls to a help screen for that menu, a return command, and space for additional choices. For the specification of the initial prototype, simply fill in the blank spaces in subsidiary menu templates for data entry screens and reports with modules to create the net inputs and net outputs specified by the essential functions dataflow diagram. Using this technique, initial prototypes will all be about the same size (regardless of ultimate application complexity) and take about the same amount of development effort (one to three weeks).

Variations on a Theme

While the cookbook approach to rapid analysis just outlined will work for many types of projects, it cannot be applied successfully without modification to all types of problems. Modifications to this approach are required when

- The size of the ultimate application (in terms of number of functions to be performed) is known from the beginning to be very large
- The size is known from the beginning to be very small
- There will be many input functions but very few output functions or vice versa

Beginning with the easiest variation, small systems are easily modeled by specifying that all functions are to be callable from the main menu. The next easiest variation—a system unbalanced between input and output functions—is modeled by creating a menu hierarchy for the type of functions that will exist in abundance and specifying that calls to the few functions of the other type will occur from the main menu. Remember also that the initial CFG is not cast in concrete. If a particular menu level becomes too crowded during prototype iteration and refinement, several similar types of functions called from that menu can be combined and called from a lower level menu. The boxes on the CFG that specify calls to these functions will then be replaced by one box specifying a call to the newly created menu.

The most difficult application variation, for rapid analysis purposes, is the large complex system. Mentally visualizing a comparison between the standard essential functions diagram just described and a large complex system, it is quite obvious that the net input and net output dataflows shown on the diagram will have to be decomposed through many levels to accommodate the numerous functions ultimately necessary to capture or produce a large volume of information. The analogy of an automobile represented by an engine on a platform with wheels cannot serve as an intentionally incomplete model of the key aspects of system functionality for large systems. If the application being considered is as complex as, say, an aircraft carrier, a prototype equivalent to a shell that floats with an engine and a propeller will be of questionable value as an experimental laboratory.

Different approaches to rapid analysis of large applications may be used depending on resources available to the developer and the amount of information about the key aspects of system functionality that are known with certainty. Fortunately, dataflow diagrams lend themselves to strategies that work with each of these conditions. Dataflow diagrams were, after all, developed as a means for reducing complexity to terms understandable by the average human being.

Let us introduce the concept of *unit* net inputs and outputs. Such dataflows are exemplified by information capture or retrieval processes that are functionally indivisible. An example of a unit input is a data entry screen. An example of a unit output is a report. On the essential functions diagram for a large system, such units may have to be combined to prevent the diagram from becoming overly complex, and represented by dataflows which are in fact a collection of data entry screens or a collection of reports. Thus, if much information is known about the key aspects of desired system functionality, the problem of application largeness will become apparent when the essential functions diagram is attempted.

Here is a useful guideline: Only prototype from an essential functions diagram on which the net inputs and net outputs are unit inputs and outputs. This means that when you discover during rapid analysis that you are dealing with a large system, you must decompose at least one more level. As you decompose from the essential functions diagram, you may consider each process on the diagram, together with its interfaces to other processes and externals, to be a context diagram for a prototype for that portion of the system. Carry the database on down to the next level set of diagrams and show the database on each new diagram—all functions for all of these subprototypes will still access one common database and will still not require file sharing or parameter passing between processes for the initial prototype.

There are several major advantages to this method of rapid analysis for large applications. First, it will help users and prototypers to better understand exactly how much is known about application size from the beginning. Second, it reduces a complex problem to pieces of a size amenable to the cookbook approach recently outlined. Third, separate prototyping teams may be used to develop each of the subprototypes, thus limiting team size and thereby limiting communications and speeding up turnaround time between prototype iterations. Fourth, it virtually eliminates most of the leveling, balancing, and partitioning problems that are common in the early stages of a large development project when using a more conventional prespecification approach. It will not, on the other hand, help to solve any of the configuration management problems common on large projects. Configuration management for prototypes and subprototypes will be no more and no less complicated than it is with traditional development.

Although it does not make good management sense to attempt very large projects with very small development teams, this phenomenon often occurs in research areas or when management perceives that there is a large risk associated with a newly proposed application. In these cases, prototyping may be used to provide a dynamic feasibility study, the successful completion of which may result in the provision of additional resources. Here, instead of many teams developing many subprototypes, a small team would develop a single subprototype to demonstrate an initial capability.

Whatever the size of the entire development team, it is usually a good idea to begin a prototyping project by using a small team. For large projects, the initial team can prototype the main menu and the database structure. If teams subsequently added to the project are required to interface with this starting point, this will help with configuration management—changes to the database and main menu structure will be made only by the initial team. Large systems are effectively prototyped as small chunks. Modern prototyping tools make the integration of completed chunks prior to delivery an easy matter.

Rapid Analysis Summary

What exists at the end of rapid analysis, for a medium-sized project, is a few (about seven) pages of diagrams, using the graphics conventions of structured analysis and design. These diagrams should only take three or four days to prepare. The project plan, context level DFD, essential functions DFD, high-level CFGs and ERDs can be the products of a joint application design session. One or two walkthrus and some revisions should produce a viable blueprint for prototyping in less than two weeks. For large projects the rapid analysis period might consume up to five weeks.

Because the models are based on structured techniques, they will be very easy to evolve into more conventional structured specifications. When the need for additional system functionality is discovered through prototype demonstration, additional processes can be added to the dataflow diagrams and additional decomposition levels added. As new data requirements are discovered, the ERD can be expanded to include more entities. When the users approve data content, a complete data dictionary or encyclopedia can be specified. As new functional modules are added to the prototype, they can be mapped on the CFGs. During the tuning phase of prototype evolution—to be discussed in the next chapter—control flow graphs can easily be converted to structure charts to describe program modules to be included in the system, and dataflow diagrams can be modified to show data being passed directly between system processes. The final system specifications will not differ in format from conventional structured specifications. The requirements specifications, however, will more closely correspond to true user requirements, as they now describe a user-approved working model of the system. The design specification will be more accurate as it has been derived from a correctly functioning working model.

DEVELOPING THE INITIAL PROTOTYPE

Now we are finally ready to sit down at a workstation and begin prototyping. Our immediate objectives are as follows:

- Get an experimental model of the key aspects of the proposed system in front of the user quickly
- Make sure that this working model is as easy to modify as the paper models produced by conventional structured prespecification

- Include user-familiar data in the initial prototype so functional and data requirements will be easy for the users to verify
- Use a data storage structure that will be easy to modify as user information requirements evolve during prototype iteration

To accomplish these objectives, we must use an adequate prototyping toolkit. Such a toolkit will consist of a truly relational database management system with integrated fourth-generation language, visual programming, and application generation capabilities, as described in Chapter 3. The following sections of this chapter will give some examples of how such tools would be used to develop the application described in the preceding rapid analysis sections. As you read through the examples, keep in mind that they do not describe the command syntax or operational procedures of any particular system. The examples are intended only to provide the general concepts of usage for these types of prototyping tools, not to train you in the use of a particular system.

At this point in prototype development, all of the necessary paper models have been completed. It is time to quickly move toward the creation of an on-line model that can be exercised by the user. The fastest and easiest way to do so is to

- Create a relational database
- Create tables within that database
- Copy existing data into the tables, if possible; create test data if not
- Create menu screens
- Create the high-level functional modules to be called from the menus

Storing Application Data in an RDMS

Creation of the relational database is usually a quick, one statement command naming the database to be created. Creation of tables within that database requires knowing which tables should be present and what data to put in them. If the ERD was constructed with care, there will be one table created for each entity on the diagram. Remember that entities are conceptual groupings of data, or things about which we store data. An entity can be thought of as a file or, in an RDMS, a table.

Continuing to use the simplified example of the study group, there were five entities: study group; research and support staff; work group; research project; and research staff. Thinking of the "project" entity, we need to figure out what information to retain about a project. In relational database management terms, any single piece of information that describes an entity is called an attribute. We will stay with that terminology because it has become widely accepted. Some attributes that might be associated with a project are a project identifier, a customer, several study group identifiers, several workers, a priority, and a due date. At a later point in the project, the developer will be concerned about primary keys and concatenated keys,[9] but right now the goal is to rapidly bring up a prototype, readily admitting that it will be less than perfect. However, where it is obvious that a small and fast change would obviously improve the original prototype database design, then it should be done. When we look at the project table, we see that the data structure might look like Table 5.1.

TABLE 5.1

Project ID	Customer	Task-ID	Staff ID	Priority	Due Date
AG-BILL 123	CONNALLY	1	73955	HIGH	5/17/89
AG-BILL 123	CONNALLY	1	45280	HIGH	5/17/89
AG-BILL 123	CONNALLY	2	46898	HIGH	5/17/89
AG-BILL 123	CONNALLY	2	06631	HIGH	5/17/89
FM-BILL 534	WHITE	3	92556	MED	5/24/89
FM-BILL 534	WHITE	3	78746	MED	5/24/89
FM-BILL 534	WHITE	4	37287	MED	5/24/89
FM-BILL 534	WHITE	4	71248	MED	5/24/89
FM-BILL 534	WHITE	4	99103	MED	5/24/89

The obvious problem is that there is redundant information in the table and it would be more efficient (and cause fewer problems in updating) if some of this information was moved to other tables (Tables 5.2 to 5.4).

This process is called normalization. Virtually a whole science has been built around this concept, which is a good idea since normalizing a database can improve retrievals and lend confidence to updating and changing of data. The reasons for wanting to normalize databases include reduction of redundancy, inconsistencies, and opportunities for lost data. To really know how to normalize, you need much, much more than is presented here. Chapter 12 provides a little more and many of the

TABLE 5.2

Project ID	Customer	Priority	Due Date
AG-BILL 123	CONNALLY	HIGH	5/17/89
FM-BILL 534	WHITE	MED	5/24/89

references listed give excellent advice on normalization.[10,11,12,13] Figure 5-10 shows some attributes that might be assigned to the entities so the tables in our example may be created. The attribute list shown for each entity does not include a unique identifier, nor does it include identifiers used to support the relationships shown on the ERD. These critical attributes are assumed for the moment while we concentrate on the application-related information related to each of the entities we want to include in the prototype. Ideas for these attributes can come from user interviews or may be creatively generated by the prototyper. The attribute list for a prototype database table is not required to be complete or correct.

TABLE 5.3

Task-ID	Project-ID
1	AG-BILL 123
2	AG-BILL 123
3	FM-BILL 534
4	FM-BILL 534

TABLE 5.4

Staff-ID	Task-ID
73955	1
45280	1
46898	2
06631	2
92556	3
78746	3
37287	4
71248	4
99103	4

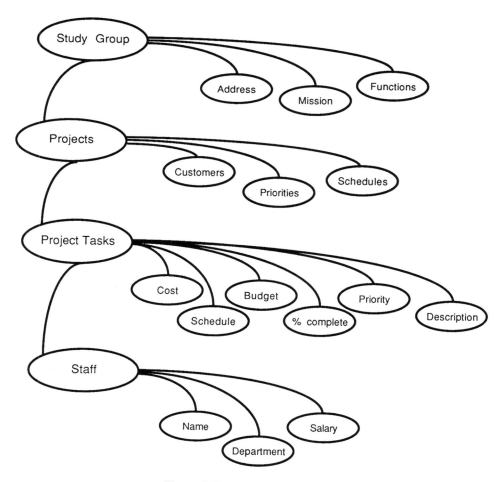

Figure 5-10 Entities and attributes.

To construct a database with these four tables, we would simply name the tables to be created and list their attributes. In some systems, the command syntax to accomplish this might appear as the following:

```
CREATE GROUP   (GROUP_ID = i2, ADDRESS = C20, MISSION = C120,
               FUNCTION = C60)
CREATE PROJECT (PROJECT_ID = C11,  CUSTOMER = C20,
                PRIORITY = C4, BEGIN_DATE = C8, END_DATE = C8,)
CREATE TASK (TASK_ID, = C5, PROJECT_ID = C11, STAFF_ID = i4,
            COST = F8.2, BEGIN_DATE = C8, END_DATE = C8,
            BUDGET = F8.2, COMPLETE = F2.0, PRIORITY = C4,
            DESCRIPTION = C60)
CREATE STAFF (STAFF_ID = i4, GROUP_ID = i2, NAME = C30,
             SALARY = F8.2)
```

In the CREATE STAFF command, "STAFF" becomes the table name, "STAFF__ID" is an attribute of integer type with a length of 4, "NAME" is an attribute of character type with a length of 30, "SALARY" is an attribute of floating point type with length of 8 and 2 decimal places. Once the initial database tables have been built, the next step is to copy into those tables any user data existing in electronic form. There will rarely be a one for one match of existing data elements and newly defined table attributes, but few relational systems are bothered by that problem. Most systems allow the user to specify the input file format and how it relates to the target table structure. As with the foregoing CREATE commands, one simply names the target table, then lists the attributes and their formats as they exist within the input file format.

If, for example, an electronic file currently existed with project task information, this information could be loaded into the newly created task table. In some systems, the command syntax to accomplish this might appear as

```
COPY TASK(TASK_ID, = C5, PROJECT_ID = C11, STAFF_ID = i4,
          COST = F8.2, BEGIN_DATE = C8, END_DATE = C8,
          BUDGET = F8.2) FROM ARCHIVE_FILE
```

Any data that can be loaded in right away have several advantages: they may exist in large volumes, so some of the database stress testing can occur right away; they are "live" data, subject to all of the peculiarities that real data can involve; they are familiar to the user, so problems are more easily spotted than with developer-concocted test data. Whether existing application-related user data are available or not, it is useful to immediately create a set of unload-reload procedures for every table in the database. When the iterative phase begins, restructuring of the tables must take place rapidly and a few developer-created utilities will speed the process. It is quite likely that discoveries will be made about how to correct data types or lengths, adding and subtracting attributes and other refinements during the time the user exercises the prototype. Unloading the "good" test data to preserve it, destroying the incorrect table, creating a new table and reloading the good data for continuation of the prototype may be accomplished swiftly when procedures are in place. In some systems, the command syntax to unload and reload a table might appear as

```
CREATE TEMPORARY (old task table attribute list)

APPEND TASK (attribute list) TO TEMPORARY

DESTROY TASK

CREATE TASK (new attribute list)

APPEND TEMPORARY (matching attribute list) TO TASK

DESTROY TEMPORARY
```

To understand how such a routine would work during prototype iterations, let us begin by considering the CREATE TASK command. This command would simply be edited to include new attributes, delete existing attributes, or change the names and formats of existing attributes. These modifications could be made at will without worrying about damaging the database structure or losing any of the presently stored data. To preserve data stored in the task table, a temporary table is first created with the same attributes as the present task table. Next a command is executed to copy existing data from the task table to the temporary table. The task table can now be deleted in its old form and immediately re-created with a new attribute list. Then, a command is executed which matches attributes from the temporary table to be copied to attributes in the newly structured task table. Finally, the temporary table can be destroyed and the routine is ready for the next revision cycle. Each time this procedure executes, some simple text editing will accomplish the database revision—there are no logic or database architecture concerns. Total revision time for one cycle would be a few minutes.

Developing the User Interface with Menu Control

Once an initial database with tables has been developed, the user must be provided with a way to reach the test data and execute input and output functions. Rather than providing the usual temporary "drivers" (throwaway software to test the lowest level modules of a system), prototypers now have the tools necessary to build the menu drivers in a form that may evolve into the final system. Such tools comprise what we have been referring to as "application generators." Visual programming techniques and fourth-generation command languages available in many RDMS packages make menu-driven systems easy to create. Just as with the CFG paper model, the on-line menus will be navigated by user control of functional execution. Using a fourth-generation command language, the prototyper may write a statement like the following to create menu choices that will be displayed on the terminal screen. In some systems the command syntax for implementing the control flow indicated on a CFG might appear as

```
HELP = call screen input_help

SERVICE          = call screen add_change_request,
                 call procedure new_request

BUDGET           = call screen add_change_budget,
                 call procedure new_budget

ESTIMATE         = call screen add_change_schedule,
                 call procedure new-schedule

COST             = call screen enter_effort,
                 call procedure new_effort

RETURN = return
```

Execution of this command string would cause the menu choices HELP, REQUESTS, BUDGET, SCHEDULE, EFFORT, and RETURN to be displayed on the user's workstation screen. Selection of one of them by the user during prototype demonstrations will cause the associated screens and procedures to execute. If the user selects RETURN, control will return to the preceding higher-level menu from which this menu was called. These kinds of commands can be used to call display and help screens, data entry screens, screens with retrieved information, data transformation procedures, conventional programs, and other menus. The way in which they are set up and in which the user can traverse the menus is according to the architecture mapped out in the CFG.

Using visual programming techniques, developers can work with users to cosmetically improve the appearance of a menu screen until a pleasing and informative one is created. For example, text may be added as in Figure 5-11. In some systems, the visual programming commands might appear as shown below the dotted line in Figure 5-11. In other systems, a pointing device such as a mouse might be used to move things around the screen and insert-edit text. In either case, when the menu appearance is cosmetically acceptable to the prototyper, the cosmetic appearance and the control flow specified by the 4GL (as in the preceding example) combine to provide a menu driver module for the initial prototype.

Visual Programming and 4GL for Function Development

At this stage in prototype development, the user may travel up and down menu hierarchies as mapped out in the CFG(s) by actually executing the prototype interactively. Next, the user team will want to see some functionality behind the menu shells. It is fairly simple, using visual programming and fourth-generation languages, to set up ways to capture data into the system, change data loaded in from existing automated files, retrieve data to the terminal screen, and create longer test reports for system printers.

If, in our example, the user wanted to enter test data about study group project tasks, then the prototyper could comply by devising a screen with the attributes of

Study Group Information Input Menu

Select one of the following options from the menu at the bottom of the screen (typing only the first letter of the word is sufficient)

HELP   for an explanation of how to enter information about
            Service, Budgets, Estimates, or Cost

SERVICE   to enter new or updated information about requests for
            service by the Study Group. Service information involves
            what research is requested, who is the customer making
            the request, and what tasks will be involved in completing
            the request.

BUDGET   to enter new or updated information about how much
            budget (person-effort, supplies, etc.) is alloted to a
            requested project or to specific tasks comprising a
            requested project.

ESTIMATE   to enter new or updated information about estimated
            target dates for the delivery of research projects or
            specific tasks comprising requested projects.

COST   to enter the amount of time Study Group employees
            have expended toward the completion of a specific
            task comprising requested research projects.

RETURN   to return to the preceding (main) menu.

- -

HELP   EDIT   MOVE   OPEN   DELETE   UNDO   SAVE:

Figure 5-11   Visual programming for menu creation.

the task table. The default screen might look something like Figure 5-12 from the prototyper's point of view. Using the visual programming tools supplied by the RDMS, the developer can modify the appearance of the table until it seems easier to use. Working in a "what you see is what the user is going to get" mode, this is more likely to happen than when screens are developed with conventional programming tools.

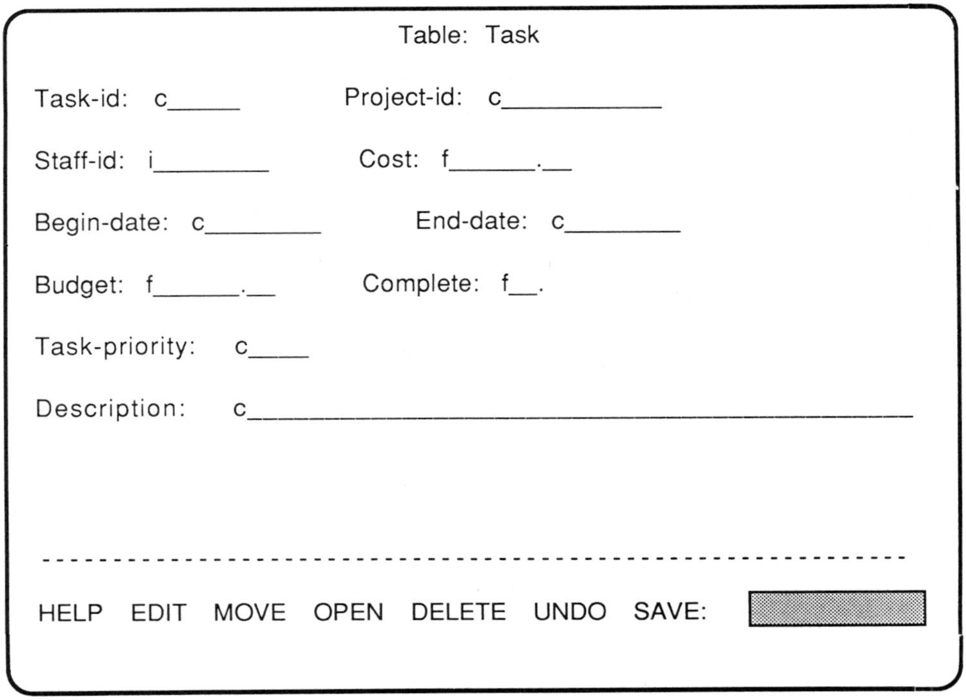

```
┌─────────────────────────────────────────────────────────────┐
│                        Table:  Task                          │
│                                                              │
│   Task-id:  c_____        Project-id:  c_____         │
│                                                              │
│   Staff-id:  i_____     Cost:  f_____.__                │
│                                                              │
│   Begin-date:  c_____     End-date:  c_____            │
│                                                              │
│   Budget:  f_____.__     Complete:  f__.                   │
│                                                              │
│   Task-priority:    c____                                    │
│                                                              │
│   Description:     c_____│
│                                                              │
│                                                              │
│                                                              │
│   - - - - - - - - - - - - - - - - - - - - - - - - - - - - -  │
│                                                              │
│   HELP   EDIT   MOVE   OPEN   DELETE   UNDO   SAVE: ▒▒▒▒▒▒    │
│                                                              │
└─────────────────────────────────────────────────────────────┘
```

Figure 5-12 Visual programming for function development.

Visual programming techniques applied to input functions such as data entry screens can accomplish more than simply providing a cosmetically pleasing appearance and on-screen help. Many systems allow the creation of data edit-audit criteria and other functionality in a visual programming mode. By providing system-requested information in on-screen dialogue boxes or forms, the prototyper can quickly accomplish such things as specifying

- Field highlighting (boxed, reverse video, or color)
- Retention of previous values (often called "sticky" fields)
- Mandatory fields (value must be entered by user)
- Display-only fields (values cannot be changed by user)
- Default values (the initial value for a new data entry)
- Data validation checks (within range or existing in other table)

By adding these specifications, the prototyper is able to create a complete and nontrivial input function instead of just a simple data entry screen. Notice that no lines of code (other than some simple 4GL command syntax) have so far been written. Thus, what is now in place has been rapid to create and will be very easy to modify if (or should we say when?) prototype demonstrations do not meet with complete user approval. There will be no system or software module logic to unravel before making modifications. Because of the very modular nature of the menu driver system created by the application generator, there will be no ripple effect to worry about when adding, deleting, or modifying functional modules.

When the prototyper has completed modifications to the default screen shown in Figure 5-12, the revised screen in the prototype demonstration might appear to the user as it does in Figure 5-13. The sequence of events would be the user signs on to the system and sees the main menu screen; the user selects "Supply Information" from the main menu; the user sees the input information menu; the user selects "Service" from the input information menu; the user sees the data entry screen shown in Figure 5-13. Notice that the visual programming commands shown in Figure 5-12 have disappeared. During execution pf the prototype, development utilities are replaced with utilities provided by the RDMS.

Most RDMS products allow users to interactively add, modify, and delete information in the database. Information can be retrieved on the basis of values entered in fields on screens such as the one shown in Figure 5-13. The commands to achieve such data retrieval and modification are typically supplied as menu-like choices by the RDMS. Thus when visual programming techniques are used to produce data entry screens, the resulting input function, when executed by the user during prototype demonstrations, will include executable RDMS commands. Thus

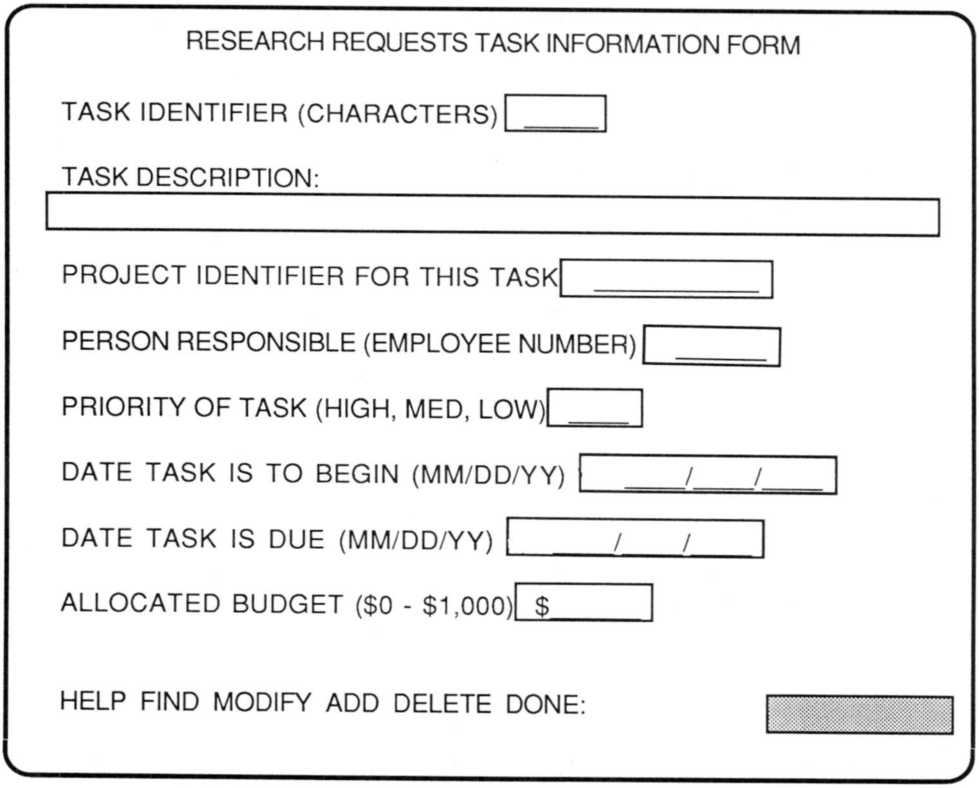
RESEARCH REQUESTS TASK INFORMATION FORM

TASK IDENTIFIER (CHARACTERS)

TASK DESCRIPTION:

PROJECT IDENTIFIER FOR THIS TASK

PERSON RESPONSIBLE (EMPLOYEE NUMBER)

PRIORITY OF TASK (HIGH, MED, LOW)

DATE TASK IS TO BEGIN (MM/DD/YY) / /

DATE TASK IS DUE (MM/DD/YY) / /

ALLOCATED BUDGET ($0 - $1,000) $

HELP FIND MODIFY ADD DELETE DONE:

Figure 5-13 A completed prototype screen.

the screen shown in Figure 5-13 shows user-selectable commands to find, modify, add, and delete data. Help at this level would relate to the use of these commands and would typically be a help function built in to the RDMS. Selection of "Done" from this screen would cause control to return to the prototyper's menu structure—back to the menu from which this screen was called. It is transparent to the user that such commands are supplied to the application by the RDMS at no cost in effort to the prototyper. This is a very powerful aspect of rapid prototyping using an integrated RDMS toolkit—free is about as rapid as you can get.

Other input functions would be created for the initial prototype in the same way. Each input function specified on the data entry CFG would be prototyped using the default screen that represented the table into which the data were to be input and applying visual programming techniques. The real power of visual programming is that, since the prototyper is constantly exposed to the appearance of the user interface during prototype creation and modification tasks, there will be few surprises during prototype demonstrations—regardless of user actions or reactions. Aborts and system crashes will not occur. Screen appearances, results of user actions, and control flow of functional execution will be very familiar and predictable to the prototyper.

Once some actual data are in the database, the developer can begin to supply some of the more fundamental functions. A trivial example would be that once actual effort expended by an employee toward the completion of a task is entered into the database, an automatic updating of the "total effort to date" attribute of the project table can be accomplished with the new information. Likewise, the amount of effort can be rolled up using the task table, since requests are composed of tasks. In this fashion, management will always have an up-to-date figure of actually expended effort costs for any research project, for the tasks that comprise that project, and for any employee for any given time period.

The final step in prototype development is to create output functions that report the results of such data transformations. Output functions often make use of a relational concept called a *view*. In relational terms, a view is a temporary (created at run time and deleted after execution) combination of information from multiple database tables. This is where the ERD created during rapid analysis comes in handy once again. Views can be defined for table combinations only where they have critical attributes to support the relationships indicated on the ERD. Did you create an ERD prior to beginning prototype development? Were database tables created such that they will support the relationships indicated on the diagram? If so, you will be in good shape for creating output functions.

Information may be retrieved from either a database table or a view using the RDMS 4GL query language. In some systems, the command syntax might be something like this:

```
RETRIEVE TASK (list of desired attributes)
WHERE PROJECT_ID EQUALS '' AG-BILL 123''
```

Execution of this command would result in the temporary creation of what is usually called a *results* or *selection* table in relational jargon. Included in the list of desired attributes could be computed fields such as COMPLETE-

((COST ∗ SALARY)/BUDGET) ∗ 100. The only other step necessary to create a 4GL report script is to write a print statement such as the following:

```
PRINT TASK (list result table attributes with associated output
            formats)
```

Output functions can also be created using visual programming techniques similar to those described for creating input functions. The prototyper operates on a default output screen generated by the RDMS, based on the default structure of a database table or prototyper-defined view. The default screen is modified to give the desired appearance of a prototype report—report by example. Again, dialogue boxes or RDMS-generated screen forms may be filled out with requested information to provide additional functionality such as column totals and other statistics.

We have discussed only visual programming and 4GL query commands as means for creating prototype functional modules. There are many other ways to include functions in the initial prototype. Some systems allow graphic output to be automatically generated based on the data found in tables or views. With a flexible application generator, calls to programs in a standard program library or existing operating system utilities can be included in the prototype menus. The authors have found that the vast majority of initial prototype development can be effectively accomplished through the use of a 4GL and visual programming. We have found these tools to be very quick for developing functional modules and that those functional modules are very easy to modify during prototype refinement.

It is also nice to have the flexibility provided by a powerful application generator when neither 4GLs nor visual programming will do the job. Program libraries can prove valuable in prototyping when they are known to include modules that need not be modified for any new system. Be careful about including conventionally developed software in a preliminary prototype and then making "a few slight modifications" to tailor that software to the new application—this seems a bit like the quick and dirty school of prototyping. The golden rule of evolutionary rapid prototyping is to make sure that all modules included in the initial prototype will be just as easy to modify, without introducing psychological complexity, as the paper models of conventional structured analysis and design.

The example used in this chapter was a fairly small system with simple requirements, but it would be a mistake to conclude that prototyping is only applicable to small, simple problems. Simple problems do not require prototyping—the conventional approach will work fine. We felt the preceding "how to" material would be easier to grasp with an example, but we did not want the example to be so complex as to obscure the principles being taught. We hope you will be able to use your imagination to extend these principles to apply to the types of software development projects you are involved with.

As an example of complex system prototyping, the NASA Goddard Space Flight Center commissioned a prototyping effort to provide a proof of concept demonstration of a Flight Dynamics Analysis System (FDAS). FDAS, a user-oriented research tool, supports spacecraft mission analysts, providing computational assistance in planning mission profiles, examining various computational strategies, and performing related flight dynamics ground support activities. FDAS provides a new user-friendly system for the space flight analysts to use and yet remain separated from the complex support software require.[14]

In addition, the Defense Advanced Research Projects Agency (DARPA), on its third year with the Strategic Computing Program in 1986, lists as its fundamental goal, ". . . to advance machine intelligence technologies by emphasizing research in several scientific disciplines." One of the four tasks primary to that goal is to build ". . . the elements of infrastructure needed to support research on advanced computing technologies, such as rapid prototyping methods for system development, large-scale emulation facilities, and access to new generation computers as they become available." Among DARPA's Strategic Computing Program projects are the Autonomous Land Vehicle, Navy Battle Management, the Pilot's Associate simulator for combat pilots, and the Army's Air/Land Battle Doctrine, all of which may employ some concept of prototyping and none of which are small or trivial systems.[15]

REFERENCES

1. Robert Block, *Politics of Projects* (New York: Yourdon Press, 1983).

2. Edward Yourdon, *Managing the System Life Cycle: A Software Development Methodology Overview* (New York: Yourdon Press, 1982).

3. Milton D. Roseanau and Marsha D. Lewin, *Software Project Management: Step-by-Step* (New York: Van Nostrand Reinhold, 1986).

4. E. Yourdon, *Structured Walkthroughs*, (New York: Yourdon Press, 1978).

5. M. Fagan, "Design and Code Inspections to Reduce Errors in Program Development," *IBM Systems Journal*, 15, no. 3, 1976, 182–207.

6. Meilir Page-Jones, *The Practical Guide to Structured Systems Design* (New York: Yourdon Press, 1980).

7. Stephen M. McMenamin and John F. Palmer, *Essential Systems Analysis* (New York: Yourdon Press, 1984).

8. James Martin and Carma McClure, *Diagramming Techniques for Analysts and Programmers* (Englewood Cliffs, NJ: Prentice Hall, 1985).

9. James Martin, *An End-User's Guide to Data Base* (Englewood Cliffs, NJ: Prentice Hall, 1981).

10. Betty Salzberg, "Third Normal Form Made Easy," *Sigmod Record* ACM, 15, no.4, December 1986.

11. C. J. Date, *An Introduction to Database Systems* (Reading, MA: Addison Wesley, 1986).

12. James Martin, *Computer Data-Base Organization* (Englewood Cliffs, NJ: Prentice Hall, 1977).

13. B. Salzberg, *An Introduction to Database Design* (Orlando, FL: Academic Press, 1986).

14. V. E. Church, D. N. Card, W. W. Agresti, Q. L. Jordan, "An Approach for Assessing System Prototypes," Collected Software Engineering Papers, volume IV, Software Engineering Laboratory Series, SEL-86-004, NASA Goddard Space Flight Center, Greenbelt, MD, November 1986.

15. Defense Advanced Research Projects Agency Strategic Computing Program Second Annual Report, Arlington, VA, February 1986.

6

Evolving a Rapid Prototype into a Deliverable System

After the steps described in Chapter 5 have been completed, a rapid prototype has been created. The project is only a few weeks old. Does this mean we are finished with prototyping? On the contrary, prototyping has only just begun. If we were prototyping to experiment with design concepts or to test the validity of process specifications, we might soon decide to abandon the prototype and begin to develop the real system. Using evolutionary prototyping tools and techniques, however, we have a solid foundation upon which to build the complete system. Let the system evolve from this foundation, rather than discarding it and starting over. This chapter describes the steps involved in such evolution.

Because we did an intentionally incomplete job of prespecification and prototype development, we have some information about the user's functional requirements but certainly not enough to develop a complete system. What we do have is a vehicle that can be used for dynamic discovery of user requirements. All we have to do now is demonstrate this crude model to the user and ask where and how it is inadequate. Inadequacies can be dealt with simply, a few at a time, in a series of iterations—

(demonstrate → specify changes → modify prototype → demonstrate)

—until the user is completely satisfied with the functionality embodied in the refined prototype. At this point, but not until this point, we will know what the user's true and complete functional requirements are.

Even when we have accurately defined system requirements through prototype iteration, we have not finished prototyping. There is still no deliverable product. Chances are very good that the functionally approved version of the prototype will not perform adequately in terms of response time if exposed to real volumes of users and data. Performance weaknesses must be discovered and corrected before the system can be pronounced adequate as a final product.

And, even when the prototype has been tuned for performance, if we are lucky, we may still not be finished prototyping. A delivered product that has been prototype-developed using the evolutionary approach may retain enough of the original flexibility of the initial prototype that prototyping techniques can be used on into the maintenance phase after delivery. Evolutionary rapid prototyping is the only approach to prototyping that can be applied to every phase of the software life cycle; as such, it is the most cost-effective approach. A little money is saved during development—due to evolving the prototype rather than throwing it away. A lot of money is saved during maintenance — because the more user-acceptable system requires fewer modifications and also because the system is easier to modify than conventionally developed software.

PROTOTYPE ITERATION

Having completed the steps in Chapter 5, Figure 6-1 shows where we are currently in the rapid prototyping process. We have built an intentionally incomplete working model and we (users and developers working together) are now ready to experiment with it. The objective of these experiments is the same as the objective of conventional requirements analysis—to find out what the user wants the system to do and to provide a means for building this functionality into the final product.

In Chapter 5 we showed how structured techniques could be used during rapid analysis to produce an adequate blueprint for prototype development. Then we showed how an integrated RDMS prototyping toolkit would be used to create a physical database and populate it with user-familiar data, develop a menu-driven modular control structure with an application generator, and create functional modules with 4GL and visual programming techniques. These steps in prototype development were illustrated by using the hypothetical "Study Group Research Request Tracking System" as an example. Having begun, we will continue using this example to

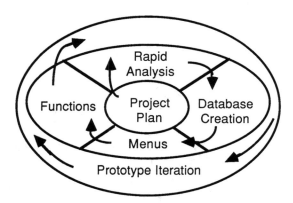

Figure 6-1 The prototyping process to requirements definition.

illustrate the steps in prototype evolution described in this chapter, fully aware that the application could be thought of as trivial.

Preparing for a Prototype Demonstration

The 18 modules specified by the control flow graphs in Chapter 5 would provide enough material for about a one-hour demonstration of these modules to users. One hour is an appropriate time frame for a prototype demonstration—it fits almost everyone's span of attention at a console and provides just enough feedback for rapid turnaround of the next demonstration. The philosophy of prototype demonstrations is similar to that of structured walkthrus—during the review period, the objective is to find defects, not to fix them. A one-hour demonstration will provide enough requests for modifications to the prototype to keep developers busy for a week or two. By having demonstrations at frequent intervals it is easier to keep users involved in the project by giving them a sense of continuity.

To make sure that all the material intended for the demonstration is covered, it helps to prepare and rehearse a demo script before the users' arrival. A script for demonstrating the prototype developed in the study group example might read as follows:

1. Show main menu
2. Have user invoke main menu help
3. Use help screen as an aid to explain the prototype
4. Have user invoke data entry menu
5. Have user invoke data entry help screen
6. Have user invoke and experiment with each of the three data entry screens
7. Return to main menu
8. Have user invoke reports menu
9. Show reports help screen
10. Have user invoke the brief interactive screen-display reports
11. Have user invoke a large hardcopy report
12. Pass out samples of the large hardcopy reports that you prepared in advance

In addition to the hour's worth of experimentation, users should be required to take samples of all reports away with them and study the information on the reports for errors. Stipulate that they have no more than 48 hours to bring back their findings—remember this is rapid prototyping and we are in a hurry.

Such a session may be a developer-run demonstration or an actual exercise of the prototype by the users. In the latter case, it has been found that users will learn much more, uncover many more errors, and have more pride of ownership if they are the operators of the prototype. Developers then assume the roles of "coach" and "facilitator" at such sessions and do not actually become involved in running the prototype.

Prototype Refinement Based on User Feedback

All prototype demonstrations will show about an hour's worth of added or modified functions. At each demonstration the prototypers will ask

- What additional functions would you like to see included?
- Which of the current processes are not correct?
- Have problems identified at the last demonstration been corrected?
- Have modifications resulted in the insertion of any new defects?

By recording and publishing the answers to such questions, either by using a form such as the one used for regular walkthrus or in a memo, much thrashing and mind-changing will be avoided and the prototype iteration loop can eventually be closed. One of the most difficult problems with the prototyping approach is knowing how and when to close what is potentially an infinite loop—prototype iteration. The loop tends toward the infinite when the rapid inclusion of one additional function always leads users to think of something else they would like the system to do, as depicted in Figure 6-2.

Rapid prototypers can build the Porsche the customer really wants instead of the Dusenburg that prespecification might lead to, but they cannot build a Lamborghini for the price of a Porsche. There is little doubt that prototyping will foster creative thinking on the user's part—a positive tendency from the quality viewpoint but possibly negative from the budgetary viewpoint. Chapter 7 presents some metrics and heuristics that will help to control this problem.

Returning to the study group example, suppose that the initial prototype demonstration resulted in the following feedback from the users:

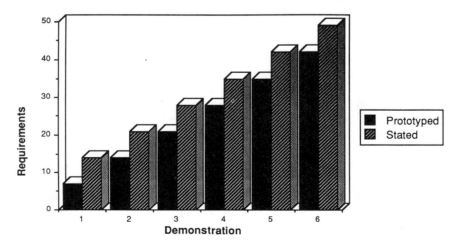

Figure 6-2   The more they get, the more they want.

- Apparently there is no way to capture effort spent on tasks as a project progresses—the task data entry screen is fine for creating new tasks, but how is the cumulative cost attribute of the task table to be updated?

- If there are errors in the cumulative cost field (some errors exist in the current data), reports sent to the customer will be wrong and this will be embarrassing—there needs to be a way for management to revise actual cost data when reports turn out wrong

- There is a need for multilevel security—staff members do not want other staff members looking at data regarding their tasks, project leaders do not want other project leaders accessing their project data, study group managers do not want other managers to see their study group information, and top corporate management wants access to everything in the database

What modifications would be required to the prototype to respond to these criticisms? How would these modifications be accomplished?

Most such modifications will involve one or more of the three high-level rapid analysis documents—DFD, CFG, and ERD. Because these documents exist only as a handful of paper documents, updating them is really no problem. Simply pencil in the changes or quickly resketch the document. However, for prototypes evolving into the final system, the refinement of these early documents will be retained as an important part of final system documentation. For that reason it is best to begin early managing such changes with a CASE tool.

To accumulate actual costs as a project progresses, we could create a new function for data entry of actual effort against tasks, calculation of the cost of that effort, and adding of the current period costs to cumulative costs for each task. How did this oversight occur in the first place? We might begin by looking at the essential functions diagram, Figure 5-7. This diagram correctly specifies a process for capturing staff effort, so that is not where the defect was inserted. If we look at the ERD (Figure 5-8) however, we can see (with hindsight) that there is no entity that could reasonably have a weekly-effort-by-staff-member attribute without containing a repeating group. Further investigation of the rapid analysis specifications reveals that the CFGs contain no call to a module for data entry of periodic effort spent on tasks by staff members.

It would be proper to begin the prototype revision cycle by first correcting the specifications. A new entity, perhaps called *timesheet* might be added to the ERD. The timesheet entity would have a relationship with tasks (one to n from the task's point of view) and another relationship with employees (one to n from the employee's point of view). This would require the timesheet table in the database to have the critical attributes Staff__ID and Task__ID. A week-ending date would uniquely identify a specific timesheet (assuming the reporting periods are to be weeks) and an attribute for effort expended would complete the table definition. Thus we would execute a 4GL RDMS command such as

```
CREATE TIMESHEET (STAFF_ID = I4, TASK_ID = C5, WEEK_END = C8,
                  EFFORT = F4.1)
```

Next it would make sense to revise the CFG for the data entry menu to include a call to a new module for weekly task effort data entry. This means the menu screen for the prototype would also have to be modified. A text editor would be used to add new lines to the 4GL command string which would specify something like

```
TIMESHEET = call screen timesheet,
            call procedure accumulate-cost;
```

The appearance of the menu screen would be modified using visual programming, then the new modules "timesheet" and "accumulate-cost" would be prototyped. Figure 6-3 shows what the new timesheet screen might look like.

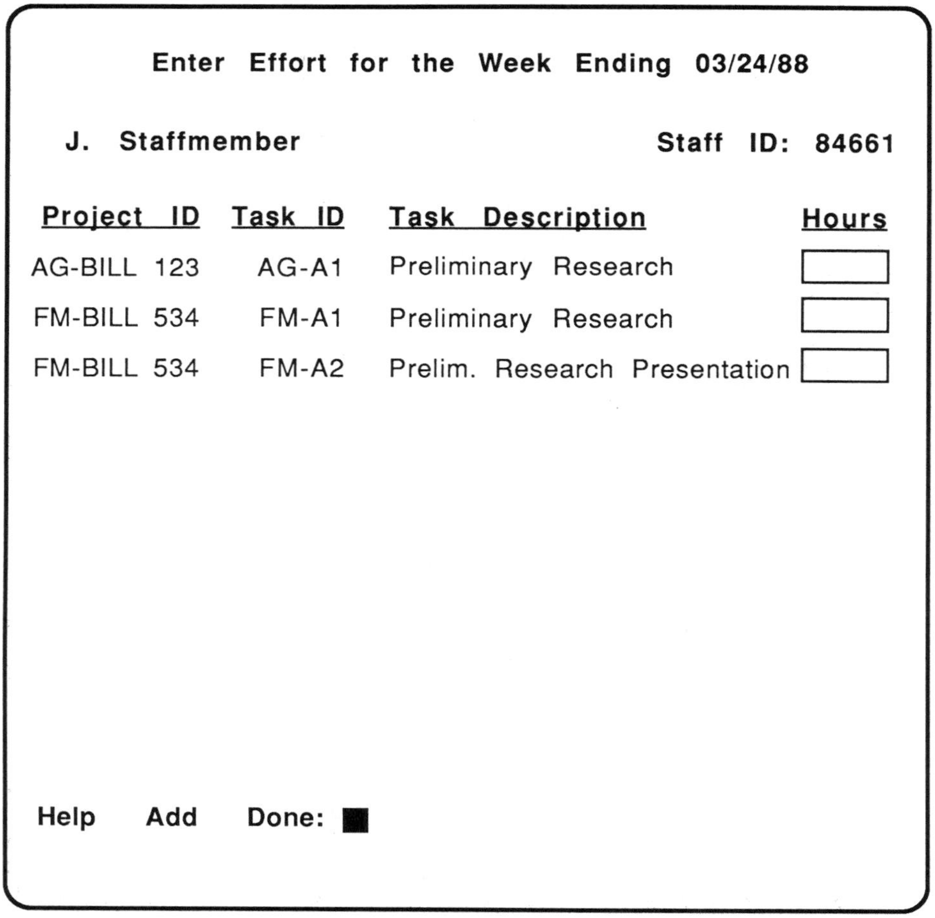

Enter   Effort   for   the   Week   Ending   03/24/88

J. Staffmember		**Staff ID: 84661**	

Project ID	Task ID	Task Description	Hours
AG-BILL 123	AG-A1	Preliminary Research	▯
FM-BILL 534	FM-A1	Preliminary Research	▯
FM-BILL 534	FM-A2	Prelim. Research Presentation	▯

Help   Add   Done: ■

Figure 6-3 Timesheet screen.

The actual timesheet screen could be prototyped in at least two different ways. The simplest would be to use visual programming on the default timesheet table. This would require staff members to know their employee identification number and the numbers of all tasks they are currently working on. To complete a data entry session on effort for the week, staff members would have to complete a screen for each task worked on that week. This does not provide much in the way of helpful information about tasks and projects that exists elsewhere in the database and does nothing toward guaranteeing that the data entered are reasonable—for example, total at least 40 hours. A more elegant solution would be to create a view combining attributes of the project, task, staff, and timesheet tables. The timesheet table attributes would be included as what are sometimes referred to as "table fields" or "subforms"—basically repeating groups. Visual programming would then be performed on the defined view rather than the timesheet table itself. The "accumulate cost" procedure would be a 4GL command string that multiplies effort in the timesheet table by a weekly cost calculated from the staff table salary attribute and then adds that cost to the cumulative cost attribute in the task table. It makes little difference if prototypers choose the simpler or the more elegant of the two preceding choices. The true test of correctness will occur at the next prototype demonstration when further requirements for modifications will become evident.

The requirement for a capability to correct errors in historical cost data (the second bullet in the foregoing example of user feedback) has some political overtones. Certainly there may be cases where reports show that the database contains incorrect data. But why should managers be allowed to make the corrections? Do managers have the best information on who worked how many hours on what task? Wouldn't it be more appropriate to ask the staff to make these corrections on the following week's timesheet? Is there a hidden agenda where managers have a desire to "cook the books" so reports always look the way they want them to regardless of actual data? What will such a capability do to the usefulness of historical data for future contract estimating purposes?

The prototyper of the system in our example may be torn between doing the "right" thing (disallowing management access for changing historical data) and doing what the customer wants (allowing it). If the prototyper uses a relational database, the opportunity for a creative solution to the dilemma exists. A "revision" table—exact duplicate of the task table—could be added to the database. A data entry screen could be created and added to the menu structure to allow managers to modify the data in this table. An example of such a screen is shown in Figure 6-4. At the time the revision module is invoked, data could be appended to the revision table from the task table. Customer reports could be produced from the revision table, while internal reports could be produced from the task table to provide data for historical metrics. Staff members would then be allowed to make corrections to unadulterated data on future timesheets. The effectiveness of such a compromise would be tested at the next prototype demonstration.

The requirement for multilevel security is perhaps the easiest to accommodate. Most modern relational database management systems have a one-line 4GL command to modify database access privileges. Such modifications can limit access

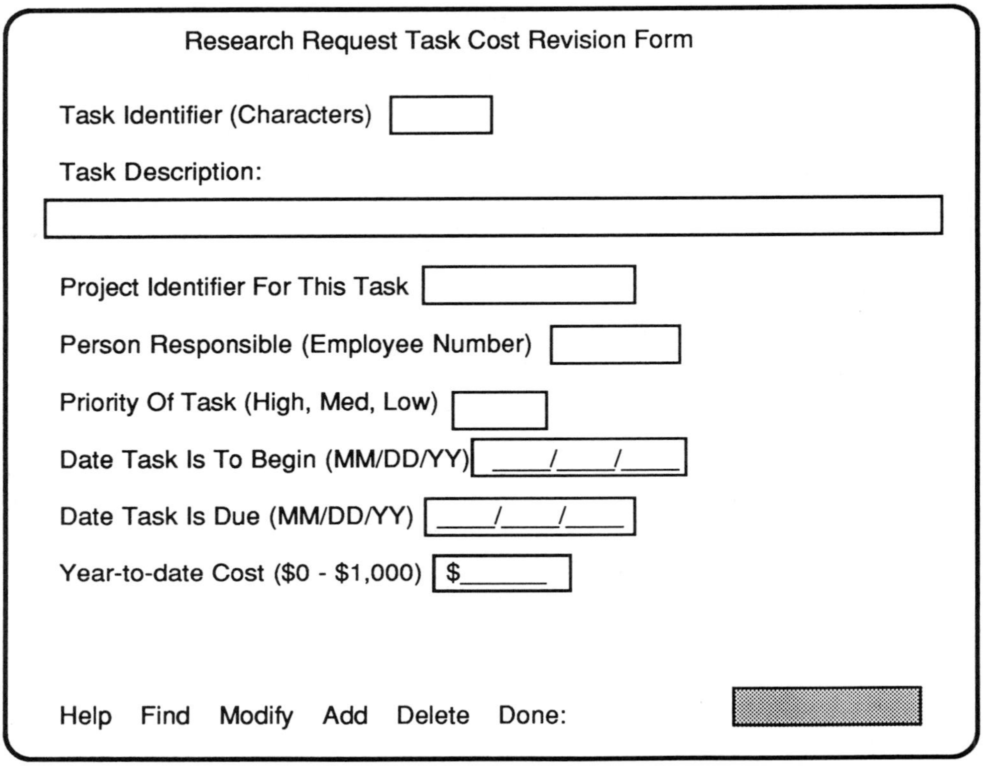

Research Request Task Cost Revision Form

Task Identifier (Characters) [_____]

Task Description:

[_____]

Project Identifier For This Task [_____]

Person Responsible (Employee Number) [_____]

Priority Of Task (High, Med, Low) [_____]

Date Task Is To Begin (MM/DD/YY) [____/____/____]

Date Task Is Due (MM/DD/YY) [____/____/____]

Year-to-date Cost ($0 - $1,000) [$_____]

Help   Find   Modify   Add   Delete   Done: [▓▓▓▓▓▓▓▓]

Figure 6-4   The revision data entry screen.

to certain tables, to certain rows in a table, and even to certain attributes in each row. The privileges can specify classes of users, times of day, input device identification, and other considerations. To accommodate the study group application security requirements, prototypers would simply set access privileges on the appropriate tables. The task table could be modified, for instance, so a staff member could only access rows where their log-in ID was equal to the value of Staff_ID for those rows. Some RDMS vendors provide *locking* at the row level, some at the table level. Most do not have attribute locking capabilities, but we can look forward to those kind of enhancements as the products mature.

The importance of user involvement during prototype iteration cannot be overemphasized. If the users and the developers coexist in the same location, prototyping is easier to accomplish than if users are spread out over multiple sites. In the case of multiple user sites, prototypers must visit the various sites at rapid intervals or user representatives may be brought in. It is imperative that users and developers are all present for the creation of the project plan and the creation of the rapid analysis documents. Again, these documents can be the products of a two- or three-day intensive session resembling a joint application design (JAD) session. Once begun, the iterative process must not be slowed by distance. With distributed processing and electronic mail, it is quite possible to ship prototype versions and related documentation. Teleconferencing is another solution for reviewing prototypes from remote sites. No solution is quite as effective as user exercise of the prototype with developers present.

User Approval of Prototype Functionality

The heading for this section is the milestone that indicates that prototype iteration is over. At this point, the user is happy with everything the prototype does—not necessarily with how fast it does it. Working together, prototypers and users have discovered what information the system must capture and produce to make it optimally useful. They have also worked out the most operationally intuitive way to invoke this usefulness. The prototyper has discovered what internal data transformations must take place within the system to produce required outputs and what data must be stored internally. Thus the system functional requirements have been worked out from the user's point of view. The user's view of functional requirements consists of the set of operational interfaces with the system and the information produced by the system. The details of how this information is produced are appropriately transparent to the user. In other words, prototype iteration is over when the user says, "This version of the prototype does everything I would like the system to do and does it just the way I would like things done."

It may sound like the prototyper's work is finished at this point but, as you can see, you are only halfway through the book. The biggest danger of prototyping is, in fact, that there will always be a temptation, at the point in time when the user approves prototype functionality, to deliver the prototype as the final system. It may be difficult to say to users, "No, you can't have this system with which you are perfectly happy—yet." It may be difficult to say to management, "No, this does not present an appropriate opportunity to reallocate resources to other projects." It may be difficult to say to developers, "Let's postpone the postdelivery celebration until we have finished documentation, stress testing, and performance tuning."

A functionally approved prototype is not a deliverable system. It is not adequately documented for future maintenance purposes at this point. We don't know yet how it will perform under future loads of data and user volumes. All we have at this point is a dynamic functional requirements specification. On the plus side, we do have an *accurate* requirements specification. We have not been faking requirements analysis. We know what the system should do because we have a working model that does just that—the user says so. The user is sure we have the requirements right because this can be verified from output based on actual user-familiar application data.

Armed with this powerful new knowledge we can proceed to publish a final system requirements specification. This specification has been evolving right along with the prototype from the days of rapid analysis. All we need do at this point is remove the word "draft" from the cover and (easily) obtain the user's signature of approval. If we haven't done so yet, we will also want to finalize detailed process specifications and the data dictionary. As we proceeded through prototype iteration, we added data definitions to the data dictionary as our functional model became progressively more refined—right? We added process specifications whenever the user gave approval to a functional module—right? There should be little to do in the way of a final cleanup of the requirements document at this point. If organizational policy also requires a formal system requirements review, we can conduct such a review with confidence. We can stand up in front of anyone, regardless of managerial level, and say without fear that we know what the detailed functional requirements of the system are. We have the user's support on this.

There is one other activity that is appropriate at this point—conducting strategy sessions regarding prototype evolution. You should know enough about prototype performance and target environment at this point to make a go or no-go decision. Can the prototype evolve into the final system, or should the actual software be completely replaced with code written in a lower-level language? Are we suggesting that sometimes it is appropriate to do throwaway prototyping with evolutionary tools? In fact, there are cases where prototype evolution might be completely out of the question, but prototyping still serves a useful purpose. Some examples of nonevolutionary situations are

- Completely embedded software—for example, an elevator control system, where there is no place to host the RDMS in the target environment
- Contractual requirements for use of a programming language that does not support (is not compatible with) use of an evolutionary prototyping toolkit
- Contractual requirements for exclusive use of a lower-level programming language
- Performance requirements for real-time applications that will obviously require the exclusive use of a lower-level language

Even in these situations, what we have accomplished so far has not been a waste of time or money. By accurately defining functional requirements through prototyping, we will avoid the massive amount of postdelivery software modification effort that is typical using conventional prespecification approaches. Also, just because we were using evolutionary prototyping tools does not imply that prototyping effort was more expensive than if we had been using throwaway prototyping tools. Good evolutionary tools are just as fast and easy to use as throwaway tools—they simply provide a path for *possible* prototype evolution.

DESIGN DERIVATION

What is a discussion about design doing at this point in the description of prototype evolution? Doesn't acceptable software engineering practice call for design before coding? Haven't we actually been designing the system as we went along? Can we design something that has already been built? The answer to all these questions is, "yes." Although it is certainly appropriate and advisable to code from a detailed structured design, we haven't exactly been coding yet. What we have been doing is dynamically defining functional requirements using a working model of the system. Since this model—built using a relational database, visual programming, and 4GL command strings—is just as easy to understand and modify as conventional paper prespecifications, we have not violated "acceptable software engineering practice." We have, however, avoided undertaking a detailed structured design while at the same time engaging in some "design-ish" types of activities such as specifying the data storage structure and the system control flow.

Next, in the evolution of the prototype to the final system, we may want to engage in some conventional coding using a lower-level language. We may want to introduce some inflexibility into the data storage structure by specifying keys or indices and creating files external to the database. The extent of such activities will result in replacement of portions of the functionally approved prototype. The percentage of replacement will vary from zero to 100 percent depending on the results of the strategy sessions recently described and the stress testing described next. To the extent that replacement is less than 100 percent, we can say that we are doing evolutionary prototyping. To the extent that replacement is greater than zero, we can no longer say that the system will remain as flexible as the paper specifications. Thus, in the case of all but the most trivial applications, we must adopt a new attitude toward prespecification at this point. When the stage of design derivation is reached, prespecification becomes a worthy activity.

If we are going to write conventional program code in a lower-level language, we need to assure, for purposes of future maintainability, that we will write structured, well-documented code. If we are going to create relatively inflexible storage structures, we need to assure that those storage structures are accurately defined and documented. We need an "as-prototyped," detailed, structured design before proceeding to the next phase. Notice that this is different from the "build-to" design called for in a conventional approach. Now we have an effective way to bridge the typically difficult gap between analysis and design. We have a user-approved physical working model from which to derive the physical design. No longer will designers be forced to make decisions about functionality because of gaps left in the requirements specification. If you want to argue that this removes creativity from the design process—yes it does, and so be it. The objective is to design an architecture that will support user requirements, not to build an elegant solution to the wrong problem.

A complete detailed design at this point involves evolving the control flow graphs produced and refined during prototyping to become structure charts. Coupling between modules may be specified at this point. Module specifications should be written for each box. A complete attribute list should now accompany the entity-relationship diagram—that is, defined as data elements in the data dictionary. There are two guidelines to keep in mind during design derivation:

- Design documentation must accurately specify the architecture of the current version of the prototype
- Design documentation must provide everything that is required for conventional software maintenance

The reason for the first guideline is self-evident—we don't want documentation that is misleading. The reason for the second guideline is more subtle. As we move into the tuning phase and begin to undertake more conventional software development activities, what is happening begins to suspiciously resemble software maintenance—making modifications to an existing system. This phenomenon has led some cynics to describe rapid prototyping as an opportunity to do software maintenance much earlier in the life cycle. There is a grain of truth to this assertion, making obvious the need for adequate documentation. Documentation, both of requirements and design specifications, can be made adequate through verification by a walkthru team consisting of potential system maintenance personnel. Why not begin now training these people on how the system works?

PERFORMANCE TUNING

If we have a functionally approved and adequately documented system, there is just one more step to take before we can say we have a finalized software product. A big risk involved in using unconventional tools for software development is that we may not be able to predict the performance characteristics under actual use without first doing some experimentation. Will the system support enough users if it becomes popular and many more people than originally anticipated want to use it? Might increases in the user's business activity cause data volumes to mushroom? What will large increases in either the volume of data or users, or both, do to the performance characteristics of the system? It is critically important to establish the answers to these questions before we deliver the final product.

Of course, it is true that large increases in the number of users and the amount of data will degrade the performance of *any* system, regardless of the development tools used. While this is true, it is also true that experience has shown the RDMS and the 4GL to be particularly sensitive to such volume issues. This fact alone has caused some critics to say that prototyping is only practical for small systems. Vendors have been very busy in the last few years struggling to improve the performance of their products. Some relational database systems can now offer retrieval times as fast as those of any type of database system or file structure for that matter (depending on whose benchmark is used). Nevertheless, because performance problems with the RDMS and the 4GL have become "common knowledge" it is probably wise to assure that your prototype-developed system performs better than conventionally developed software to avoid any possibility of "I told you so."

Here are some things of which to be wary. During prototype development and iteration, did you

- Avoid specifying key attributes to be used as table indices?
- Give prototype demonstrations to small groups of users identified in the project plan rather than the full set of possible users?
- Use test data in some tables where actual application data were not available?
- Avoid normalization of tables in favor of quick development of screens and reports?

If you operate using the procedures described in this book you must take these approaches—they are not mistakes—they represent the way business is appropriately conducted during prototype development and iteration. During these early stages the performance of the system is de-emphasized to concentrate on functionality of the system while building a working model that is as flexible as possible. Nevertheless, these actions will have built some performance traps into the system that are likely to surface sooner or later. We recommend bringing these issues to the surface now and fixing all discovered potential performance problems before the software is delivered.

Stress Testing a Prototype

The objective of stress testing is simple—to break the prototype. Find the bounds of every functional module of the prototype, if possible, and document them. If you don't break a module, you will not know where the breaking point occurs. And if you don't have that knowledge, you will not know how much data or how many users the prototype will support. Risky business to say the least.

One breaking point of a prototype module is the point at which the user can show that, for legitimate business purposes, the response time of that module is inadequate. Theoretically, it is the point at which one fewer user or bit of data would produce response time that was just barely adequate. While it may not be possible to develop such precise benchmarks, any stress testing is better than none, and none is too frequently what many prototypes receive. How many times, in fact, do conventional development approaches use response-time stress testing? Typically, this is only done when human life or the survival of expensive equipment is at stake.

There are very few experts in the field of precision benchmarking. The issues concerning the validity of various benchmarking techniques are somewhat confusing. The bottom line would seem to be that there is no such thing as a believable benchmark. It is hard to find someone expert enough to devise a "typical database query." We frankly admit we are not. Therefore, we use the less rigorous term, stress testing. Stress testing makes use of actual application data, real users, and actual prototype functions rather than artificially developed benchmarks. Stress testing will not provide a precise breaking point as just described theoretically. Nor will it provide an absolute guarantee, upon successful completion, of adequate response times in all possible future usage conditions. It is simply a practical and common sense approach to force to the surface performance problems likely to exist in a functionally approved prototype.

Those who are conscious of the possible magnitude of performance problems that can exist in large applications often question why the prototyping approach avoids wrestling with performance issues until this late in the game. These people can often cite war stories in which an ultimate project failure could have been avoided by giving consideration to performance issues at the beginning of the project. Here is a message to these people: It is perfectly acceptable to *think* about possible performance problems at the beginning of a project. We would like to suggest, however, that many more projects have failed because developers failed to think about functionality at the beginning of a project, or because there was inadequate communication between users and developers regarding proposed system functionality.

In addition to desiring to concentrate on functionality at the beginning of a project and desiring to keep the system flexible and easy to modify as long as possible, there is another motivation for prolonging performance consideration until now. Having an example of possibly undesirable performance in place, we can ask the users to prove that they need better response time. This is a more cost-effective approach than spending much effort trying to achieve two-second response time on all functions because that was a performance requirement thought necessary by the user and therefore specified at the beginning of a project. The philosophy is functionality first, performance as needed. Worrying about performance problems at the beginning of a project can be like worrying about the sky falling or the end of the world—it might never happen. We have not written any conventional programs yet. We have probably not hosted the system in the target environment. There is still plenty of time to deal with performance issues.

Recognizing that performance can be the known problem of most critical interest at the beginning of some projects, the bottom line is that rapid prototyping, basically a dynamic functional requirements modeling technique, contributes little to the solution for performance problems. Do not try to use a wrench to hammer nails, or a hammer to drive screws. Trying to solve performance problems with rapid prototyping tools is similar to trying to model functional requirements by writing assembly language code.

As a suggestion of how to apply rapid prototyping to applications where performance problems are known in advance to be of paramount importance, try using computerized system simulations to solve the performance problems and try *prototyping the simulations*. Simulations have long been recognized as a means of solving performance and timing issues. No one ever worries about trying to evolve simulations into deliverable systems. The simulation is considered a separate product of the development project. Simulations must be run by human users and quite often have uneccessarily complex user interfaces—a problem that *can* be solved effectively using rapid prototyping techniques. Using the prototyping tools recommended in this book, simulations will be easier to develop, easier to use, and *might* sometimes be evolvable into deliverable products.

As an example of typical prototype evolution, let's consider some stress testing that might be done for the study group application. Suppose we create a test study group database that is a duplicate, in terms of tables and attributes, of the prototype database. Then we can use copy routines, as described in Chapter 5, to populate this database. Next we can either use more copy or append routines, or both, to increase the data volume in all tables (say, double it), then execute all the prototype reports and record the execution times. If these times are acceptable to the user, we would increase the data volumes and try again, repeating this procedure until we obtained unacceptable response times—the approximate breaking point. Then we have to ask ourselves and the user: What is the margin for error? Are we talking about twice the anticipated data volume expected, or only ten percent more? No guarantees, but at least we know the risk level. We can rationally decide if the risk is acceptable.

A similar strategy can be used to determine the maximum number of users the system will support. Suppose that the study groups employ a total of 100 staff members. Realistically, it is not probable that all 100 users will ever be using the system concurrently. Even if they did, it is extremely improbable that all of them would ever execute a system function concurrently. There will, however, be periods of heavy activity in future use of the system. During these peak periods there will be some occurrences of multiple function executions. These occurrences can have a dramatic negative effect on response time. During prototype iteration, there may never have been more than one or two simultaneous users, so we have no data on system user capacity.

Now we must establish breaking points for numbers of users. We could have six staff members execute a data entry module such as timesheet. When all have completed a timesheet, have them enter "save" and all hit the Return or Enter key simultaneously. Record the amount of time required to refresh the screen. If response time is satisfactory, add more staff members to the experiment and try again. Repeat until unsatisfactory response time occurs—the approximate breaking point. Perform this experiment for each interactive prototype module until all user volume breaking points are known.

The stress tests just described are somewhat artificial—they simulate but do not duplicate a production environment. This artificiality leaves some unknowns in our performance equation. We stress tested for data volume alone and then we tested user volume alone. There is an unknown and unpublished equation that goes something like this:

$$T = X U + Y D$$

Where T is response time
U is the number of users
D is data volume
X and Y are unknown nonlinear functions

In other words, response time is a nonlinear function of the number of users and the amount of data which the system must accommodate. The problem is that all the variables in the equation are unknown. No one has yet been able to derive meaningful values for X and Y. All that can be said is that there is known to be a trade-off—the more users a system must support, the less data it can accommodate and vice versa. It is also known that the functions X and Y represent steeply rising curves. For small volumes of users and data, incrementing either U or D, or both, will not increase T very much. For large volumes of users and data, unit increments of U and D will cause a dramatic increase in T. Although the precise shape of the curve is unknown currently, we suspect that it looks something like the one in Figure 6-5.

The complex interrelationship between number of users and amount of data causes the unit stress tests just described to have little useful meaning. Obviously, we must undertake stress testing of user and data volumes combined. Only empirical observation will provide any real data points. One practical way out of this dilemma would be to specify, after conducting the unit stress tests just described, the probable maximum number of concurrent users—almost pure guesswork. Then the unit data volume stress tests could be performed again, establishing for each module the maximum data volume given the probable maximum number of concurrent users.

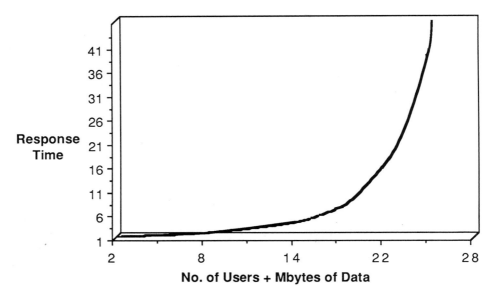

Figure 6-5   Response time as a function of users and data.

The result of such stress testing is that we at least know which prototype modules are fragile with respect to performance characteristics. What we have really been doing is establishing the performance risk levels involved in delivering the prototype as is. For some modules the risk level might be clearly too high. For other modules there might be no problem at all. Problematically, there is usually a third category where a gamble involving unknown probabilities must be taken. We encourage you to be very conservative in taking such gambles. Remember that the curves for X and Y are very steep.

Next we will examine some strategies for fixing identified performance problems. Suppose that due to the large amount of historical data loaded into the project table, with only a five percent increase in data volume and one user, it takes seven seconds between the time a command is entered to save the entry of a new project and when the screen is refreshed with a new blank research request form. The user must have at least a five-second response time with at least a 50 percent margin for error. Suppose further that, if 12 staff members try to enter and save effort data on the timesheet form, response time will be 17 seconds. Since timesheets are typically filled out during the last working hour on Friday, the user feels that a six-second response time (the result of the last test before adding the twelfth user) with a 50 percent data volume margin and 50 users would be more appropriate. Finally, suppose that a large internal report on the progress of all projects consumes six hours of CPU time with no increase in data volume at all. The user would like the report to execute in less than ten minutes with a 50 percent data volume margin.

Next we give some techniques for resolving such problems for the study group example and for real-world applications. We will give four basic techniques for improving response time, in the order of their simplicity. The reader is encouraged to try the first technique; then, if still better performance is needed, apply the second technique; and so forth until adequate performance is obtained. The last of the four techniques is appropriately labeled, "the last resort," and the reader is reminded that this technique is only recommended if all else fails.

Database Structure Optimization

Although a truly relational RDMS does not require the developer to specify the key or index for a table, most systems provide this capability as an option. This means that the creation of a database table, without specification of a key attribute, will result in a default storage structure that is known, in relational jargon, as a *heap*. The heap structure means that every time a record is added to a table, it is placed at the top of the heap, so the heap is in no particular order. A heap is not a very efficient storage structure—it requires database retrieval routines to read every row in a table before returning a result. Obviously, dramatic improvements in response times can be achieved just by specifying the key attribute for each table. Doing so will permit the RDMS to use very efficient keyed-access sort algorithms to return a result after reading only a few rows.

Specifying a key, however, places a few constraints on the developer. For obvious reasons, a table cannot contain multiple rows with the same key value. Keys must be unique values. Also, attribute list revisions, accompanied by unload-reload routines as described in Chapter 5, become more complex when keys are specified. One must be very careful not to delete the key from the attribute list during such revisions. This complexity is compounded by the fact that many systems allow the developer to specify secondary and tertiary keys as well. Thus indexing a table necessarily introduces some inflexibility into the database structure. For this reason, it is wise to avoid indexing until retrieval procedures and required attributes are well known—after prototype iteration is finished. Leave all table structures in the default heap format until user approval of prototype functionality is obtained.

When retrieval procedures are well defined, after user approval of prototype functionality, you will have a clear idea of what the key(s) should be for each table. Joins of multiple tables will have been defined and refined to produce prototype views and reports. The joins will specify a retrieval result attribute list to be produced "where *this* equals *that*"—*this* and *that* being attributes in different tables that are required to have the same value in the retrieval result. By inspecting the number of times *this* and *that* occur in such retrievals, you can verify their candidacy as key attributes for their associated database tables. It only makes sense to do this after the user has completely approved the functionality of the current prototype version. Only then do these relationships become stable.

As an example, the performance problem having to do with a seven-second response time for the data entry of new research requests might be solved by modifying the project table to index on Project__ID. In some systems, an example 4GL command to achieve this modification might be

```
MODIFY PROJECT TO INDEX ON PROJECT_ID
```

Execution of this simple command would cause the project table to be permanently indexed. To verify that this is a good idea, we note that in the user-approved prototype, the task and timesheet tables are frequently joined with the project table, using Project__ID as the common attribute, to produce views, data entry screens, and reports.

Thus, this one statement modification will go a long way towards solving not only the first performance problem, but also helping to alleviate the second and third as well. Timesheet response time will improve to the extent that required joins with the project table have been optimized. Project progress reports will execute faster to the extent that joins between the project and task tables have been optimized. These optimizations might then be carried a bit further by indexing the task table on Task__ID and the staff and timesheet tables on Staff__ID. Secondary and tertiary keys might also be specified where sensible. The task table, for instance, might use Project__ID as the secondary key and Staff__ID as the tertiary key.

There is another means for optimizing the database structure, having to do with the concept of normalization alluded to earlier in this chapter. Normalization is good because it reduces redundant attributes, reduces redundant data entry, and eliminates database inconsistency. The ultimate goal of normalization is to arrange the database such that any attribute need only be updated in one table. Unfortunately, normalization can also be inefficient because, as it increases the number of tables in the database, it also increases the amount of work the system must do to recombine tables to produce views and reports—thus increasing response time. In other words, normalization involves a trade-off between optimizing response time and optimizing data entry effort. Since data entry effort is also dependent on response time, it becomes a recursive problem. Bill Inmon is one of many experts who suggest that "denormalization" is one answer to this problem.[1]

Due to the balance necessary between theory and practice, we propose a common sense approach to optimizing the normalization trade-off, based on practical experience. Use "best normal form" rather than striving toward third, fourth, or fifth normal form. Best normal form requires that attribute values for a particular row in a database table should be dependent on the value of a unique key for that table. Also, there should be no repeating groups in any table definition. A further constraint, based on practical experience, is that the optimal number of attributes for a relational database table is, just like bubbles on a DFD, seven plus or minus two. Fewer than five attributes in each table will require too many relational joins to produce required output, thus seriously degrading response time. More than nine attributes in a table may cause too much redundant data entry if, as is often the case, the large number of attributes means that some of the nonkey attributes recur in other tables. Admittedly, following this guideline will typically result in gross violations of the classic third normal form concept. It may also cause some redundant data entry to occur in some cases. Our only justification for this nonacademic approach is that in our experience it has proven to be an optimal trade-off range. You are encouraged to view it as a rule of thumb. With normalization, the idea of having between five and nine attributes makes *no* sense for some kinds of data. Real time telemetry data, for example, may have many attributes, all dependent on the key.

When the database structure has been thoroughly optimized, perform unit stress tests once more to see what performance gains have been achieved. Some of the identified performance problems have probably dropped out of consideration. We might find in the study group example, for instance, that response time for project data entry on the research request form has improved to four seconds with a 50 percent margin for anticipated data volume. Suppose that response time for timesheet data entry has improved to the point where 30 concurrent users can obtain an eight-second response time with a 50 percent margin for data volume. Suppose execution time of the project progress report has improved to two hours with a 50 percent data volume margin. We have now solved the first performance problem, we're almost there on the second issue, and we still have a way to go on the third.

Configuration Modifications

Applications built upon a relational database, like any other application, run faster on fast processors with lots of main memory and access to more on-line storage. Thus, an effective tuning strategy can be to upgrade the hardware configuration where feasible. Hardware upgrades can be inexpensive compared to programmer salaries. Also, a one-time hardware upgrade will improve the performance of all future prototypes developed on that system where tuning will have to be repeated for each new prototype developed. Furthermore, where hardware upgrades are feasible, the prototype is allowed to remain in a more "pristine" state. Fewer modules will have to be rewritten in lower-level languages to meet performance requirements. The entire prototype will remain more maintainable. A simple cost-benefit study will indicate when upgrading the hardware configuration makes sense.

We have heard cynics say that using the hardware upgrade strategy for performance tuning of relational systems means something like buying a new machine for each new prototype-developed application. We believe this to be an overly scary generalization based on experiences in which no other tuning strategies were employed. We would only see the need for re-hosting a relational application on a dedicated processor in the case of extremely large applications developed on already overused hardware configurations. Specifically, this would mean that the machine was already hosting multiple applications before prototype development began and that the new application was much larger than anything previously developed on that machine. This might present a justification for acquisition of an additional computer. However, there are many less drastic strategies involving upgrading the CPU, upgrading RAM, or adding additional hard disk storage capacity to the system.

Suppose that we looked at the cost of hardware upgrades for the study group example and found that upgrading the CPU from an 8-Mhz processor with a 16-bit data path to a 16-Mhz processor with a 32-bit data path, upgrading RAM from 8 Mb to 16 Mb and adding an additional 500 Mb of hard disk storage would cost

50 percent of the estimated money required to pay programmers to replace the prototype timesheet and project progress report modules with low-level programs. This doesn't tell us that such a configuration upgrade will absolutely solve all our remaining performance problems, but it appears to be a sensible gamble since the upgraded configuration will also improve the performance of all future prototypes developed on this system. Suppose, for instance, that we do this upgrade and that the results are that timesheet data entry response time is now four seconds with 50 concurrent users and a data volume margin of 50 percent. Execution time for the project progress report is now 25 minutes—not bad! All problems are solved except for the last—project progress report execution time. We might even be able to convince the user to live with the 25 minutes or risk a lower data volume margin.

Data Minimization

The data minimization strategy does not really apply to the study group example. There is only so far one can stretch an artificial example to illustrate all desired points. Basically, data minimization involves realizing that since relational database systems are slowed down dramatically by massive amounts of data, it might prove effective to remove some data from the RDMS and store them elsewhere.

An example of a situation where this strategy might be effectively employed is a geophysical exploration application. In such an application, required information might deal with geological data collected at many drilling sites by instruments that take multiple readings every few inches down a hole thousands of feet deep. Obviously, the result will be gigabytes of application data. An example of a functional requirement for such an application might be to provide the user, upon interactive query, with information about at which depth a proposed drilling site might expect to encounter a particular type of rock formation. This would require the RDMS to search through all the gigabytes of stored data and possibly perform some joining operations to produce an output.

Another example of a difficult data management task might be a large text management application, such as the storage and retrieval of legal case studies for a large law firm. Such an application would require the storage of large blocks of free-form textual data with retrievals based on some key word scheme. There are specially optimized text databases for the performance of this type of task—relational databases are not particularly efficient in this area.

Fortunately, there are "work-arounds" for such massive data management applications. First we must realize that much has already been done to minimize the amount of data that the prototype database must handle. This is due to the minimalist approach we took to prespecification before initial prototype development. A comprehensive data modeling approach would require users to specify detailed data requirements in full before creating a database. The initial database using this approach would be developed from a corporate data model containing all of the attributes the users could possibly ever conceive of needing. Users will tend to be conservative when subjected to this approach, fearing that if a data requirement is not prespecified they will have no opportunity in the final system to obtain this data, should they ever need them. The result, in many cases, is a warehouse full of data, much of which will never be needed but all of which must be perpetually updated and searched to produce outputs.

Using a minimalist approach on the other hand, we begin by creating database tables that contain only the critical attributes needed to support the entity-relationship diagram model plus some preliminary guesses about a few additional attributes that might provide an interesting experimental prototype. A few of these guesses might be wrong—we will delete these attributes when it is discovered that they are never used in prototype modules. Additional data requirements will surface during prototype demonstrations—we will add these attributes before the next demonstration. These modifications will be easy to make using the RDMS. The user will become comfortable with the fact that newly-discovered data requirements can easily be accommodated as they surface during prototype iteration. The philosophy here is, "Show me why you need additional data," as opposed to, "Tell me up front about all the data you need to do your job." The former approach will lead to a smaller, more efficient database structure.

Despite the goodness of the minimalist approach, we will still sometimes find ourselves faced with an application that must manage massive amounts of data, as with the two examples just provided. When this creates performance problems—and it will—a solution is to excise the bulk of the data from the RDMS. Chapter 5 showed how easily data can be copied into the RDMS. Data can also be copied using a very similar type of 4GL command syntax—for example, replace COPY FROM with COPY TO. It is time to do this during the tuning phase when it is discovered that reports or other outputs relying on retrievals from tables containing gigabytes of data result in epic execution times.

Once the data have been moved to external files, 4GL command and report writer strings can be modified or created to use the database as a sort of "mail order librarian" that knows where to find the required data but does not actually have the information in stock. Now search routines will pull only the data required for the output at hand into the database and delete the data from the database once execution of the function has terminated. Figure 6-6 illustrates this strategy.

In the case of the geophysical application example, the detailed exploration data collected from the instruments at drilling sites could be moved to external files. The database would only contain tags or pointers to these files—for example, drilling site location. In the case of the legal case study application, the detailed textual portion of case studies could be removed to external files. Keywords would be kept in the database and case number would be used as a pointer to the external files.

The Last Resort

The last resort is obviously coding or, more specifically, the replacement of 4GL or visually programmed modules with performance-efficient low-level language programs. We give this as the last resort because it introduces the maximum in

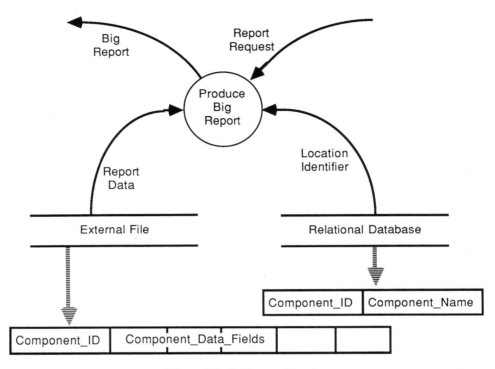

Figure 6-6 Database as librarian.

inflexibility into that portion of the system. No longer can we say that this module is as easy to modify as a dataflow diagram or a structure chart. Introducing such inflexibility will ultimately mean higher maintenance costs after delivery of the final system. There will always be at least some amount of postdelivery maintenance required—adaptive responses to legal and organizational policy changes if nothing else. There is a positive side as well as a negative side to the last resort: At least such a path is available to evolutionary prototypers, using the right kind of prototyping tools. Any remaining performance problems can usually be solved using this approach.

The replacement of prototype modules with lower-level language programs is simple once the code has been written. Simply save the program under the same name as the original prototype module and let the 4GL command string that defines the menu structure call the program whenever it previously called the prototype module. The 4GL command syntax makes no distinctions between a module created with a 4GL report writer or a program written in a third-generation language. Both are procedures known only to the prototype menu driver by their names.

This simplicity should be qualified by pointing out that some RDMS products have this capability and others do not. Products without any programming interface cannot be considered true evolutionary prototyping toolkits. Systems with this capability sometimes refer to the feature as a "programmer's interface" or an "embedded query language" or a "customizer." Whatever the name for the feature, the meaning is that programming interfaces have been implemented through the development of drivers for specific languages. Another thing to keep in mind is that this implies that not all programming languages are supported by all RDMS products. Make sure that the product you intend to use interfaces with the languages used in your development environment.

Another capability provided by a programmer's interface is to be able to incorporate reusable code as part of the initial prototype. While this approach has some appeal (free code), it is also fraught with danger in the form of inserting inflexibility into the system during the early stages of prototyping when this is the least desirable thing to do. All third-generation languages make use of control syntax: GO TO, DO WHILE, FOR. . .END, PERFORM UNTIL, and so forth. While some of these commands can be used to create well-structured programs—hopefully any "reusable" code will be well-structured—branching commands can also be misused to quickly modify undesirable performance during "rapid prototyping." The easiest and quickest way to remove a program problem is to branch around it. If much undocumented wandering branching is inserted into reusable code during prototype iterations, the final product will be overly complex and difficult to maintain.

An alternative way to use reusable code would be to create a very simplistic 4GL script as a place holder during prototype iteration, then replace the 4GL with the reusable code during tuning. Using this approach, we would be sure that we had defined functionality correctly for the target module and would not have to modify the inserted code. We would have a structured design in place, created during design derivation, as an aid to understanding how the module should function. The existence of reusable code does not free software developers from the responsibility for accurately defining system requirements or delivering adequate system documentation and maintainable software.

Returning to the study group application example, suppose that a third-generation language program is written to replace the 4GL report writer script that produces the project progress report. The coding is based on the module specification and structure chart pertaining to this function, created during design derivation. The code is then subjected to conventional unit test, using the study group database as a test bed. To integrate the new code into the prototype-developed system, the 4GL report writer script is removed (perhaps archived) and the program is renamed with the same name as the 4GL script. Now the program is subjected to unit stress testing for performance. The results show that the program will produce a report in five minutes with a 50 percent data margin.

DELIVERING THE EVOLVED PROTOTYPE

Now we have a final software product. The golden rule of rapid prototyping is: never deliver a prototype. During prototyping, you may often hear users asking, "When can we have the prototype?" or, from managers, "When are you going to deliver the prototype?" The appropriate answer to these questions is, "Never."

Make it clear, beginning with the project plan, that there are critical differences between a prototype and a final software product. A prototype is an experimental model. A final product is verified to be a long-range usable system.

A final product must include a detailed functional requirements specification document. Such a document, approved by the customer and a walkthru team, verifies that detailed requirements are in fact well known and agreed upon. It will be a valuable learning aid for future system maintenance staff. Speaking of maintenance, a walkthru team consisting of potential maintenance personnel must approve the detailed design documentation. The customer must provide explicit approval of system performance under stress testing. Developers must be sure that proposed maintenance personnel have adequate training to be able to make RDMS and 4GL modifications. With proper training, such modifications will be much easier than conventional program maintenance. Maintenance will resemble prototype iteration—fun and fast. Without proper training, maintenance can become a disaster.

Developers can create a delivery checklist based on the project plan and the activities called for in Chapters 5 and 6 of this book. Just before the system is made available to the customer for actual production use, developers must make sure that each item on the checklist has been completed. Each item must have independent verification, such as customer approval or walkthru team approval. An example of such a checklist is shown in Figure 6-7.

Delivery Checklist			
Deliverable	**User Approval**	**Walkthru Team Approval**	**Management Approval**
1. Functionally complete prototype			
2. Functional requirements specification document			
3. Performance tested and tuned final product			
4. Detailed Design Document			
5. User Guide			
6. Trained maintenance personnel			

Figure 6-7 Delivery checklist example.

MAINTAINING A PROTOTYPE-DEVELOPED SYSTEM

Now the prototype-developed system is ready for implementation. This might be a good opportunity to review what has been accomplished by using the evolutionary rapid prototyping approach in place of conventional software development. Obviously, customer satisfaction with the functionality of the delivered system is much greater. This must be true or we would not have finished prototype iteration. Unfortunately, software developers are often only secondarily concerned with customer satisfaction. Right now, if you are a software developer, you may be wondering, "But what about cost?" Figure 6-8 shows what we have found the cost differentials to be between prototype-developed and conventionally developed software.

Immediately below each set of bars in Figure 6-8 is the conventional life cycle phase being costed. Below that (in parentheses) is the equivalent rapid prototyping task. All bars indicate the cumulative effort to date for a particular life cycle phase. Keep in mind that the comparisons shown are for an average project. The rapid prototyping activities tend to be subject to more variance than conventional approaches. Prototype iteration, for instance, will vary greatly according to the types of control techniques applied to users during this phase. Design derivation

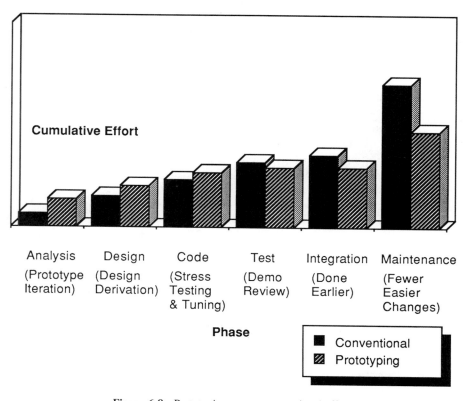

Figure 6-8 Prototyping versus conventional effort.

effort will vary according to how well the specifications were kept updated during prototype iteration. Tuning effort will vary according to how much must be done to meet performance requirements and which tuning techniques are used. Test and integration effort will vary with an auditor's requirements for these activities. Formal testing need only consist of a review of successful prototype demonstrations. Integration occurred with the development of the first version of the prototype. Maintenance effort will tend to vary in inverse proportion to the amount of tuning effort.

To some people, the disappointing message of Figure 6-8 is that the first half of the life cycle will be *more* expensive using the rapid prototyping approach instead of a conventional approach. Another way of understanding why it takes so much longer to reach user approval through prototype iteration is that with prototyping you capture all of the user's functional requirements, whereas with conventional prespecification you may be fortunate to capture half. Previously quoted statistics indicate that this is the case and no amount of wishful thinking will make it otherwise. Do you want to deliver the right system, or do you simply want to compress the front end of the life cycle by some dramatic amount? This is your binary choice.

It is perfectly acceptable to be primarily concerned about software costs if it is *total* life cycle costs with which we are concerned. Maintenance is half of this total and statistical evidence shows that half of maintenance costs are due to building and delivering the wrong system and then making expensive postdelivery modifications. We believe that Figure 6-8 is very conservative. Much maintenance effort can be saved due to the enormous reduction in psychological complexity of prototype-developed software.

Modifications to a 4GL script are an order of magnitude simpler than the same functional changes to a conventional procedural program. If this was not true, prototyping in and of itself would make no sense at all and no one in their right mind would have ever thought of doing it. In 1982, the authors conducted a series of studies that attempted to quantify maintainability of existing software by developing a set of psychological complexity metrics.[2] We concluded that the metric most strongly correlated to maintenance effort was the count of branches in a program. Although this work received some notice, we ultimately decided it lacked imagination because it was only a statistical verification of what every good programmer already knows—lots of GO TOs are not a very good idea.

The basic difference between a 3GL and a 4GL, by our definition, is that one cannot write any but the most trivial 3GL program without using control logic and, therefore, branching. A true 4GL, on the other hand, makes branching unnecessary and impossible by not allowing for it in the syntax. A 4GL script cannot branch, no matter how much the developer might want it to. This means our psychological complexity metric for any 4GL script would be zero, thus yielding the ultimate, or ideal, in maintainability. Not only can you not write a GO TO (or any other kind of branch) in a 4GL script, you cannot insert a GO TO during maintenance activities. Experience as maintenance programmers and managers of maintenance programmers has taught us that the average maintenance programmer operating in a crisis mode in the middle of the night will frequently insert an undocumented GO TO as a quick fix to a difficult problem: Isolate the problem, write a replacement module, branch around the problem to the new module. This, coupled with our research into psychological complexity, led us to conclude that, over time, maintenance will erode the structure and maintainability of even the best structured program.[3]

How much money can be saved due to this reduction in psychological complexity? Our studies showed that as much as 70 percent of the variance in maintenance effort could be explained by the variance in the number of branches in programs. How much money you will actually save will depend on the extent to which you can successfully evolve, rather than replace, prototype modules.

REFERENCES

1. William H. Inmon, "Optimizing Performance with Denormalization," *Database Programming & Design*, 1, no. 1, December 1987, 34–39.
2. Linda Brice, J. Connell, and J. Taylor, "Deriving Metrics for Relating Complexity Measures to Software Maintenance Costs," *Proceedings of the 1982 Computer Measurement Group International Conference*, CMG, Inc., Phoenix, AZ, 1982, pp. 134–41.
3. John Connell and Linda Brice, "Prolonging the Life of Software," *Proceedings of the 1984 NCC*, AFIPS Press, pp. 243–49.

7

Managing the Rapid Prototyping Process

Chapters 5 and 6 presented an approach to development of a rapid prototype and an explanation of how to evolve the prototype into deliverable software. That presentation was aimed at software developers. This chapter is aimed at software development management. Management is responsible for staff and resource acquisition and allocation, measuring and controlling progress, and customer relations. These responsibilities take on some critically different aspects when a rapid prototyping approach is used. Management must understand these differences and be able to cope with them for a rapid prototyping project to be successful.

REQUIRED SKILLS FOR A RAPID PROTOTYPING PROJECT

Armed with the methods described in Chapters 5 and 6, you may feel you are ready to undertake a rapid prototyping project. Before jumping into such an undertaking, ask yourself if your current staff has the skills needed to successfully complete the project. The manner in which you have conducted business in the past may not have required the same skills required for a rapid prototyping project. You may have analysts and designers, but they may not be practicing structured techniques. You may have a crew of programmers, but they may not be familiar with fourth-generation languages or visual programming. You may have database administrators, but they may not have experience with relational databases. If the majority of your staff is of the "old school" where they do not believe in team work, are not convinced of the expense of maintenance, think that anyone worth their salt would "do it right the first time" anyway, and believe that everyone is smart enough to decipher "clever but efficient" code, then you should probably plan on educating them before assigning them to a prototyping project.

The job descriptions within a prototyping team will minimally include systems analyst, system designer, database administrator, prototype developer, and product reviewer. Individuals may have multiple job descriptions depending on team size and organizational philosophy about division of labor. The skills needed by these personnel will include functional modeling, information modeling, control flow modeling, relational database management, visual programming, and structured quality assessment. Programming skills may be required during the tuning phase. A skill matrix, showing which skills are needed by which types of individuals, is presented in Figure 7-1.

To interpret Figure 7-1, consider the set of dots below each job category to comprise the minimum set of skills required of that type of professional. There is absolutely no problem with a professional having more skills than those required for the job at hand. Thus an analyst would need at least functional modeling skills to prepare the functional model during rapid analysis and functional requirements specification tasks. Likewise, a designer would need information and control flow modeling skills to prepare the information and control flow models during rapid analysis and design specification. The database administrator (DBA) goes into action after rapid analysis has been performed and needs information modeling skills to be able to interpret the information model correctly to develop a database. Obviously, the DBA also needs skills with the particular RDMS being used. The developer needs all the modeling skills because he or she will be working from the models

	Analyst	Designer	DBA	Developer	Reviewer
Functional Modeling	●			●	●
Information Modeling		●	●	●	●
Control Flow Modeling		●		●	●
RDMS			●	●	
Visual Programming				●	●
Structured Walkthru					●

Figure 7-1   Required skills for rapid prototyping.

prepared during rapid analysis. The developer must also be a master of the rapid prototyping toolkit in use — exhibiting an easy familiarity with the RDMS and visual programming techniques. The reviewer must be a master of all things the project plan says are to be reviewed, in addition to having specific training in structured quality assessment.

Asking software professionals if they have the required skills is not a foolproof approach. These days, most developers claim to use structured techniques. Many claim to understand relational systems and assert that they have the ability to write 4GL routines. A hard look at these claims often reveals more lip service than actual practice. Ascertain what formal training your staff has in these new skills. Find out what previous experience they have had in applying such skills. Ask to see examples of the application of these skills to their recent assignments. Of course, management should know if new hires have the proper experience from their resumes and if senior employees have been to recent training sessions. Still, an up-to-date skills inventory can be a useful aid in selecting the prototyping team; in-depth interviews prior to final selection are a must.

If you find that many of your staff do not have all the required skills, a training plan is in order. Fortunately, training in all of the skills shown in Figure 7-1 is readily available. Excellent training courses in the understanding and application of structured analysis and design techniques are available from the same sources listed in this book as publishers of textbooks on those subjects. There are courses with titles such as "Structured Analysis and System Specification," "Structured Design," "Real-Time Structured Analysis and Design," and "Structured Quality Assessment," to name just a few. Many vendors of the better relational database management systems offer comprehensive training in the use of their products. These courses teach students how to write 4GL routines, how to create functions with visual programming, and the fundamentals of database creation and modification. Once a database management system is procured, users' association meetings help with designing similar applications in different organizations. Professional seminars and conferences lasting usually two or three days are available on a large number of prototyping-related topics. One group of academicians and practitioners has recently begun to meet semiannually to study the rather narrow topic of entity-relationship structures.

TOOLKIT SELECTION CRITERIA

Do you have the right hardware and software tools for rapid prototyping? Chapter 3 described the critical features of such tools. Prepare your own checklist that expands on these features to meet the requirements of your development environment. For the types of applications you develop, performance may be critical. You may have special portability requirements for prototypes and final products due to a mix of hardware configurations throughout your organization. In certain environments, security requirements or fault tolerance may be paramount. The relative importance of such criteria will vary from one organization to another. Thus you must develop your own unique checklist with each desirable tool characteristic weighted according to the specific needs of your development environment. Figure 7-2 is an example of how such a checklist for selection of an RDMS might look for one specific organization.

Criteria	Weight	Score	Weighted Score
Application Generation	10	5	50
Function Generation	9	9	81
Truly Relational	8	9	72
Performance	7	4	28
Security	5	9	45
Portability	4	0	0
Total		36	276

Figure 7-2 A sample RDMS evaluation checklist.

It will probably not be possible to find tools that score perfectly in all categories. In the imperfect world we live in, it seems that trade-offs and compromises are frequently required. Thus it is extremely important to accurately set the weights on checklists such as the one shown in Figure 7-2. Be certain that the weights really reflect the relative importance of the desirable features to your organization. Otherwise, evaluations may be skewed out of true proportion and you will end up with a product that does not meet your true needs. On any checklists for evaluation of an RDMS to be used for evolutionary rapid prototyping, for example, there will always be three features that must be weighted relatively more important than any other features: application generation, function generation, and true relationality. Without a strong implementation of these features, you will not be able to accomplish evolutionary rapid prototyping. What may vary from one organization to another is the relative weightings between these categories and how much higher they are weighted than other critical features.

To select software tools because they just happen to run on the hardware configurations currently available or because they will run on hardware deemed desirable seems a bit like the tail wagging the dog. When talking about big productivity gains and cost savings, in addition to dramatically increased customer satisfaction through the application of the evolutionary rapid prototyping approach to software development, why not select the best software tools first and then acquire the hardware necessary to host the tools? In short order, the benefits are guaranteed to outweigh the cost of new hardware acquisition. If you use this approach, hardware selection is easy. There is only one critical criterion: Does it host the selected software tools? Only in the case where there are a variety of machines that will host the selected software do other criteria such as price and performance become important.

Do not evaluate hardware or software from advertising or sales claims alone. Be aware that all vendors have features which they refer to as "checklist items." Vendors know you will be evaluating their product against a checklist. Certain features show up on most checklists, so vendors make sure they have at least a minimal implementation of these features so the item will be checked off on all evaluations. Just because a hardware vendor states that your selected software will run on their machine does not mean that the version of the software they support is equal in capability to versions running on other machines. The only way you can tell the difference between a checklist item and a fully supported feature, is to insist on a hands-on trial period or, minimally, a hands-on demonstration. Do not score critical features with a "yes" or "no." Instead, use a range of values, say from one to ten, indicating the relative robustness of a feature's implementation. For a good example of an objective product evaluation approach, see the referenced Palmer & Associates paper.[1]

MEASURING AND CONTROLLING RAPID PROTOTYPING PRODUCTIVITY

If you have an appropriately skilled staff ready to undertake a prototyping project, and they have the appropriate prototyping tools at hand, you can initiate the project as described in Chapter 5. Shortly thereafter you will find yourself trying to evaluate progress toward completion and attempting to control interactions with users. How do you know how close your prototypers are to obtaining user approval of prototype functionality? How do you prevent users from continuing to request desired enhancements in an infinite loop of prototype iteration? Are there objective and accurate means for estimating effort in an environment where concurrency and iteration are the primary characteristics?

There are special problems related to measurement and control within the rapid prototyping domain. Most quantitative software development estimating and control models assume sequential development phases and tasks. Many of the more widely used models rely on metrics based on estimated lines of code. Effort estimation metrics based on lines of code will be of little use since coding will be held to a minimum. It is difficult to know how many iterations of a given prototype will be necessary. If the prototype is to be used to verify user satisfaction with functionality, then it must be iterated until it accomplishes this goal. A means is needed for assuring convergence, within schedule and budget limitations, on a system solution and user approval.

Barry W. Boehm is probably the most respected expert in the area of software cost estimating. He was instrumental in developing the COnstructive COst MOdel (COCOMO) in use at TRW and other large installations. His model, developed with a great deal of experience and expertise, can be used in basic, intermediate, and detailed versions.[2] While COCOMO has earned a great deal of respect, we do not recommend it in its 1987 state for use per se on prototyping projects. It requires some knowledge of the number of "delivered source instructions" and it is based on the traditional waterfall life cycle model. As has been stressed in this book, it is a goal of prototyping to hold the number of delivered source instructions to a minimum. And, where source code is necessary to evolve the prototype into a delivered system, that coding activity is done toward the very end of the project, in the prototype tuning phase. The number of delivered source instructions cannot be realistically estimated at the beginning of the project when the entire set of primitive functions is probably unknown, and the subset of functions to be rewritten for efficiency purposes is almost certainly unknown. Because COCOMO depends on the traditional life cycle waterfall model, it does not fit easily into a prototyping environment. Recall that in that model, "system feasibility" is followed by "software plans and requirements," which is followed by "product design," followed by "code." Each step of the process allows a return to the previous step until that step's product is either validated or verified. Prototyping, on the other hand, follows the iterative approach so development of a function may be followed by restructure of a database, more analysis, more menu creation, or another function, depending on user reaction to the exercise of the prototype version.

Boehm suggests that the accuracy of software cost estimation improves as a project moves through phases as they become nearer to project completion. During the feasibility study, the accuracy of the software cost estimation depends so heavily on uncertainties (Who is the system for? What do the data look like?) that they can vary by a factor of four (on the high side or low side) 80 percent of the time. Since Boehm is known to be interested in prototyping — his *spiral model* is beginning to receive a great deal of press — and since TRW is involved in prototype projects,[3] there will no doubt be a future version of COCOMO that will be compatible with prototyping.[4] The preceding material was not meant to be critical of the COCOMO products but rather to advise caution in applying them to a prototyping project before exploring recent innovations.

Estimating software development effort is a difficult subject, even with conventional approaches. Software estimates have a documented tendency to always be low.[5] The tendency for the low bias in software estimates is due, in part, to the optimism of the developer, compounded by the encouragement of management to deliver low estimates so customers will be happy and sign the contract.[6] Many organizations do not use quantifiable estimating metrics, but rely instead on the ego-biased bad guesses of developers. We do not intend to solve all the problems associated with this phenomenon in this book — it is not a book on software estimating. Instead, let us pretend that there are no problems with conventional software estimating. Therefore, our only concern becomes the areas where there are additional estimating and control problems arising from application of the rapid prototyping approach. We will assume that, if you know how to prepare an accurate estimate for a conventional software development project, you will be able to use the following information to successfully estimate, measure, and control effort and progress during a rapid prototyping project.

Defining Prototyping Effort Requirements

Chapter 5 asserted that the first critical task in initiating a rapid prototyping project is the preparation of a project plan that tailors the conventional life cycle methodology to permit successful application of the evolutionary rapid prototyping approach.

Once published, such a plan must not be archived and forgotten — it becomes a valuable management tool that contains critical benchmarks against which effort and progress may be measured and controlled. A rapid prototyping project plan contains descriptions of the life cycle phases and tasks along with crude preliminary estimates for effort required to complete the tasks. The problem is, how can such estimates be made objectively and reliably?

At the beginning of a project, with very little information from which to derive quantitative metrics for estimating, it is certain that estimates in a project plan will not be accurate to within a few percentage points. Nevertheless, we would like some assurance that estimates are as likely to be high as they are to be low. We would like the mathematics used for quantitative estimating to contain metrics that are based on historical data and thus are unbiased. We would like the formulas to be modular so actual numbers derived from measured performance can be plugged in at the end of each project phase, thus steadily improving the accuracy of estimates as the project moves toward completion.

Most software projects have some interaction with users prior to preparation of either a project proposal or project plan, or both. These interactions are usually sufficient to give developers some crude idea of what the customer has in mind for key system features. Preproject rapid analysis might be undertaken, based on these preliminary interactions, to develop rough models for proposed functionality, stored information, and control flow. Such models need not be accurate enough to provide a prototype basis, but will contain the information needed to prepare unbiased quantitative estimates. Preproject modeling need only consume a few hours, given some state-of-the-art automated tools for computer-aided drawing. The models and the estimates can be refined as more information becomes available.

Building contractors always use metrics based on standard construction units. If a brick wall is to be built, there are metrics available regarding the average amount of time required to lay one brick. Estimating the time required to build a wall then is reduced to simply calculating the number of bricks required from the wall's dimensions and multiplying that number by the current metric for brick laying. Software development estimators have long been searching for the equivalent to a brick in their profession. Progress to date has indicated that a line of code is probably not an extremely useful equivalent to a software brick. DeMarco states that functionality to be developed is probably a much more meaningful metric.[5]

The control flow graphs produced during rapid analysis on a rapid prototyping project specify the functional modules to be included in the initial prototype. They may therefore be used for preliminary metrics related to functionality to be delivered. Chapter 5 explained that a box on a control flow graph might become a menu, data entry screen, report, display screen, or a transparent process. For lack of a better cohesive term, we will refer to all such modules as prototype functions. Therefore, if we know (because we have measured it) how long the average function takes to develop, we have a metric that can serve as the prototyping brick. We can multiply boxes on the CFG times the metric to derive development time. Do not confuse this process with the concept of *function points*, an area where Capers Jones has produced some fine work.

Solutions will not be provided for all the problems associated with software estimating. Instead, suggestions are offered to compensate only for the new problems associated with estimating that may arise due to taking a prototyping approach to software development. Maintaining that stance, it can be stated that the primary differences will be encountered during the activities of prototype development, prototype iteration, and system tuning — the development activities — rather than during the specification activities of analysis and design. Use whatever metrics you currently have available for estimating specification effort. Use the following metrics for estimating prototyping effort.

Total prototyping effort, E, consists of the effort required to develop the initial prototype, P, plus the effort required to iterate the prototype to user approval of functionality, I, plus the effort required to tune the system to user approval of performance characteristics, T.

$$E = P + I + T$$

Prototype development, P, is equal to the number of functions included in the initial prototype, F_1, multiplied by a metric that reflects the average amount of time required to develop a prototype function, K_1.

$$P = F_1 * K_1$$

Prototype iteration, I, is equal to the number of functions in the functionally approved prototype, F_2, times a metric that reflects the average amount of time required to iterate a function to user approval of functionality, K_2.

$$I = F_2 * K_2$$

Since the number of functions will not change during tuning — only the performance of functions will be altered — a new estimate for number of functions does not have to be derived for this task. Tuning is equal to the number of user-approved functions, F_2, times a metric that reflects the average amount of time required to tune a function to user approval of performance, K_3.

$$T = F_2 * K_3$$

Now let us consider how to obtain values for F_1 and F_2. F_1 can obviously be derived from the control flow graphs of rapid analysis. There may not be a one to one correspondence, however, between boxes on the CFG and functional modules in the initial prototype. Prototypers often discover during prototype development the necessity for additional modules. A formula might therefore be used stating that functions to be included in the initial prototype, F_1, are equal to the number of boxes on the CFG B times a metric that reflects the average number of initial prototype functions per CFG box K_4 — a ratio.

$$F_1 = B * K_4$$

The number of functions that will exist in the user-approved prototype F_2 is equal to the number of user-approved prototype functions per function in the initial prototype K_5 — also a ratio.

$$F_2 = F_1 * K_5$$

It can be observed that one of the problems with this estimating approach is that the estimate for prototype iteration effort, I, is dependent on an estimate of user-approved functions, F_2, and that is in turn dependent on an estimate of functions to be included in the initial prototype, F_1. An estimate that depends on an estimate that in turn depends on a third estimate cannot be extremely accurate. In fact all of the elements of the equation $E = P + I + T$ are estimates that depend at least on a second estimate.

The good thing that can be said about the foregoing metrics is that they are unbiased — they are at least as likely to be high as they are likely to be low. Therefore, they are likely to provide estimates that will not guarantee the typical software project budget overruns and slipped schedules. Furthermore, it is not necessary or advisable to hold developers to the preliminary estimates included in the project plan. Preliminary estimates can be vastly improved, in terms of the probability of matching ultimate actuals, by including actual data in the preceding formulas as such data become available.

For instance, as soon as development of the initial prototype is finished, which may be as soon as two or three weeks into the project, actual numbers are available for substitution into these formulas in the place of F_1 (functions in the initial prototype) and P (effort required to develop the initial prototype). This means that inaccuracy in the estimate for prototype development is eliminated but, more important, inaccuracies in the estimates for prototype iteration and system tuning are vastly reduced since each contains an estimate of user-approved functions, F_2, which was formerly dependent on an estimate of initial prototype functions, F_1, but is now based on the actual number of initial prototype functions. In a similar fashion, but much further along in the project, the estimate for system tuning can be further improved by substituting the actual number of user-approved functions at the end of prototype iteration for F_2 in the formula $T = F_2 * K_3$ (tuning is equal to the number of user-approved prototype functions times the average amount of time required to tune a function). Thus, estimates can be made to continually converge on ultimate actuals if the estimates are revised at each major project milestone.

An additional remaining problem with the foregoing estimating approach is that you will need to have good numbers for the metrics K_1, K_2, K_3, K_4, and K_5 — based on historical data. For your first few prototyping projects, such numbers will not be available. In fact there has not yet been enough general experience with the rapid prototyping approach to be able to cite any useful industry statistics. You will have to develop your own metrics, and your estimates will not be very accurate until you do so.

In the mean time, what should you do about rapid prototyping project estimates? New and potential rapid prototypers always want to know about case studies relative to effort requirements. Such information can be extremely misleading since effort is so dependent on widely varying environments. Metrics for conventional software development also vary widely by domain. Estimates for development in a COBOL programming environment are derived from metrics that are extremely different from those used in an Ada programming environment, for example. Metrics for real-time system development are very different from metrics for business application development. Rapid prototyping just makes this domain-dependent problem worse by adding the confusion of a vast array of different types of rapid prototyping tools with wide variances in ease of use.

With the preceding caveat, the following statements are based on our experience. The average amount of time required to develop a prototype function has been 15 minutes to 4 hours, depending on the tool being used and the complexity of the application. The average amount of time required to iterate a function to user approval has been 1 to 10 hours, depending on the same factors plus certain personality traits of the users involved. The average amount of time required to tune a function to user approval of performance has ranged from one to 80 hours, depending mostly on the type of application, number of users, and amount of data. Does this kind of imprecise information give you an indication of the significance of domain-dependent metrics? Obviously, you will not be able to use the numbers just given for your own metrics, and you will have to make do with guesses until you have collected your own historical data. Your most valuable piece of information will be found in the tracking system of your own shop. Find and use the productivity factor representing average effort for producing an elementary process in your environment as your *software brick*.

Managing the User's Expectations during Prototype Iteration

Perhaps now you have been convinced to begin your own program for measuring prototyping effort, but you would still like some hints about how to control prototyping projects until such time as meaningful historical measurement is a fait accompli. During those first few projects, what do you do about controlling users and developers during prototype iteration to prevent the process from going into an infinite loop? Assuming a lack of available historical data, a heuristic approach is offered next for specifying a date for user approval of the prototype in the project plan and then using an audit trail technique to assure that iterations are converging on that date.

Heuristically (and very roughly) speaking, we can observe from experience that prototype development and iteration tend to consume a little more effort than traditional analysis and preliminary design specification activities for projects of the same size. This phenomenon may be in part because prototyping has the same goals and places many of the same requirements on developers as traditional prespecification. This means that if you think you can develop accurate estimates for traditional prespecification for a project, you can use those estimates to specify a date for user approval of prototype functionality in the project plan.

Use a date for specification of user approval of prototype functionality. Do not specify how many iterations will be required. The latter will depend on how difficult the individual iterations are — a factor that cannot be predicted until user feedback from prototype demonstrations has been obtained. Then use an audit trail approach to work toward convergence on a solution by that date. Take notes during each prototype demonstration regarding what changes the user requests. Obtain agreement from the user as to the contents of the notes at the end of the demonstration. Have the notes typed up as a memo after the demonstration. The memo will be from the user attendees at the demo and addressed to developers, development management, and user management — you prepare the memo, the leader of the user group signs and sends it.

At each prototype demonstration after the first one you will go over the memo from the previous demonstration, attempting to obtain user agreement that the requested changes have been made and are acceptable. This at least tends to prevent the thrashing that sometimes occurs when users change their minds about whether or not certain functions should be included. Using this approach, such thrashing becomes highly visible to user management and is demonstrated as the user's doing. On the other hand, valid requests for changes tend not to be ignored by developers since such requests are made known at frequent periods to the developer's management. The entire iteration process becomes a responsibility shared equally between users and developers.

As the demonstration memos begin to create an audit trail showing that problems identified with the prototype are being solved satisfactorily, convergence on a solution will begin to happen. Both users and developers will be aware of the approaching deadline for approval of prototype functionality, and both camps will feel equal responsibility for meeting this deadline. A final mechanism for meeting the deadline within specified schedule and budget constraints is to specify in the project plan a time frame just prior to user approval of prototype functionality during which a "last chance" prototype demonstration will occur. At this second-to-last prototype demonstration, users will be made aware that they must be prepared to present a final wish list. If the prototype performs according to the desires expressed on this final list at the next demonstration, they are obligated to approve prototype functionality. This may not always happen according to plan, but, when it doesn't, the problem is as likely to lie with the user group as with the developers, and management will have the information about where the responsibility lies.

SUMMARIZING THE RAPID PROTOTYPING MANAGEMENT PROCESS

Management of a rapid prototyping project is a process in many ways similar to the development and evolution of the prototype itself. In both cases the process involves much concurrency and iteration. Therefore, a model for rapid prototyping management looks somewhat like a meta model of the process model presented in the earlier chapters of this book for rapid prototyping. Figure 7-3 is such a model.

The rapid prototyping management process is founded on having an adequately trained staff of rapid prototypers. At a minimum, they should all have read a book like this or read some of the many recent trade journal articles or have had some formal introduction before the first project begins. Rapid prototypers must have an adequate prototyping toolkit at their disposal. Acquisition and continual upgrading of such tools is a management responsibility. An ongoing educational program is important in filling gaps in the knowledge of new hires and to assure that the currently used approach remains state-of-the-art. Both tools and educational offerings must remain under constant reevaluation to stay abreast of the rapidly changing technological advances in this field.

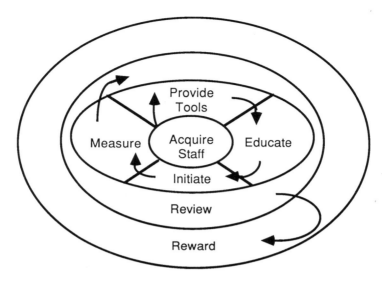

Figure 7-3 The rapid prototyping management process.

When projects are initiated, management has the responsibility to see that a project plan is in place that will be an adequate mechanism for ongoing control of project progress. As the project proceeds, management must assure that adequate effort measurement procedures are being followed so future projects will have improved metrics available for estimating. Review procedures must be set up and followed in a manner that will tend to produce convergence on a solution and the meeting of critical milestones specified in the project plan.

Finally, a word about reward mechanisms is appropriate. Prototypers often do many things "right" even though the iterative process sometimes makes it appear that work is continually being thrown away. It is wise for managers to see the glass as half full instead of half empty when the struggle for correctness is in mid-course. There are many opportunities to praise the developer other than just when user approvals are obtained or milestone dates are met on schedule. Prototyping provides so many opportunities for developers to obtain negative feedback from users that even the strongest of egos can take a beating. Managers can compensate for this by congratulating developers for unearthing and fixing problems so early in the life of the project. Every prototype demonstration should give management an opportunity to verbally reward developers. "Congratulations for having a demonstrable prototype ready so fast!" "Congratulations for presenting a prototype that was so successful in eliciting user feedback (positive and negative)!" "Congratulations on getting those user-identified problems from last week's demo fixed so fast!"

When the project runs into trouble, remind developers of how easy it is to recover from mistakes when using a rapid prototyping approach. Nothing is ever locked in. Everything remains flexible. When users appear unhappy with progress, remind developers that it is better to have unhappy users early in a project than to have unhappy users after the software is delivered. Correctly prototyped software products almost always produce happy users in the long run.

REFERENCES

1. Palmer & Associates, Inc., "Relational Database Management Systems for Personal Computers, a Benchmark Comparison, Informix SQL, INGRES, ORACLE," Deluth, Georgia, February 1987.

2. Barry W. Boehm, *Software Engineering Economics* (Englewood Cliffs, NJ: Prentice Hall, 1981).

3. Barry W. Boehm, T. E. Gray, and T. Seewaldt, "Prototyping versus Specifying: A Multiproject Experiment," *IEEE Transactions on Software Engineering*, May 1984.

4. Larry L. McLaughlin, Lance Valt, and Scott Overmeyer, "Tutorial Notes — User Engineering and Active Prototyping," 1986 Fall Joint Computer Conference Professional Education Program, Dallas, TX.

5. T. Demarco, *Controlling Software Projects* (New York: Yourdon Press, 1982).

8

Causes of Failures during Prototyping

This chapter documents problems encountered with prototyping. If this book is meant to convince readers of prototyping's merits, then this chapter is meant to convince readers that there are hidden dangers as well. Prototyping is not a panacea for all problems associated with software development. Not only are there some problems which rapid prototyping does not solve, there may be some new problems created by using a rapid prototyping approach.

To reemphasize an earlier statement, rapid prototyping is not an inherently risky approach. Basically, rapid prototyping reduces the overall risk of project failure. Most projects that fail do so because they produce the wrong system—a situation prevented by prototyping. This does not mean, however, that prototyping projects cannot fail for other reasons.

The motivation for including this somewhat negative material is due to the high levels of misunderstanding about rapid prototyping in the software engineering community. Such misunderstandings encompass what rapid prototyping is, how to do it, what the benefits are, and what type of tools are appropriate—almost always causing project failure. These misunderstandings are shared by widely read authors, researchers, high-level managers, and both experienced and inexperienced software engineers. Almost all causes of prototyping project failures are rooted in such misunderstandings. Project leaders who allow prototyping projects to proceed according to a manager's mistaken preconceptions of rapid prototyping will be doomed to failure. Such failures can be avoided if the suggestions in this book are followed: Agree upon a definition; create a project plan and stick to it; involve the user; follow all phases of the model, including tuning; and provide developers and users with the proper tools.

If you have found this book helpful, then you can, of course, recommend the methods outlined in it to others. Send as many people from your organization as possible to seminars and workshops on the topic. Most important, prepare a project plan for each new prototyping project. Use such a plan as an educational tool. Head off the possibilities for misunderstandings about the approach by obtaining agreement on the details in the project plan. Assume the worst: that any new prototyping project attempted may encounter all of the problems discussed next. Then, prevent such problems from turning your project into a disaster by explicit prohibition in the project plan. The chapter attempts to document many known causes of failure during prototyping projects, and suggests a specific solution for each. The general solution to all such problems, however, is education.

MISUNDERSTANDINGS BETWEEN USERS, MANAGERS, AND DEVELOPERS

The importance of an adequate project plan to project success cannot be overemphasized. Such a plan is a communication vehicle that can be used effectively to head off misunderstandings and to prevent potential disaster by reminding managers and users of their respective responsibilities. Lack of proper planning frequently causes critical misunderstandings between users and developers regarding development techniques. The following communication problems have been observed on various projects.

The Role of Structured Techniques

Some users and managers still object to the use of structured analysis and design because they never became familiar with the techniques. Others object to the use of structured techniques because they had unfortunate experiences when those techniques were oversold as a means for assuring software quality. While it may be argued that such cases represent incorrect application of a methodology, such an argument will do little to alter the damaged perceptions. Some people think of rapid prototyping as a means for escaping the necessity for structured analysis and design, reading the definitions presented here with their own interpretations. They may attend a seminar or workshop on rapid prototyping and only hear what they want to hear.

There is a widespread misconception that rapid prototyping means an end to "analysis paralysis" because it means no prespecification and minimal documentation. If you are still unclear about the appropriate role of structured techniques in rapid prototyping, then please reread Chapters 4, 5, and 6. When prototypers simply develop a working model and then iterate out the problems with the user, they have found that most systems were too large and too complex to follow such a simple formula. This "quick and dirty" approach led to confusion and lack of control. The paper models of structured analysis and design are necessary because they provide a clear and concise picture of the total system architecture as opposed to the dynamic working model of a prototype which only reveals a "chunk" of a system at a time to the observer. Looking at one module at a time can be confusing, in terms of grasping an entire architecture, when there are more than a dozen or so modules. The two models (working model and paper model) must coexist to present the customer with an understandable view *and* to provide the developer with an accurate build-to design.

Imagine that a vice president or director in your organization or in the customer's organization reviews a project plan and reacts negatively to the use of structured techniques during rapid analysis, prototype iteration, and design derivation. Suppose these executives attempt to dictate that structured analysis and design will not be used on a prototyping project. It is important to make the significance of these techniques understood if your project is to be successful. It is not possible to undertake structured specification in secret after having given the appearance of being cooperative and signing a project plan where those elements are absent. As soon as you agree to one, the schedule and budget will be cut by the amount you estimated for specification tasks. Figure 8-1 shows about what portion of each prototyping project phase must be devoted to specification.

Why the insistence on structured techniques? There is a close correspondence between the structured methodologies and the way rapid prototyping tools are most effectively applied. Dataflow diagrams, particularly the top three levels, are very useful in helping to conceptualize the functional requirements of a system. When using an RDMS as a prototyping tool, they are also useful in modeling functional interfaces to a data store. The entity-relationship diagram is widely used to model a relational database structure. Control flow graphs are an optimal means for depicting a menu-driven control structure. These or similar structured tools are the most rational approach to planning and controlling prototyping activities. They are also the most efficient way to document a prototype-developed software system architecture.

There are negotiable and nonnegotiable items in any prototyping project plan. The use of structured techniques is nonnegotiable. A project without the use of

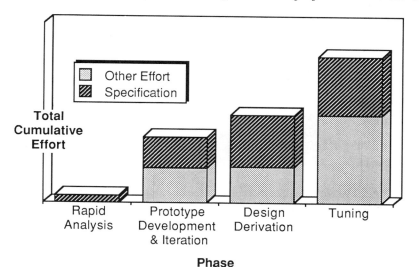

Figure 8-1 Specification as a percent of total effort.

these techniques stands very little chance for success. You can, of course, always refuse to undertake a project without agreement on the use of structured specification techniques. You can also write a memo stating that you refuse to take responsibility for project success if a structured approach is not acceptable.

Design First versus Prototype-Derived Design

It makes no sense to specify requirements and design in detail before prototyping when the purposes and benefits of prototyping have to do with discovering require ments. The idea of *deriving* a detailed design (DFDs to primitive levels, a complete data model, and so on) from a working model is foreign to many users and software development managers. Because it is so difficult for most of us to think in a manner seemingly contrary to years of training, many of us have trouble seeing a prototype as a dynamic requirements model. We often want to insist on a design review before any development activity is allowed. Of course, a design review implies the existence of a design document and all of the work that led up to its creation.

This group has the opposite mindset from those just described who are afraid of analysis paralysis. The design first group is skeptical about the ability of prototyping to produce quality software without first producing a detailed design. A person in authority, operating under this misconception may say, "You may produce a prototype, but only after you have completed thorough requirements analysis and detailed design." This viewpoint has the backing of most published methodologies, auditors, and publications on software engineering—it is simply 180° off course when applied to prototyping.

Detailed complete specifications will only mean costly revisions as a result of prototyping discoveries. Detail design driven prototypes are very similar to the old way of doing business: Produce a complete, but wrong, system and then modify it (and the specifications) until it meets with user approval. Prototyping uses tools that allow more rapid modification to the working system than conventional tools, but it does not provide anything that makes specification revision more rapid.

Are you thoroughly confused at this point about the role of specification in a rapid prototyping project? The idea is not to prototype from a detailed design nor to prototype without prespecifying. There is instead a fine line the prototyper must walk: Specify a little bit, prototype a little bit, specify a little more, prototype a little more—until a complete system model is in place. It is not a new concept, as those in favor of incremental development have advocated "build a little, test a little" for years. The complete system model will, at the time of user approval, consist of detailed paper specifications and a fully functioning working prototype. This fine line is not well understood by today's software engineers, managers, and users. The approach is sensible, it works, and it produces quality systems—if it is done as prescribed.

The impact of giving in to management or user pressure for a design first approach will be a much more expensive prototyping project. It will still be possible of course, to produce a quality system, but only if the paying customer is willing to endure the expense of specification revisions necessitated by prototype revisions and the expense of replacing prototype modules developed from inaccurate specifications. Building a complete prototype, based on a complete design, before the first iteration will mean that you will ultimately have to produce about twice as many prototype modules before user approval is obtained. Your options, with a design driven approach, are that the project will cost twice as much or the results will be unsatisfactory to the customer.

The solution to avoiding this problem is to make very clear in the project plan when the final requirements review and the first design review will happen—after user approval of prototype functionality. Explain the prototyping approach to design in the plan and explain it again at the preliminary requirements review held after rapid analysis. If auditors or managers external to the project get wind of what you're up to and want to interfere by inserting their misconceptions about the role of design in a prototyping project, bring out the project plan and show them the signatures of your manager and your chief user.

When to Have Formal Reviews

When to place project review gates on a prototyping project often causes difficulty. Many managers are simply not comfortable without lots of frequent formal reviews. To these managers, early reviews represent an opportunity to discover whether or not schedule and budget are slipping before it is too late to take corrective action. The problem is, formal reviews serve no useful purpose during prototype iteration. The prototype iteration phase contains no discrete tasks which can be proven complete. Thus there is no way to schedule meaningful milestones in the middle of prototype iteration.

The scheduling of formal reviews is a negotiable item. If your manager insists on frequent early reviews, give in on this point. A mid-iteration review will serve no useful purpose, but it will do little harm. At worst it will slow down the weekly iteration cycle a bit for the week of the review. Just be careful what you call these superfluous reviews. Don't claim, for instance, to know what the requirements are before you have completed prototype iteration. This means that the formal *System Requirements Review* cannot be held until after user approval of prototype functionality.

There are alternatives to scheduling superfluous reviews to pacify nervous management. The first alternative is to have a preliminary requirements review very early in the project. This review presents the results of project planning and rapid analysis. Managers and users get a feel for what will be prototyped, which tools will be used, what the deliverables will be, and what the preliminary schedule and budget are. The second alternative is to point out during the preliminary requirements review that each prototype demonstration during the iteration phase is like a mini review. The results of each demonstration will be written up and forwarded to management. In this way, management will be kept up-to-date on project progress.

Minimal Coding

During one prototype demonstration, a customer asked, "How many lines of code do you have in that prototype?" The answer was, of course, "virtually zero." The customer response was an angry one. Most organizations, as standard procedure, estimate projects and charge customers based on the lines of executable code to be delivered. After all, lines of code are the only tangible measure of productivity we have. Thus, if a system with 200,000 lines of code are worth x, then a system with 400,000 lines of code must be worth $2x$. The obvious extension of this philosophy is that a prototype with zero lines of code must be worthless. The concept of minimal coding causes users accustomed to paying by the line of code to feel they are being cheated.

One can argue, of course, that there are a few lines of 4GL in the prototype. Furthermore, menus, data entry screens, and reports created using visual programming will ultimately be executed by 3GL code generated by the RDMS. Even so, prototyping is based on the concept of minimizing code writing. Managers and users must be educated to understand that the reason for code minimization is to produce a dynamic requirements model that is as flexible as conventional paper specifications. Do users ever ask, "How many lines of code are in that requirements specification?"

Another opportunity for misunderstanding may arise when the final system is delivered. The customer may ask, "Now, how many lines of code are in the system?" If the prototyper has done a good job of avoiding the replacement of prototype modules with 3GL modules during the tuning phase whenever possible, there will still be far fewer lines of code per dollar spent than one would expect in a conventionally developed system. Somehow we must educate customers to understand that they are really paying for what the software does for them, rather than for the lines of code included. A line of code does not automatically provide any utility to the end user.

DIFFERING DEFINITIONS OF PROTOTYPING

Project members holding differing definitions of prototyping is the number one cause of prototyping project failures. When the team of users, developers, and managers subscribe to more than one approach, problems are sure to arise. Some of the more commonly known approaches were presented in Chapter 2. No one approach is completely good or bad, but trying to combine them is confusing and nonproductive. Everyone involved with a prototyping project should have the same answers to the following questions:

- Is the prototype simply the first version of the final product?
- Will a prototype module be as easy to modify as a dataflow diagram?
- Is the prototype to be used only to experiment with various design alternatives?
- Are we prototyping to test the requirements specifications?
- Will the prototype use actual data and allow the user to test what-if scenarios during demonstrations?
- Will there be any possibility of evolving the prototype into the final product?

The answers to these questions must be contained in the project plan. Before beginning a prototyping project, pose these questions to your management, to your development team, and to your users. If they are answered according to the guidelines presented in this book, then the understanding among the three groups is good enough to proceed with the prototype.

If preliminary discussions about project objectives and approaches indicate that the prototype is thought of as the first version of the system, to be produced as a result of conventional prespecification and development, then a test model prototype as described in Chapter 2 is being considered. Users and managers must be made aware that such an approach will not be cost-effective in helping to define correct requirements. Iterating such a prototype will be painful and expensive, regardless of the tools used to produce it. The extra effort will be due in part to the necessity of documentation revision.

Which tools will be used to produce the initial prototype? If developers are talking about prototyping in a language that uses control logic syntax, a third-generation language, then the prototype modules will not be easy to modify. Easy modification is what makes prototyping an acceptable alternative to total prespecification. The end result of prototype iteration using programming languages will be a system of patchwork code, modified many times with branching statements inserted as needed to modify functionality. These modifications will ultimately produce a system very high in psychological complexity and the impact on the customer will be exorbitant maintenance costs. This is the quick and dirty prototyping approach described in Chapter 2. The cumbersomeness of iterating a prototype developed in a language that uses control logic syntax is typically compensated for by skimping on specification and documentation tasks. Thus, this approach is particularly insidious because during prototype iteration it appears to be as fast and successful as a structured evolutionary prototyping approach. The failure of the quick and dirty approach often does not become evident until after delivery of the final system.

Many vendors sell what they call prototyping products that are, in reality, display-only model generators. You can call such display-only models prototypes if you wish, but such a prototype will not provide verifiability of functional requirements. The user will not be able to see what happens to familiar application data as a result of transformations performed by the prototype. The discriminator between such tools and a true rapid prototyping tool as described in Chapter 3 is this question: Will the prototype contain actual application data and will it perform transformations on the data as a result of user invocation of prototype modules? Display-only model generators can be fun and easy to use. Within a limited scope, they can even be useful in working out details of the user interface. They will never provide an all-encompassing approach to software development as described in this book.

There is another class of prototyping tools that, while allowing the fast creation of a prototype that uses actual application data and performs user-invoked transformations of data, does not provide any path for evolving such a prototype into the final product. This is typically because the commands created with these tools are interpreted by the computer at run time as opposed to a system that compiles and executes an object code application. Eventually, for systems of any size, the prototype will have to be abandoned for performance reasons. At the time of prototype abandonment, the system will have to be rewritten using a conventional programming approach. The result may be a system that really does satisfy the user's functional requirements, but it will have cost more to produce than a conventional system and will be just as expensive to maintain. This is the throwaway approach to prototyping described in Chapter 2.

Frequently, the most disturbing aspect of throwaway prototypes is that the user interface will not be identical to that in the final system. If the prototype is developed with one set of tools and the final product is implemented with a totally different set of tools, you run the risk that user familiarity with the "look and feel" of the prototype will not transfer well to user acceptance of the "look and feel" of the delivered system. This is particularly true when a very friendly prototyping environment is replaced by a more cryptic production environment for performance reasons.

Throwaway prototyping is not always bad and does not necessarily lead to project failure. Evolutionary prototyping tools can be used effectively to produce throwaway prototypes with great benefit to the end user in terms of identifying functional requirements. If you are using a throwaway approach, however, it is important to clarify for management and users what the cost difference and end result will be. In other words, acknowledge in the project plan that a throwaway approach will involve a development cost add-on rather than a cost savings and do not overstate the possible maintenance cost savings. The bottom line is that the customer must be willing to pay a slightly higher cost to receive a more useful software system.

None of these alternative approaches to prototyping is wrong if management and users are made fully aware, using a project plan, of exactly what the trade-offs are before authority to proceed is granted. The point is that there are many approaches to and philosophies about prototyping. If the end results of a prototyping project are to be universally viewed as successful, everyone involved in a proto-typing project must have a common understanding regarding approach, philosophy, appropriate tools, probable costs, and possible benefits. Figure 8-2 illustrates the trade-offs involved with the various prototyping approaches, benchmarked against the conventional software development approach.

Figure 8-2 needs some explanation; it is not statistically verifiable with data available at this time, but it can be substantiated by common sense. As shown, the most powerful capabilities for defining requirements are with throwaway and evolutionary prototyping because they both use actual application data and working functions and are applied during the requirements definition phase. The same things could be said of quick and dirty prototyping but lengthy time lags between prototype iterations toward the end will degrade this capability. The lowest development costs will be using the quick and dirty approach, due to lack of specification requirements. A test model prototype can be as verifiable, evolvable, and maintainable as a prototyped system developed using the evolutionary approach—if evolutionary tools are used and the much higher development costs are agreed to and paid.

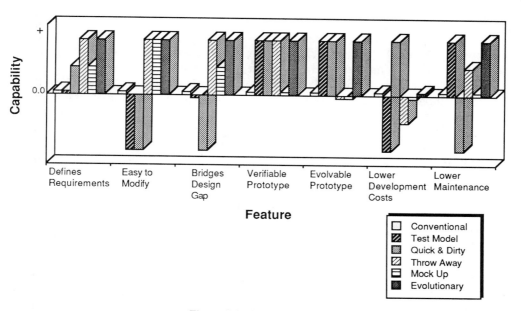

Figure 8-2 Prototyping approach trade-offs.

THE ROLE OF THE USER

On a prototyping project, the user will be an active participant on the development team, not a passive observer . Therefore, it is just as important that users understand what prototyping is all about and what their role on the project will be as it is to achieve this understanding among the developers. In most cases, users will not be involved in writing programs during the tuning phase or in preparing technical system documentation. Users may be involved to some extent in visual programming to create prototype modules and in developing interactive help screens—an approach that has been used successfully on some projects. Users will always be heavily involved in prototype review and critique and in providing direction for prototype iteration. The iteration phase will require an almost full-time commitment from the users.

An interesting aspect of heavy user involvement is that it is typically not funded. That is to say, prototyping projects tend not to prepare estimates that include the cost of user project team members' time, nor is this cost typically included in the final reporting of overall project cost. Software developers have historically failed to include user time in software development cost figures and thus carry that syndrome into prototyping projects. If you want to argue that an accurately costed prototyping project is thus more expensive than a conventional software development project due to heavier user involvement, you have a good point. In the few cases of projects where user time was considered in total cost figures, we have found that the customer was perfectly willing to pay the additional cost. Prototyping is fundamentally an approach directed at achieving maximum benefit for the user from the money spent on development. Thus, the additional cost is easily justified from the user's point of view. Figure 8-3 shows the appropriate level of user effort, relative to developer effort, for each prototyping project phase.

Ideally, users who will become project team members should be positive contributors, not presenters of roadblocks due to possible misguided preconceptions about prototyping projects. Some of these misconceptions have been discussed. Now let us examine the possible misunderstandings that can arise about the appropriate functions of user team members during the course of the prototyping project. It is critically important to resolve such misunderstandings as early as possible during the course of a project or they will cause project failure.

Getting Past Imperfect Prototype Demonstrations

The demonstration of the initial prototype provides the first opportunity for a sometimes violent airing of misunderstandings between developer and user project team members. The initial model will, intentionally, not demonstrate complete functionality. Early prototypes may not have good response time to user actions. On rare occasions, users may say, "It's great that we will address functional issues before worrying about performance." More frequently, you will have to remind the users that these are the legitimate objectives, as stated in the project plan, of the initial prototype because at the first demonstration you may be faced with angry users. While the central idea behind prototyping is to make customers happy, remember you are walking a line between two extremes. On the one hand, they are pleased to see progress demonstrated by the initial prototype (as opposed to the usual six-month delay with seemingly no action while developers write specifications in a vacuum). On the other hand, they are accustomed to receiving software that is intended to be fully functional the first time they see it.

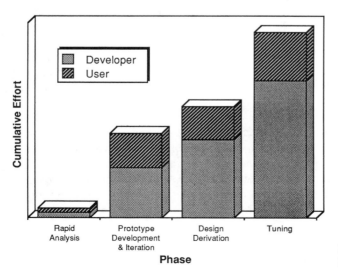

Figure 8-3 Appropriate user effort levels.

The initial anger of users at early prototype demonstrations may be a shock to first-time prototypers. You will want the customer to realize the quality and amount of hard work involved in having a working system demonstrable with only a week or two of effort. Users do not typically have much appreciation for what is involved in software development. Many of them believe that software developers spend most of their time going to meetings and writing unintelligible documentation. All they know is that, historically, what they first see of a working system is likely to be very close to what they will get in the final product and that modifications always consume many expensive months of effort.

A benefit to having users directly involved in performing some of the easier visual programming development tasks is that it will help them to understand that modifications to the initial prototype will be trivial. If you do not use this approach, you can try asking your angry users to trust you for one week. When they see many of their initial objections dissolved at the next prototype demonstration, with only a week's worth of effort, they will become more comfortable with remaining prototype imperfections. Slowly you will be able to convince them that the initial prototype is a very flexible experimental model, not intended to be a correct image of the final product.

The danger of these early demonstrations is that users will be so upset that they will clamor for management to shut the project down due to the evident incompetence of the development team. This is why it is so important to explain specifically in the project plan what the initial prototype will and will not do and what its purpose is. Just because a user signs the project plan does not mean they will remember what they signed up to when the first demonstration occurs, but at least the agreement has been documented and you should be able to get past the initial anger to the second demonstration. Be consoled by the knowledge that it is better to have irate users on your hands at the beginning of a project than as a result of delivering a useless but expensive final product.

A conventional software development project begins with a high level of user confidence in the ability of developers to do the right thing. This confidence level continues as users see analysis and design milestones being met successfully, although there is usually some slight degradation when specifications are delivered in a jargon unintelligible to the user. If the user completely understood the specifications, there would probably be a more drastic drop in the confidence level. During the coding phase, users completely lose visibility regarding project progress. The developers seem very busy, but is anything productive being accomplished? Programmers often say they are about 90 percent done for a very long time. This uncertain period often seriously erodes user confidence. The wall of truth is typically encountered during system test when users get their first peek at a working system. Now comes the same level of anger that prototypers typically experience at the first prototype demonstration. This anger level intensifies when users are asked, when the final product is delivered, to live with remaining system imperfections until postdelivery tuning is accomplished. The inverse curves of user confidence levels between a conventional project and a prototyping project are illustrated by Figure 8-4.

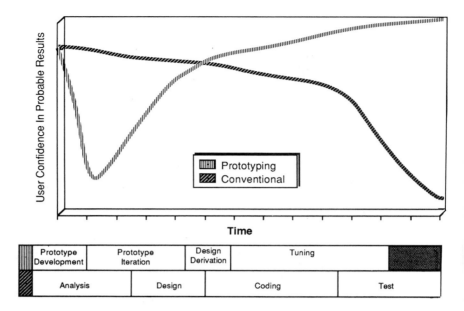

Figure 8-4 Inverse confidence curves.

Defining User Responsibilities

For users to be productive members of a prototyping team, there must be a clear understanding regarding their responsibilities. These responsibilities are spelled out in the project plan and may vary appropriately from project to project. For trivial projects with well understood requirements, 100 percent of all development work may be performed by either the user or the software developer, working alone. For larger, more complex projects, users and developers must work together for the project to be a success. This means there must be an agreement from the beginning regarding who will perform what tasks.

Users may participate somewhat in—and certainly will make a contribution to—specification tasks, but these tasks are basically the developers' responsibility. Users may perform some prototype development tasks, but the responsibility for prototype development and modifications will usually fall mainly to developers. Tuning phase modifications will also be mainly developer responsibilities. Since these three categories encompass most of the activities described in Chapters 5 and 6 regarding prototyping project tasks, a conclusion can be drawn that there is little left for the user to do: a mistaken conclusion.

Users must agree to have the right representatives of the user team at the right weekly or biweekly prototype demonstrations. These representatives typify the sort of person who would be likely to use the prototype modules being demonstrated after delivery of the final system. These demonstration attendees will be asked to experiment with the prototype and find its flaws and missing elements. Their responsibility is to be able to state clearly what the prototype is doing wrong. Which functions are difficult to use and why? Does the present user interface suggest possibilities for a better interface? Are critical data missing from the output? Are certain data transformations being performed incorrectly so resulting output contains mistakes? What additional functionality is needed to make the system useful? Finding these defects is the responsibility of the user team members; the amount of effort is not trivial and the responsibility is not light.

Often the users will be unable to find all defects within the one-hour time frame allotted to a prototype demonstration. This is particularly true in the case of large complex reports. For this reason, such reports should be passed out at the end of a prototype demonstration rather than perused and critiqued during the demonstration. The users should be given one or two days for finding the errors and missing elements in the reports and providing this feedback to developers.

Users are also often asked to experiment interactively with the prototype during the time between demonstrations, but this is not always a good idea and it can backfire on developers. Leaving the prototype in the hands of users during iteration may create an overload for developers. Suggestions for changes may come in much faster than they can be accommodated. The fact that change requests will now come at random times, perhaps over the telephone, rather than at regularly scheduled prototype demonstrations, will have a disruptive effect on the project and will create many opportunities for thrashing and mind-changing. There is also a danger that users may begin to use the prototype to perform regular work tasks. This will create configuration management problems and may create problematic pressure from the user community for premature delivery of the prototype. Such a scheme can work only if there is a clear understanding that users may experiment for a given period of time, collect suggestions for changes during that period, and submit them all at once at the end of the period. A new "version" of the prototype is then released with all changes incorporated.

The project plan must make it clear that convergence on a solution to functional requirements definition is the equal responsibility of both user and developer team members. Chapter 7 provided a memo audit trail technique for assuring that this aspect of user responsibility is enforced during the course of a prototyping project. Prototype iteration is fun, but it cannot continue indefinitely. The objective, as with any software project, is to deliver a useful system at some justifiable expense level, not to deliver the most powerful software system known to mankind.

LOSS OF FLEXIBILITY AND MAINTAINABILITY DURING THE TUNING PHASE

Much of the good work done towards building a flexible low-maintenance system can be undone during the tuning phase. A programmer looking at a 4GL script will often recognize that the module could be made to execute faster using a lower-level language program. If managers offload all the analysts and prototypers and onload programmers during the tuning phase without any more clear direction than, "Tune the prototype for performance," there is danger of a wholesale replacement of prototype modules with programs.

Remember why we decided that prototyping was an acceptable alternative to conventional prespecification in the first place? Using the right kind of prototyping tools, the prototype will be just as easy to modify as any paper model of the system. Wouldn't this ease of modification be nice to retain through to delivery of the final product? Such flexibility would certainly lower the costs of ever-present adaptive maintenance chores. If you justified the prototyping approach based on lower maintenance costs, the justification can evaporate during the project's tuning phase if unanticipated amounts of programming occur.

EFFICIENCY AT THE EXPENSE OF MODIFIABILITY

If programmers are given wholesale license to tune the prototype, they may unnecessarily replace prototype 4GL modules and visually programmed screens with conventional programs to achieve unrequested gains in response or execution times. They may think they will be rewarded for such efforts. The result will be a less flexible end product that will require more effort to modify after delivery. Faster is not always better and even when it is, Chapter 6 showed how some very effective tuning can be accomplished without programming. We described how hardware configurations can be adjusted, some relations (tables) may be replaced with flat files, and other measures can be taken for efficiency. Programming should be the last resort during the tuning phase.

Performance requirements must be approached from the "prove you must have it" direction rather than the "isn't this nice?" direction. Don't let the user require at the beginning of a project that all functions must have n-second response time. Don't let programmers decide during the tuning phase that shaving seconds off current response time is the goal regardless of degradation in flexibility. For some functions, a response time of many seconds may be acceptable. Any improvement over the previous system should be considered a positive gain. What postdelivery cost benefits would be achieved by faster response time and how does this compare to the cost of lost flexibility?

PROGRAMMING WITHOUT THE BENEFIT OF DESIGN

If unnecessary programming is combined with shortcuts in the postapproval design phase, the result may be unstructured, unmaintainable programs. This can lead to postdelivery disaster in terms of maintenance costs. Programmers are often impatient with documentation chores, and design specifications may seem unnecessary when all they have to do, apparently, is write programs that mimic prototype functions. This approach will lead to lack of structure within programs, a documented cause of high maintenance costs.[1]

There are times, of course, when a few programs must be written during the tuning phase, and this in itself can cause problems. More frequently these days, prototypers are not programmers. They are specialists in fourth-generation languages, visual programming, and relational databases. They don't like the tedium of writing conventional programs and in many cases have technically lost touch with how to write programs. If a programming specialist is called in during the tuning phase to write one or two small programs for a large complex system, that person may have a difficult time grasping the architecture of the overall system. Even if a detailed design specification exists, the temporary programmer may have a difficult time understanding the design and thus be tempted to write his or her programs ignoring the design.

The only answer to this dilemma is careful management during the tuning phase. Know what your tuners are up to. Make sure there is a walkthru of the tuned products. Keep some prototypers on the project to the end. Make sure that the goal of the project stays focused on delivering a low maintenance system by leaving this responsibility in the hands of those who have a good understanding of rapid prototyping concepts.

PREMATURE DELIVERY

The following material defines when delivery is premature in a rapid prototyping project, explains the forces which create pressure for premature delivery in this environment, and describes the likely impact of succumbing to such pressure. These are lessons learned from experience. After you have finished reading about premature delivery, you may feel that it so violates the properties of common sense that you will be incredulous the possibility could even exist. Be advised that it is a rare case where the recommendations included in this book are followed precisely from start to finish. In many other cases there were some aspects in which the software was delivered prematurely and procedures called for in the original project plan were not adhered to.[2]

Perhaps the tendency to prematurely implement prototype-developed software is due to the word *rapid* or the overuse of the term *prototype*. These words lead developers to want to see how *rapidly* they can deliver the *prototype*. This motivates us to repeat the following: A prototyping project is not necessarily supposed to be more rapid than conventional software development. The only significance of the word *rapid* in this context is when applied to development and modification of a dynamic requirements model; it does not refer to the time required to produce a deliverable software product.

The following material does not intend to imply that all premature deliveries are failed projects. Sometimes you get lucky. On the other hand, any degree of premature delivery has an attendant risk level of project failure and one failure is all that is necessary to discredit the concept of prototyping in your organization. Think of the following material as things to be aware of if you want to reduce your risk level, rather than a warning that premature delivery will always result in failure. Don't succumb to pressures or temptation for premature delivery if you can help it, but sometimes this phenomenon will not be entirely under your control.

Coping with User Pressure for Premature Delivery

Pressure for premature delivery is the most frequently encountered problem on prototyping projects and when such projects fail it is the single most common cause of failure. Users are often the primary instigators of this problem.

The increase in popularity of the prototyping approach to software development is due to user satisfaction. At last users can request and receive systems they like within a reasonable time frame. The excitement level in the user community at the end of a successful prototype iteration phase runs quite high. At this point, nine out of ten users will say, "I like it. Stop the project now and give it to me."

Have you ever seen an advertisement for or demonstration of a commercial software package that made you feel you simply couldn't stand to be without that product one more day? Have you ever felt frustration when your boss said that such a package could not be acquired without a several-month trade study and formal evaluation period? Then you know how users feel at the end of the prototype iteration phase. They are looking at and interactively experimenting with software they know will solve a major portion of their current job problems. They will be very impatient with your reminders that they signed up for several more months of development activity in the project plan.

The most unfortunate aspect of this problem is that users often have direct control over the funding of a project. If you get obstinate about the project plan, they may just cut your funding and stop the project. Your only recourse in this case is to document what is happening. A prototype is being delivered rather than a final software product. Chances are great that the prototype will not survive heavy usage over a long period of time. Write memos documenting these facts and referencing the original signed agreement, the project plan. Do not, however, get involved in a memo war. The idea of prototyping is to cut through the bureaucratic red tape and deliver better systems faster. Normally, the project plan, faithfully followed, is adequate for documentation of project progress. If the users succeed in a premature delivery maneuver, then it will be necessary to make it clear to everyone associated with the project that you don't think this is a very good idea.

When is Prototype Delivery Premature?

If you are delivering a prototype, the delivery is premature. Do not deliver prototypes—deliver long-range usable software products.

During prototype iteration, the objective is to modify the prototype until it exemplifies all of the user's true and complete set of functional requirements for the final system. During a long iteration phase with a hard-to-please user, this objective can seem very illusive. When the date arrives when you said you would be finished with prototype iteration, will you be willing to slip the schedule and overrun the budget if the user has not expressly approved system functionality? Particularly for fixed price contracts, many managers may at this point rationalize that the user will get as much functionality as they paid for and not more. Just as with freezing paper requirements specifications before they are correct, this will produce a system of poor quality with which the user will not be satisfied. If the user is not satisfied with system functionality at the end of prototype iteration, there is very little chance they will ever be satisfied.

Prototype-developed software cannot survive under heavy usage if it has not been stress tested and tuned for performance. While this may seem intuitively obvious after the discussion in Chapter 6, it is amazing how many projects neglect this task. Perhaps this is because most conventionally developed software has typically never been stress tested for performance. Nationally, there are few qualified experts trained to perform the job of rigorous performance benchmarking. Even informal stress tests such as those suggested in Chapter 6 are typically neglected unless human life or the survival of expensive equipment is at stake. And even under such serious circumstances, software has been placed into production incompletely tested. The testing phase of a conventional software project typically only tests the software for functional correctness. In 1987, there was a lawsuit pending against the manufacturers of a radiation therapy machine for deaths allegedly caused by operators using an unexpected sequence of commands which resulted in the machine's software failing to access appropriate calibration data. If courts choose to view software as a "product" (as opposed to a service, where willful negligence must be proven), then product liability standards will apply—vendors will be held strictly liable for injuries caused by defects. The fact that software is intangible may not disqualify it from being labeled a product for legal purposes. After all, it can be owned, sold, and have defects which can be corrected. The suggestion here is that testing as we have known it is not enough—rigorous testing must take place and must include performance stress testing and tuning as critical steps of prototyping projects. Not only should we do it, we had better get used to doing it or be prepared to face the courts.

As with prototype iteration, express user approval of the results must be obtained for stress testing with large volumes of "live" user data to be meaningful. It requires hard work on the user's part to validate the results. This, again, is more common when dealing with hard-to-please users—the kind who always want everything to be faster. The questions to ask these users are

- Faster than what (how is the information obtained currently)?
- To serve what legitimate business purpose?
- At what acceptable level in additional maintenance cost?

An inappropriate approach is to close out the tuning phase when *you* think performance is fast enough. If the user has a legitimate complaint about performance during artificial stress testing, the problem will probably get worse under actual usage.

Inadequate Documentation

Because the detailed system design is derived from the functionally approved prototype, design becomes an exercise in documenting an existing system. Because documentation is one of the least favorite tasks of most software developers, there is often a temptation to skimp on this activity. A detailed design should be in place before proceeding with the tuning phase to assure that any coding that occurs will flow from and exist within a structured architecture. Sometimes a professional, accurate, and understandable user guide can be produced with relative ease by printing input and output screens and menus and adding some accompanying explanatory dialog. A detailed design of system procedures and control flows must be added.

For a system to be easy to maintain, descriptions of its architecture and control sequences need to be published. Unfortunately this step is often skipped when delivery is premature. Later, if problems with running the prototype in a production mode surface, they are not easy to remedy without the proper design documentation. If a project plan is properly prepared and adhered to, the detailed design phase will be accomplished. Remember that the project plans are to be agreed upon by users, managers, developers, and their peers.

Adequate requirements documentation consists of dataflow diagrams decomposed to the primitive level, process specifications for each primitive level function, and a data dictionary or encyclopedia including correct definitions for all dataflows and data elements. If the system contains real-time processes, there may also be state transition diagrams and control flows on the dataflow diagrams, specifiying the sequence and conditions under which processes are activated. If the procedures recommended in Chapter 6 are followed, the final requirements document may be published immediately after user approval of prototype functionality.

Adequate design documentation consists of entity-relationship diagrams describing the final database schema, complete entity attribute lists with corresponding data dictionary definitions for each attribute, structure charts evolved from prototype control flow graphs, module specifications for each structure chart module, and structured logic charts for each existing program. The final detailed design may be published immediately after user approval of the performance-tuned final product.

To a certain degree, the contents of adequate documentation will depend upon the size, complexity, and nature of the application being documented. The best way to decide what adequate documentation should consist of for each application is to let a walkthru team make this determination. This walkthru team should consist of persons who are likely to be responsible for system maintenance after delivery. The team can review the plan for documentation components promised in the original project plan, and for reasonableness. The team can be recalled as documents are about to be published to review them for adequateness for maintenance purposes.

Why Do Premature Deliveries Occur?

There are three possible sources of pressure for premature delivery of a prototype: users, managers, and developers. In other words, anyone who has anything to do with a prototyping project can have motivations for wanting to deliver the system before it is really ready. Often, pressure for premature delivery can come from a conspiracy of users, software development managers, and development staff—all agreeing on immediate delivery. If you are the project leader knowledgeable about the risks of premature delivery, you may find yourself faced with heavy opposition.

During the second half of a prototyping project, when a working system exists with which users seem quite pleased, managers will frequently sense an opportunity to divert resources from an apparently successful project to projects which may be experiencing painful budget, schedule, or user satisfaction problems. If some of these projects have a higher corporate priority than the prototyping project, support for re-allocation of resources may come from upper management, regardless of what the project plan says.

As has been pointed out earlier, it is quite easy to oversell users on the benefits of prototyping. As soon as the user team members see something they like, the majority of them will be severely tempted to clamor for immediate delivery. If these same users have control over project funding, they may have the needed leverage to force immediate delivery at this point.

In one case, a prototype was turned over to all potential users for hands-on experimentation. Even the skeptics had a chance to exercise it. This was useful for obtaining user feedback regarding desired changes, but there were some undesirable side effects. On-the-job usage served to raise expectations to unrealistic levels. It appeared a production system was in place that was being modified to meet true user requirements. Surely this system would be released soon to replace the current one and solve all problems. Much goodwill was lost with this user community when the functionally approved prototype was not immediately delivered, and even more was lost when it was finally delivered prematurely, due to user and management pressure, and then quickly scrapped (pulled out of production) due to performance problems and lack of adequate documentation.

The strongest pressure for premature delivery will come when the development staff is faced with design derivation. At this point, a system exists which meets all the users' requirements. The development staff is looking at remaining tasks which appear to be a lot less fun than prototype iteration: documentation and performance tuning. There is typically a large backlog of requests for new applications, creating additional pressure to complete the current project as rapidly as possible. It is easy for the development staff to succumb at this point either to management or user pressure, or both, for immediate delivery of the prototype. The development staff thinks, "We could take care of documentation and performance tuning at our leisure after the system is in production."

The final, but perhaps strongest, motivation for premature delivery is that prototyping projects tend to be hot. In our experience, most of the prototyping projects we have seen are attempts to solve, using the new prototyping approach, an extremely difficult application problem that a software organization has repeatedly been unable to solve using other approaches. This difficult problem is also typically critical to the overall organization's operations. Thus, a prototyping project of this type will have very high corporate visibility. High-level management will be watching the project closely to see if this new prototyping approach will produce any positive results. Because of the high visibility of the project and the critical nature of the application, any partial success, such as user approval of prototype functionality, will create enormously powerful pressure for immediate delivery.

A word of advice about this last factor is in order. We do not recommend that your first experience with prototyping be on such a highly visible, difficult, critical application development project. When you are first learning to apply rapid prototyping techniques, you will probably make many mistakes. Use a simple noncritical application as a learning experience first before you try to solve really tough problems, even though you may have some that have been pending for a long time and may be hoping that prototyping will provide the proper solution for them. If you have a successful experience (or two or three) using the new techniques on simple problems before you try to tackle a really difficult problem, you will begin to be recognized as the local expert on rapid prototyping and your opinions about premature delivery will be more widely respected.

What Is the Impact of Premature Delivery?

If prototype iteration is terminated before express user approval of functionality is obtained, the delivered system will not satisfy user needs. This defeats the purpose of prototyping in the first place. If the prototype is delivered without adequate stress testing and tuning, the system runs a high risk of exhibiting severe performance problems during actual use. If the system is put into production without adequate detailed design documentation, approved by a walkthru team consisting of maintenance personnel, the system may accrue high modification costs during operation and maintenance. Because of the typically existing pressures for premature delivery just discussed, prototype-developed software often exhibits one or more of these characteristics. If any of these factors are severe enough or if several factors combine to create a severe problem, the delivered prototype may be pulled from production.

When prematurely delivered prototypes are pulled from production use, rapid prototyping may be discredited in the affected organization as a development approach. This is a very real danger because, for any new technique, there are always cynics who would prefer to see business conducted as usual. These cynics are just waiting to say, "I told you so."

In one case where prototyping failed due to premature delivery, the tendency was to blame the techniques used for the failure, instead of mismanagement. Finally, in a post mortem, the real causes for failure surfaced: improper project management and the incorrect *application* of rapid prototyping techniques, not the techniques themselves. The skeptics, however, now say that rapid prototyping means inadequate design and slipshod testing and they advocate the return to conventional software development. Therefore, the failure of one rapid prototype for a critical application could mean that future users and developers would lose the availability of all of rapid prototyping's advantages.

During the prototype iteration phase, functions may be redefined, menus may be added, deleted, or modified, and, more likely than not, the database structure will be altered (although this activity will probably peak during tuning when restructuring is done for performance reasons). The point must be made that the system is not fully fleshed out at this point and should not be delivered as soon as it meets user approval for functionality. A great deal of time can be lost by prematurely putting a prototype system on the floor for everyone to use for real work. The skeptics will criticize every minor problem as though it were a fully tested system instead of a refined prototype, and the proponents will like it so much they will be incredulous that the system could be scrapped. Much goodwill stands to be sacrificed in both camps due to improper definition of a prototype to the entire project.

STAFF RESISTANCE

The maintenance staff unfamiliar with rapid prototyping techniques may be skeptical about them. When a prototype fails, they may take the opportunity to say, "I told you not to deviate from our current procedures." Courses offering instruction in prototyping techniques may be offered within organizations as one way of making maintainers feel part of the team. They would be consulted about issues of system maintainability early in the life cycle—perhaps as early as project planning and certainly no later than design derivation. They can be made to see that maintaining prototype-developed software can be more interesting than conventional software maintenance because the new way of maintenance strongly resembles the prototype iterations conducted during the analysis phase of development.

A rapid prototype involves the application of fairly radical techniques incorporating fourth-generation language and relational database tools. Maintenance personnel with a third-generation coding and conventional file structure background will be hard pressed without adequate training to understand a system developed with rapid prototyping techniques. In a highly technical field, lack of understanding is threatening to one's professional stature; there is a tendency to belittle techniques with which one is not familiar.

THE IMPORTANCE OF TRAINING

The best way to clear up misconceptions about rapid prototyping is with an in-house training program. Unfortunately, such training is not always easy to obtain from commercial sources. A possible method of implementing such a program within an organization is to select a successful rapid prototyper and place him or her in charge of designing the training program. If no such person is available, then it might be wise to reconsider using rapid prototyping techniques only after adequate training can be obtained. The misuse of rapid prototyping can yield more disadvantages than the benefits to be gained from its proper application.

REFERENCES

1. Linda Brice and John Connell, "Deriving Metrics for Relating Complexity Measures to Software Maintenance Costs," *Computer Measurement Group Conference Proceedings*, 1982.

2. John Connell and Linda Brice, "The Impact of Implementing a Rapid Prototype on System Maintenance," *AFIPS Conference Proceedings*, National Computer Conference, 54, 1985, 515–24.

9

Case Studies in Rapid Prototyping

Prototyping is certainly not an entirely new idea, having evolved from a need to more completely specify user requirements during the system development cycle. The desire to accomplish those goals has really been with us since the beginnings of programming. More than likely, it has been discussed only since the early 1980s because we simply did not have the tools until then. Not one of us really wants our systems thrown away, not used, or tuned forever. Attempts to formalize some scientific approach toward achieving correct systems began around 1968 and was loosely called *software engineering*, a term which sprang from a NATO conference held to address the problems in software development. In 1970, W. W. Royce introduced what we now know as the waterfall life cycle model; Barry W. Boehm reintroduced that model in 1976. The model would probably have looked quite different if the tools we have available now had been available then; it may well have included a prototyping phase. As this trend continues, the process model presented in this book will no doubt change in the future to accept an ever-expanding toolkit.

In 1978, Tom DeMarco brought us the book *Structured Analysis and System Specification*, and Edward Yourdon and Larry Constantine published *Structured Design: Fundamentals of a Discipline of Computer Programming and Systems Design*. These books, along with Page-Jones' *The Practical Guide to Structured Systems Design* and a few others, helped to bridge the gap between "structured programming" and "structured analysis," making use of then-available tools and paving the way for "structured rapid prototyping." Dataflow diagrams are advocated in the writings of this period, and they continue to be useful. Yet we realize that if modern prototyping tools had been available then, those books might have been written a little differently. They might have dealt less with modeling the current system and more with getting something quickly in front of the user.

In 1984, McMenamin and Palmer wrote a book called *Essential Systems Analysis,* which admonished us to forget about concentrating so much on exactly what method is used to implement a system (its incarnation or physical manifestation) and focus our thoughts more on discovering the true essence of a system—the most important, albeit the most difficult, part.[1] This idea was reiterated by Fred Brooks in a 1987 article titled "No Silver Bullet—Essence and Accidents of Software Engineering."[2] Brooks reminds us that software construction involves both essential tasks—fashioning the complex conceptual structures—and accidental tasks—representation of these abstract entities in the machine. He points out that we have had some help with the accidental tasks (high-level languages and programming environments for instance), but that the essential tasks have been largely ignored. One of the things that can be done to alleviate this inequity is to rapidly prototype for specification requirements, allowing the client to test the conceptual structure for consistency and usability.

The concepts of incremental system development and top-down design and implementation have been around quite a long time. "Build a little, test a little" has been advocated for many years, yet those phrases take on new meaning with the advent of better tools for building and with the view that the user is the tester.

In addition to these historical contributions of some of the pioneers in software engineering, particular experiences in prototyping have also helped to shape the methodology presented in this book. The case studies presented here are examples of some approaches that worked and others that were not totally successful. Each project made a unique contribution to the thought process concerning what rapid prototyping should be. These projects were undertaken at various companies and are real-life true stories about rapid prototyping.

The following case studies in prototyping will be covered:

1981–1982

- A profit and loss reporting system to detail a division's financial status more finely than corporate reports—it shows the power of examining user interfaces as a window into further examination of functionality
- A corporate planning system used to provide five-year plans for an 8,000-person laboratory—it describes how some "difficult" users with continually changing requirements can be dealt with effectively using prototyping
- A compensation analysis system used by managers to allocate raises and promotions—the beginnings of simplifying the development process
- A billing, or "recharge" system used by the graphics arts department of a large organization—it points out the danger of turning users loose with queries
- A database or data dictionary detailing interrelationships among software applications, used by a data processing division—it describes how developers can make use of tools for themselves as well as for their users

1983–1984

- A litigation support system requiring large amounts of textual data, used by attorneys in six states—it describes how prototyping was the way to serve, in a hurry, users not familiar with computers
- A law firm management system used to handle the internal information processing requirements of the firm—it describes how the user grew up on prototyping and is unaware of any other type of system development activities
- A project management system, also used for trend analysis by a data processing division—it points out how a good prototype with potential to evolve can fail in the "evolving" phase due to improper management

1985 and Beyond

- A system to provide a computer-aided software engineering environment
- An embedded, real-time, artificial intelligence application
- A glimpse into prototyping on a Strategic Defense Initiative project

THE BEGINNINGS OF RAPID PROTOTYPING: 1981–1982

During this period, experiments with fourth-generation languages having RDMS foundations were taking place, but a prototype was almost always something to be discarded once system requirements had been accurately defined. A mixed approach began to evolve whereby some parts of the system would be developed with RDMS tools and other parts would be coded in a conventional programming language. Figure 9-1 shows the approach used at that time. The difference between Figure 9-1 and the more mature prototyping model is in the center ellipse—in the early stages the importance of project planning, rapid analysis, and menu development had not been recognized.

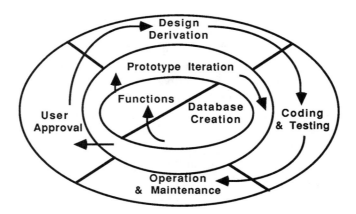

Figure 9-1 Early prototyping.

A Profit and Loss Reporting System

Work on this project began in 1981. Initially, the development tools used were structured specification techniques, a minicomputer, a COBOL compiler, and a network model database. The objective of the project was to develop a financial application for a particular division of a company that would provide more detailed information about that division's activities than the corporate accounting reports provided, but at the same time would reconcile accurately with the corporate reports. This was a medium sized project involving about a dozen users and 200,000 data records, and had been estimated at 4.5 person-years of development effort.

Proceeding in a traditional fashion, the first step was to have a series of weekly meetings with the users wherein the details of a structured analysis specification based on dataflow diagrams, process specifications, and a data dictionary were worked out. The structured analysis model was iterated based on feedback from the users as if it were a paper prototype. This seemed at the time a very state-of-the-art way to proceed. It seemed as though it was bound to produce better results than the traditional approach of producing a lengthy prose style requirements definition.

A red flag was raised at one of the weekly user-analyst meetings. A high-level user exclaimed, "I took these process specifications home and showed them to my wife last night and asked her if it wasn't amazing how closely computer programs resembled English these days." The process specifications were written in structured English to remove ambiguities. Each "mini-spec" was a rigorous statement of user policy for what primitive level functions were to be performed by processes, thereby accomplishing the required data transformations. This user evidently misunderstood and thought he was looking at lines of source code. If this level of misunderstanding existed, another level could exist regarding whose policy was contained in the specifications or exactly what was being specified.

This red flag caused a more careful examination of this user's understanding of the existing version of the structured specification. As it turned out, he had an elementary level of understanding, but no evident feeling that complete and total understanding was necessary. Often, elements of the structured specification were being approved simply because they existed: They were promised and then delivered on schedule—a good sign from this user's point of view. The paper model was supposed to be a communications tool but was poorly understood by the user and was viewed instead as a design tool for developers—appropriately incomprehensible to the layperson. This was another case of an analyst assuming that user approval of structured specifications is based on a complete understanding of the specifications.

In this case, every effort had been made to lead the user gently, step by step through the specifications. When that approach failed to produce a complete understanding, a mock-up prototype of the system was created by using a text editor to produce static examples of data entry screens and reports. Application control was not prototyped, nor was it possible to produce a prototype that used actual application data or responded in any interactive way to user actions. Nevertheless, the mock-up of the appearance of the proposed system's pieces turned out to be much more useful in eliciting feedback from the user than the structured specification alone had been.

The user immediately understood that this is how we intended his system to look upon delivery. Printed copies of proposed screens and reports were soon covered with red user ink.

The moral of this story is not that structured analysis is a poor medium for communication with users. Indeed, dataflow diagrams must be prepared before mock-ups of proposed screens and reports, or the tendency is to lose track of the point of the screens and reports—the big picture. The moral of the story is rather that shopping for software functionality by examining interface examples can be a very powerful technique from a user's point of view. This is the basic thesis of rapid prototyping, and in 1981 it seemed a startling discovery.

The Continuation of the Profit and Loss System

The second case study is actually a continuation of the first, as it happens that the profit and loss system project was also one where a relational database management tool, a fourth-generation language, and visual programming were used. When the original system was delivered to the users, it was discovered that static mock-up prototyping had not been conclusive in verifying the goodness of the user interface. The users actually had a lot of trouble figuring out how to *use* the system. The result of their confusion was that much bad data had been entered into the database, causing continual requests for system maintenance to correct erroneous reports. Frequently, attempts to make the system more usable required changes to the database schema. These changes were not trivial due to the network model of the database product being used. The system was consuming as much programmer effort during maintenance as it had during development.

In 1982, the user acquired an organizational standard minicomputer as a result of the trend away from the mainframe and toward distributed computing. In addition, the organization acquired a site license for one of the then-new relational database products.

The users of the profit and loss system were being pressured to have their system converted to the new minicomputer. The conversion cost would have to come out of their department's budget, so there was some resistance to this pressure. At the same time, the members of the software development department were being trained to use the new RDMS in a one-week hands-on in-house training course. The natural thing seemed to be to learn by prototyping the profit and loss system. By the end of the week most of the functions of the actual system had been duplicated and could be demonstrated using actual application data. The *way* the prototype system functioned, however, was much different. The difficulties of the user interface were concentrated on in the prototype, making an attempt to create a more user-friendly system.

At this point it was discovered that the primary value of using an RDMS for prototyping was the ease with which data storage structures could be modified. Schema changes that would consume one or two weeks' worth of programming effort using the network structure DBMS could be performed in minutes using a text editor with the RDMS. No more writing complex COBOL programs to attempt reloading precious data into a new schema, only to obtain an error message saying,

"Sorry—some chains and pointers have been broken and the database was destroyed and all data lost."

A demonstration of the prototype produced during the training class convinced users that the potential of this new tool was worth a feasibility study to see if there might be a cost benefit in converting their system to the new hardware-software environment. The study showed that conversion cost would be lower than the original development costs and that the resulting product would have much lower maintenance costs—a net cost benefit would accrue after six months. A significant part of the conversion proposal was that *prototyping* would be used to establish a more user-friendly interface.

The profit and loss system that resulted from the conversion accomplished the same results as those intended by the original system—a financial application that provided detailed information about the division's activities and reconciled accurately with the corporate accounting reports. The difference was that the new system was much easier to use. Users made fewer mistakes, and much less maintenance effort was necessary to correct data integrity errors. The converted system was a hybrid. Half of the modules were COBOL programs and the other half were RDMS routines. The RDMS routines were either report writer scripts or visually programmed data entry screens. The RDMS, at that time, did not include a menu-driven application generator or a report by example feature. All the data for the application resided in the RDMS. There were fewer performance problems than with the network structure DBMS. Software maintenance consumed about half the resources of the old system.

A Corporate Planning System

The purpose of this system was to provide five-year financial plans for review by the board of directors. Obviously, one of the characteristics of this project was high visibility. There was really only one interactive user—a person identified as the corporate planner. She would use the system to pull together information from many existing corporate financial systems and present the information in a series of reports to the board. She had done this job for many years and was the nemesis of many programmers. This was the classic difficult user—never quite satisfied with anything you developed, always insisting that the changes you made were not the ones she asked for, and breathing down your neck while you tried to implement her latest need ("the CEO *must* have the report for an impromptu meeting first thing in the morning," and more . . .).

The application had evolved over the years from a manual system to a word processor to a COBOL-mainframe system to a minicomputer system to an RDMS-based system. Each conversion entailed burning out a few programmers due to the difficulties involved in attempting to please this particular user. This is the point at which the new technique of rapid prototyping was called on to alleviate the pressure. In fact, what had already transpired over the years was actually slow prototyping of the worst kind—iterations involving changes made to the COBOL programs were typically one to six months apart. Now, there was no way to make this user more pleasant to deal with, but at least the iterations could be forced to happen faster and the inevitable changes could be made less painful through the use of a then-new RDMS toolkit.

The discovery made with this project was that, with some users, prototype iterations only serve to spawn more ideas for changes. Developers still had the same problem with this user that the changes made were allegedly never what she had requested. The difference was that, since it was apparently so easy to make changes, she felt this gave her license to request even more—requesting changes became her full-time job. She was having so much fun she even put in some unpaid overtime. The developers were tearing their hair out and polishing up their resumes.

At the point when the project looked as though it had gotten into an infinite loop, top management was called in to provide some resolution to the problem. A solution was for the developers to take notes at each prototype demonstration regarding the changes requested by the user. At the end of the demo, developers would read the notes back to the user to see if she agreed that these were her requests. Developers would then draft a memo, based on these notes, from the user to themselves with copies to the user's boss and the developers' management. They would ask the user to sign and send the memo. Each memo after the first would have a checklist showing that problems identified in the previous memo had been fixed. This established an audit trail that prevented thrashing. It became very publicly embarassing for the user to change her mind too often, so she didn't.

Eventually, the user and the developers and their managers felt that covergence on a final solution was imminent enough that a "last chance" demo could be scheduled. The objective of this demonstration was to establish a final list of requested changes—hopefully a few minor changes which, if made correctly, would cause the user to grant approval of prototype functionality at the final demonstration. This actually worked. The system was delivered to the user for production use. She was more satisfied with system functionality than ever before.

There is also a happy epilogue to this story. Some months later, the software department decided to offer in-house rapid prototyping workshops. Both users and programmers could sign up for the courses if they first satisfied the prerequisite of having completed the in-house RDMS course. Our difficult user, pleased with the results of prototyping, signed up for the course to see if she could learn to do it for herself.

The instructor offered two types of course completion certificates. The first certificate said, "*Student__name* has *satisfied* the basic requirements for completing the Rapid Prototyping Workshop by attending all sessions." This certificate had imprinted on it a picture of a subcompact economy car. The second certificate said, "*Student__name* has *exceeded* the basic requirements for completion of the Rapid Prototyping Workshop by developing an outstanding prototype during the course of the workshop." Imprinted on this certificate was a picture of an exotic Italian sports car. Guess who earned one of the exotic sports car certificates?

Some of the programmers in the class, tending to spend the entire week in rapid analysis trying to get the specs right before proceeding to development, were shown up by new computer users. Those users, typically impatient with specification, were anxious to dive right in to prototype development and therefore most of the user-students had something up and running by the end of the course. Does this mean that users make better prototypers than software professionals? Of course not. But, nothing separates users from developers hereditarily. Users can become expert prototypers with significantly less training than that required for a degree in computer science.

A Compensation Analysis System

This was not a very complex application, but it has the distinction of being one early system produced and delivered using only RDMS-based tools. There were 4GL report writer scripts, visually programmed data entry screens, and automatically generated graphic analysis of data. Application control was menu driven and created using 4GL and visual programming application generation tools, then packaged for the first time with the RDMS. This meant no more writing of job control language.

The system had quite a few users. Most managers responsible for raises and promotions used the system to study relationships between experience, education, performance evaluation, and compensation. There did not have to be concurrent users. The system was capable of copying in only that data from corporate personnel files that related to a particular department, for review by the department manager. This limited the amount of data that had to be managed at one time by the database, and the number of concurrent users was never more than one. These limitations were actually very fortuitous security requirements levied on developers at project onset.

This was a successful prototyping project from all aspects. Very few specifications were produced, so development time was shorter by almost an order of magnitude than what would normally be expected using conventional tools. Users from the highest levels of management were very enthusiastic about the usefulness of the system as prototyping began to gain corporatewide acceptance. The absence of branching statements in the prototype-developed modules meant that strange, unexpected events did not occur when the system was put into production. This, coupled with functional acceptance on the part of users, meant that required maintenance effort approached zero.

Prototyping tools now appeared powerful enough to produce many types of small applications without programming. For a while, prototyping ran amuck at this organization. It appeared to be so much faster and more powerful than conventional software development that users were encouraged to break up a request for large system development into several requests for small prototype-developed systems to do the same job. Many successful systems were prototype-developed during this period without writing any third-generation language programs.

Graphics Arts Recharge System

The graphics arts department was a service organization that recovered their costs from other departments for the provision of labor and materials used to prepare artwork for proposals, presentations, and so forth. An automated system was desired to provide operation cost information on scheduled reports with easy data entry and ad hoc query capability. In the early days of relational database systems, RDMS products were sold primarily on their ability to make ad hoc queries easy for the end user. This was a moderately large system with four working groups of end users, 20 database tables, and 35 reports in the final product.

During the development of this prototype, a menu-driven application generator was not available, so the production system contained 45 job control files. Most of the modules in the delivered system remained as RDMS modules after user approval of prototype functionality. All data entry screens were based on visual programming. Almost all of the reports were produced with a 4GL report writer. There were only two small COBOL programs in the entire application. Once again, there were no performance problems because this was a one-system machine—the users owned the mini and used it only to run this application.

The lesson learned with this project had to do with ad hoc queries. The users quickly discovered that the RDMS had been oversold on this count. Any retrieval of interest posed serious problems for end users in formulating a retrieval command that would produce the expected and correct results. Sometimes poorly structured query commands would cause valuable data to be transformed into worthless nonsense or to be entirely deleted.

Various unsuccessful attempts were made to solve this problem. Individual users were interviewed and difficult queries were categorized. More job control command files were created to help in standardizing queries. New users of the system were required to attend formal RDMS training. Refresher workshops were offered focusing on ad hoc retrievals. None of these approaches really solved the problem. The only workable solution to this problem is to create applications so retrievals and updates by users are restricted to the reports and data entry screens created by developers. These end users found themselves in trouble when allowed ad hoc query access to a production database.

A System Information Database

This project demonstrated that prototyping can be used to generate requirements which the users did not know existed. The application was a system for managing information about software development and maintenance for use by the software department.

In the absence of full analysis and user interviews, all that was really known was that there were always some basic elements of documentation needed for any software application:

- The basic purpose of the system
- Identification of the customer
- How the system runs (tasks, procedures, call files, jobs, and so on)
- How execution of modules begins and ends
- What languages are used and how they are invoked
- Which functions are performed
- What files exist and where they are used
- How data are processed and by which tasks or programs
- What input and output formats look like
- Who is responsible for which portions

It was also known that documentation was unpalatable to programmers who at minimum required automated documentation tools. CASE tools and system-corporate encyclopedias were not widely available in 1982.

When first approached, management of the software department thought such a tool sounded nice but was not worth the effort or dedication of scarce programming resources, especially since no official cost-benefit study had been performed. In a compromise, it was agreed that two person-weeks could be devoted to development of a rapid prototype to demonstrate the concepts involved in the proposed system. An RDMS was available for the inventory and management parts of the documentation function. It was used to structure tables to receive live data from a hierarchical database on a separate computer and from files that programmers had set up to keep track of various systems for which they were responsible. Many programmers, disappointed with the manually maintained central files, had taken steps to record data about software applications in a more usable state, creating a hodgepodge of data sources.

As the pilot system progressed, automated retrievals replaced manual documentation such as the Visual Table of Contents (showing the organization of the modules of a system and how they interrelate), the Hierarchical Input Process Output (showing where, how, and by what module data are transformed), indices of programs, indices of files, indices of tasks, and catalogs of application systems.

When shown prototype modules, developed within this short time frame, which replaced current labor-intensive procedures, management granted approval for a full-scale project to proceed. The programming staff became the users, suggesting additional functionality thought to be useful in maintenance efforts. User approval of prototype functionality was obtained through a survey that indicated almost overwhelming approval of the system.

The system was devised with the intent of helping programmers to map present and future systems. Once in place, however, it provided some fringe benefits. A matrix describing system identifiers and associated responsible programmers, previously maintained on word processing equipment, was made available via a simple merge of relations. A similar matrix detailing the application system, organizational section where the functional responsibility for the application resides, and responsible programmers for an application was also reproducible as a new and more detailed report to management.

While the primary intent of the database was to serve the programming staff who maintained present systems and developed new ones, the functions could be expanded to include the operations side of systems production. Run and recovery instructions, file access and permits, account restrictions, job setups, file retentions, expected outputs, and other operations data could be appended to system, task, program, file, or data element relations as appropriate. Operations information was a natural addition because operators and production controllers were also interested in employee system responsibilities and system functional descriptions, which were already present in the prototype database.

Since this project, pilot model prototypes have been used several times to convince managers, users, and customers of the validity or effectiveness of certain concepts. Contractors have found prototyping useful during proposal phases of major contracts—to demonstrate a superior system concept to the customer. The same concept of prototyping requirements which users do not know exist can be carried forward into the prototype iteration phase. Prototypers are free to insert suggestions for what they feel would be useful functionality into prototype versions, to be validated or rejected by users at demonstrations.

EVOLUTIONARY PROTOTYPES: 1983–1984

Around 1983, conventional wisdom was that relational databases in general and rapid prototyping specifically were not suitable for applications with large numbers of users or huge amounts of data. Systems were classified as suitable for prototyping or unsuitable, based on size. Figure 9-2 shows the approach to prototyping typically used during this period, characterized by minimal planning or specification and no formal testing. The difference between Figures 9-1 and 9-2 is the addition of "Menus" in the center ellipse of the model. Menu development became possible as a prototyping step when RDMS vendors offered software package tools to set up menus which called other menus and ultimately called processes and painted screens.

In this way, the structured evolutionary approach to prototyping was worked out. The RDMS tools were beginning to allow the creation of turnkey RDMS-based applications. DeMarco's *Controlling Software Projects* was published and contributed the concept of a multidimensional approach to requirements modeling.

A Large Litigation Support System

A comprehensive on-line litigation support system prototyped in 1983 continues to be used by a national network of attorneys. The users recognized a need for rapid communication among their sites and to be able to share large volumes of

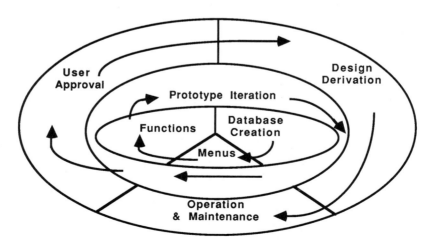

Figure 9-2 Toy system prototyping.

information to support litigation occurring in six states. The users, none of whom had previously used any type of automated system, were aware that, due to the magnitude of the information, a computerized system was absolutely necessary. Volumes of information spanned 1940 through 1963 (about 50 four-drawer filing cabinets) and there was a need to retain everything concerning the litigation currently being produced. The attorneys strongly believed that the system had to be available within 12 months and had to function as their primary research tool.

Due to the user's inexperience and the stringent data and time requirements, rapid prototyping seemed to offer a hope for getting the project begun. A representative group of users gathered for a two-day session where the system's basic design was developed using DFDs as the communication mechanism. In this basic session, no data modeling was done (entity-relationship models), no system event path modeling was done (control flow graphs), and no screen or report formatting was discussed—partly because the prototyping methodology was still immature and partly because the entire representative set of users was available only for those two days. It seemed that the dataflow along with some basic processing concepts were the most important aspects of the system that needed to get started.

Because there was so little time for turning the basic requirements into something the user could see, available tools had to be used. The tools included a DEC VAX/780, INGRES relational database management system, an on-line office management system (ALL-IN-ONE), and a full text editor. The VAX was used because it was handy and had enough capacity to provide a prototyping environment.

The purpose of the first phase of the prototype was to get the user familiar with using automated systems. They were accustomed to law libraries and other manual systems and the developers could sense that the establishment of a common framework in which to work was necessary for deriving specific requirements. Immediately, machine accounts for 20 users were created within the office management system, and terminals and communications gear were acquired. Two analysts from the development team went to each of four initial sites to provide user training. Simultaneously, other members of the development team had acquired a representative sample of the data—several thousand pages of text—that would eventually go into the litigation support system.

The initial prototype system consisted of office management functions and a set of ten menus and retrieval screens built using the forms generation package of that system, providing a consistent system "look and feel" to the user. The initial data were processed using a full text editor, and because INGRES is really not an adequate full text management system, some code was written. The following were two areas where code appeared necessary: code to tie the text editor to INGRES for full document retrieval; and a simple parser to extract keywords from the full text to be loaded into INGRES for document indexing and retrieval.

This phase of the system work was completed in 30 days. The system development team then visited the main user's site and demonstrated the first stage of the prototype. This "demo number one" provided the user with their first opportunity to see what the final system *could* look like; it took three days and generated requests for about 50 changes. It became obvious that the demo was a success and that there was a need for continued close communication between user and developer—

developers sensed a need for expanded requirements and also sensed that the attorneys were not yet comfortable in making requests in computerese. It was decided to iterate the prototype on a two-week cycle to help the user with communication of needs. The changes in the beginning were prioritized with respect to the user's perceived needs and with respect to what could realistically be accomplished within a two-week cycle. The analysis-design team then returned to work on the list of changes.

The second prototype demonstration validated the approach with both parties. Once the user was shown the rapidity with which developers could modify the system, many of the initial 50 changes of low priority were discarded and new, more relevant requirements surfaced. These iterations continued for three months until there was a solid baseline of requirements.

As better hardware and software tools became available in the marketplace, some seemed well suited for use in updating the litigation support system. A prototype exercise of one workstation proved its usefulness, so workstations were installed in several attorneys' offices. Now, some corporate data are downloaded and maintenance of the system is performed via a mini-prototyping methodology. In 1983, the prototype budget was $750,000. The next year's budget for $2.5 million included funds for new machine acquisition. By the third year, the prototype had evolved into a "successful" system. It reached and has maintained an annual budget of $5 million.

Law Firm Management

The major participant in the successful prototype experiment just described, a large law firm employing in excess of 300 employees, realized their own need for firmwide internal automation. Impressed by the rapidity with which the multiuser automated litigation system had been developed, this firm decided to hire developers from that project to prototype their firmwide management needs. An experienced person from the litigation support system now works full-time at the law firm.

The firm was already sold on prototyping and had available a mid-range computer with excess capacity running UNIX that had been used for telephone billing. This project began with two factors critical to success already in place: the user's acceptance of the methodology due to their past experience and a wealth of software tools running under UNIX, including an RDMS.

Presently, all automated firm-management systems are developed by first developing a prototype and then moving quickly into the iteration phase with the user until the requirements are correct. In a way, the procedure could be thought of as continual prototyping whereby the systems are always evolving to meet the user's changing needs and are never really "frozen" in production. Some of the systems developed to support the law firm's internal management needs include a recruiting system; a court appearance scheduling system; a conflict of interest checking system; a personnel time-reporting system; a library management system; and an internal inventory system for such items as briefcases, overhead projectors, and conference room scheduling. The law firm is pleased enough with the results (spoiled, you might say, in that everything is prototyped and there are no lengthy waiting periods before results are produced) to order a second UNIX system and produce a long-range plan for continuing to produce management systems.

A Project Management System

In this case, a project plan was produced. It was correct in format and approved by a walkthru team consisting of peers. Unfortunately, the project plan was not followed. The budget was cut drastically, both in staff and in schedule. The project plan forecasted a demonstrable prototype in October and historical data loaded, employing experienced staff members, in January. Instead, the prototype was demonstrated and delivered in August, complete with historical data, as a final product. Only inexperienced student labor was used to produce this product.

Why was the budget so severely modified? There were a number of reasons. There was an optimistic belief that just maybe this one time the odds could be beaten through the use of the magic of prototyping. Management was in an untenable situation where a system was needed, but proper staffing was difficult to justify since the new system would have an unclear payoff, at least in the early stages. Student employment was available only for the summer, combined with only one staff member who was terminating at the same time. The belief, the real hope, was that some of the system could be implemented before the staff melted away. In that way, corporate memory could be preserved, the major functions could be used, and some time could be bought to properly staff it for completion of implementation and for maintenance.

Figure 9-3 contrasts the desired and the actual life cycle for a case study failure. It may be noted that with the failed prototype, the project plan was written but not followed, the prototype iterations involved too large a user audience, tuning was not done, delivery was ahead of schedule, and the training was inadequate. When prototypes fail, one might ask why mature project team members would deviate so far from years of experience-based knowledge. The answer is an important one; prototyping is still new as an industry tool and we are prone to misuse it. While it is the most valuable of all of the communication tools between customer and developer, and solves the problem of delivering the wrong system better than anything else known at this time, it has the potentially hazardous element of appearing to all parties—customers and developers—to have a trivial implementation since the desirable and necessary elements of a system have been defined. While identifying the problems is a large part of the battle in any problem solving situation, it is by no means the entire activity.

The project management prototype was turned over to all potential users for hands-on experimentation. Even the skeptics had a chance to exercise it. This was useful for obtaining user feedback regarding desired changes, but it had some undesirable side effects. The demonstrations served to raise expectations to unrealistic levels. The appearances were that a production system was in place that was being modified to meet true user requirements. Surely this system would be released soon to replace the current one and solve all problems. Much goodwill was lost with this user community when the prototype was not immediately delivered, and even more was lost when it was eventually scrapped.

When the system went into production, the quantities of users and data were far more than expected. The unexpected usage levels put severe strain on a system that had never been stress tested or performance tuned. Unacceptable performance

Life Cycle Activity: Case Comparison		
Life Cycle Phase	Failed Prototype	Successful Prototype
Project Planning	Adequate, but not followed	Followed precisely
Rapid Analysis	Well done	Adequate
Database Development	Adequate	Adequate
Menu Development	Adequate	Adequate
Function Development	Full functionality of all specified processes	Include non-functioning display processes
Prototype Iteration	Hands on for all users	Hands on for developers only; demo to users
Tuning	Not done	Extensive exercise and tuning of prototype
Detailed Design	User Guide + high-level paper model	Detailed physical specifications
Delivery	No checklist, not done according to plan	Checklist, done according to plan
Training/ Maintenance	No training, skeptical staff	Adequate training, enthusiastic staff

Figure 9-3 Failure versus success

problems resulted. At this point, a maintenance staff that did not have extensive training or experience in maintaining prototype-developed systems was faced with making complex modifications to a sparsely documented system based on an unfamiliar RDMS and 4GL modules. The maintenance staff complained bitterly about lack of documentation and standards violations, calling the system unmaintainable. Management listened and pulled the system out of production.

Since users were told that fourth-generation techniques and rapid prototyping were being used to develop the system, the tendency was to blame these techniques for the failure. Finally, in a post mortem, the real causes for failure surfaced: project management and the incorrect application of rapid prototyping techniques. The skeptics preached for years afterward that rapid prototyping means inadequate design and slipshod testing and they advocated the return to traditional software development.

Because the prototype had some problems due to mismanagement, the whole idea was discredited in the organization. This case, despite a disastrous beginning, actually has a hopeful ending. About two years after the failure, the concept was revived by management, with an eye to proceeding cautiously. A draft of the methodology has been placed in the standards manual as an optional systems development plan. Based on the acceptance of the draft and the frequency with which the option is chosen, it stands a very good chance of becoming the standard. Hopefully, the failure of one rapid prototype for a critical application does not necessarily mean that future users and developers will lose the availability of all the advantages of rapid prototyping. It was this project, primarily, that prompted the insertion of a prototype tuning phase in the prototyping process model.

LARGE AND COMPLEX SYSTEMS: 1985 AND BEYOND

During this period, it was discovered that structured rapid prototyping was an approach that could be successfully applied to the evolutionary development of all types of applications: transaction-oriented, real-time, artificial intelligence, embedded, many concurrent users, and complex functionality. It began to appear that the claim could finally be made that rapid prototyping was the best way to develop all software in the future. This widening of applicability was due in part to improvements in the features and performance characteristics of prototyping tools, but was also due to further refinement of prototyping techniques. The elements of project planning, rapid evolving analysis, stress testing, and performance tuning were added to the formalized approach.

Computer-Aided Systems Engineering (CASE) Environments

CASE tools, growing in popularity, are widely used to automate structured analysis and design methodologies. In mid-1984 the demand for such tools was high, but only a few commercial products with very rudimentary features existed. Many firms, particularly defense contractors it seemed, were considering the in-house development of CASE tools. Defense contractors are big users of CASE tools because they have found it useful to apply structured modeling techniques to very large projects (over 1,000 engineers) and to the modeling of entire system concepts (both hardware and software modules).

An early CASE prototyping project consisted of the creation of a comprehensive environment for application system development. The objective was the in-house development of a suite of automated tools to support the entire life cycle, from requirements analysis through code and test to operation and maintenance. Needless to say, the technology for implementing the requirements of such a system is very complex. The original estimate of effort for this project was 50 person-years.

Because the development team was small and the task was large, an incremental development approach for the project was decided upon. After developing an essential functions diagram for the entire application, the requirements analysis process (bubble) was chosen to be prototyped and tuned until a module that supported just that much of the total system functionality could be delivered. Figure 9-4 shows an annotated essential functions diagram for the initial prototype. This approach yielded some quick initial capabilities and, for the relatively low cost of 18 person-months, validated the concept of rapid prototyping in an organization where it was being used for the first time. As a result of the delivery of the requirements analysis module, the total effort estimate was revised downward to 18 person-years.

A couple of new twists were added to the structured prototyping approach during this project. Management, nervous about the downplaying of the importance of prototyping project specifications, insisted that the structured specification produced during rapid analysis be more than just a way for the developers to collect their thoughts prior to prototyping. The project manager insisted that the paper specifications evolve along with the prototype so that, as new requirements were discovered and prototyped, they would be well documented. As requirements were added to the structured specification, structured walkthrus were required to ensure the accuracy of the specifications.

The approach proved valuable. When it was time to hold a formal system requirements review, the prototyping team could simply make viewgraphs out of the structured analysis models and graphically present requirements that had already been validated by user approval of prototype functionality. During the ensuing months and years of continuing development, there was a high turnover rate among the development staff. This turnover was not due to dissatisfaction but rather to the dictates of corporate priorities. The impact of the turnover was minimized by the presence of accurate, understandable, unambiguous documentation coupled with an easy-to-evolve prototype developed system.

The prototype evolved into the final product, but not without stress testing and tuning. The tuning did not involve the writing of conventional programs, but it did require some new techniques for improving performance without writing code. It was found that the RDMS was not a good vehicle for managing large blocks of text—a necessary feature for a requirements information management system. The database was restructured such that the text blocks existed only outside the database

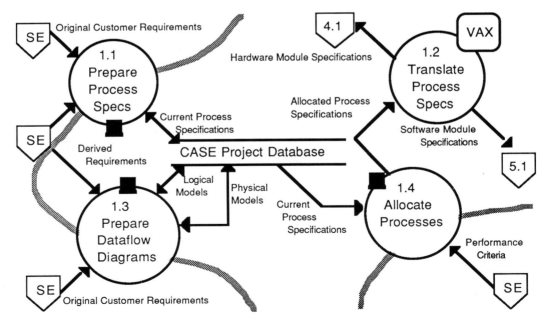

Figure 9-4 Essential functions diagram for an incremental build.

on sequential files. Each record consisted of requirements text and a requirement number that would tie the record back to information retained in the database. The database was used to provide such functionality as requirements traceability, configuration management, and document formatting. Individual requirements text was appropriately managed with a text editor. This technique of using the database as a librarian that knows where the data are but does not actually contain the data has since been used successfully to improve the performance of many other data-intensive applications.

The concept of a distributed database was also used to improve performance on this project. It seemed obvious that all 1,000 potential concurrent users would never have a need to access all of the data in the database from their workstation. Each engineer would only need information relative to the part of the system he or she was working on plus information about the interfaces to other subsystems. A concept of master and slave networked databases evolved. The original prototype was developed on a minicomputer and then ported fairly easily to a supermicro for delivery of the final product. Each supermicro (with diskless nodes) would support a work group of 5 to 25 users. All work groups would be tied together through an Ethernet local area network and a configuration management database workgroup would manage interfaces.

A wide variety of hardware and software was used within this company. Members of each project would make an autonomous decision at the beginning of the project regarding what computer hardware and software would be acquired to support project activities. Since these tools were often purchased with contract funds, they usually became the customer's property after the project was over and such decisions had to be made anew for each project.

Because of this diversity of project environments, it was difficult to foresee which ones could support the prototype-developed system. Would the environment be able to host the RDMS? The RDMS used to develop the prototype ran under a wide variety of operating systems on a wide variety of computers from mainframes and minicomputers to supermicros and personal computers. Still, it was an integral part of the CASE application and could not easily be separated and replaced with another.

Eventually, the decision was made to modify the product to be database independent. This seemingly rational decision produced strange results. The system evolved from an application with almost no lines of code to one with over 200,000 lines of C code. Database product specific things such as visually programmed screens and 4GL report scripts were all replaced methodically with programs. Even the menu-driven control structure was replaced with conventional job control routines. The only remnant of the original product that was allowed to remain was the RDMS data storage structure. One result of these modifications was successful database independence. Another, less fortunate, result was the conversion of a virtually maintenance free system into a maintenance nightmare, shunned by most project members.

An Embedded, Real-Time Artificial Intelligence Application

Here was an application that supposedly had no user interface. The software was embedded on board a vehicle that navigated itself without a human driver. The knowledge used to make navigation decisions was gained from a sensor suite consisting of devices such as a color video television camera and a multispectral laser scanner. The performance requirements for the vehicle escalated over a period of six years in six-month increments, beginning with navigating an asphalt road at three kilometers per hour and ending with off-road obstacle avoidance at 50 kilometers per hour.

The early issues that arose on this project all had to do with the appropriate application of rapid prototyping techniques to the problem at hand. What might a demonstration of prototype software (without a vehicle) accomplish? Could a capabilities demonstration be simulated in software only without using an actual physical vehicle? Which project problems might not be amenable to a rapid prototyping approach? Could a software prototype of this system evolve into the final product? A workable approach to prototyping was required because the customer had been promised in the project proposal that rapid prototyping would be used to develop an initial experimental system within six months.

Without revealing, at first, how these decisions were made, let us examine in more detail a high-level view of the requirements for this system. Figure 9-5 shows how the actual physical layout of the experimental system was conceived.

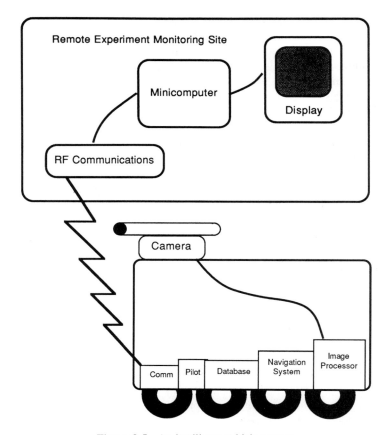

Figure 9-5   An intelligent vehicle system.

The vehicle had a set of on-board computers that included an image processor, a navigation system, a knowledge and rules database, and an electronic pilot. Each of these processors had a counterpart off the vehicle at a remote experiment monitoring site. Radio frequency communications were used to relay data between the vehicle and the monitoring site.

Prior to running an experiment, a test conductor would initialize the vehicle. The initialization process consisted of providing the system with information regarding start and end points for experiment segments, coordinates of landmarks that could be sighted along the test track, and constraints for the vehicle relative to the experiment segments. When the initialization process was complete, the operator would press the start button on a control box that had two buttons—the other button was for emergency stop.

The great hulking 20-ton vehicle would go lumbering off on its own down the test track at three kilometers per hour. The camera would begin collecting visual data. The image processor would digitize the visual data into a series of scene models as shown in Figure 9-6. The navigation system would analyze the scene models, find road edge points, calculate a center line, and compute the difference between the current trajectory and the desired trajectory. The vehicle performed skid steering by sending different velocities to the left wheels than to the right, so the pilot subsystem would use computed trajectory differences to calculate needed velocity changes and send appropriate steering commands to the wheels. As all of this occurred, experiment results could be displayed on a big screen back at the remote experiment monitoring site.

A rapid analysis of this high-level view of functionality might produce a dataflow diagram similar to the one shown in Figure 9-7, an entity-relationship

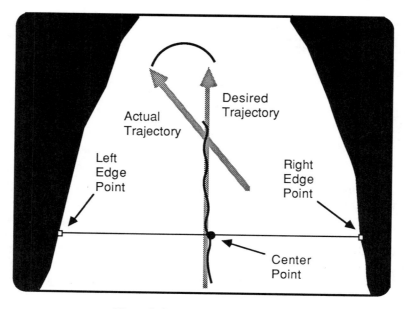

Figure 9-6   A digitized scene model.

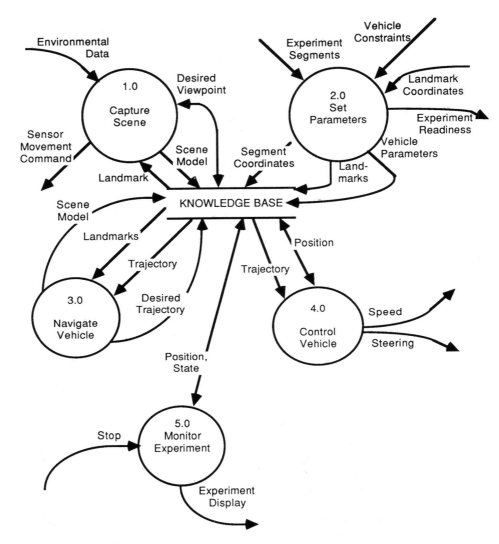

Figure 9-7 Essential functions of intelligent vehicle system.

diagram similar to Figure 9-8, and a control flow graph similar to Figure 9-9. These diagrams are, in fact, very similar to the actual diagrams contained in a long-range operations concept document delivered to the customer. They are presented here because by now the format should be familiar as a good blueprint for developing the initial prototype. The dataflow diagram shows processes interacting with a database, and only with the database—no interprocess interfaces. The entity-relationship diagram looks to be a good model for developing a preliminary database schema using an RDMS. The control flow graph looks to be a good model for developing a menu-driven control structure for the initial prototype.

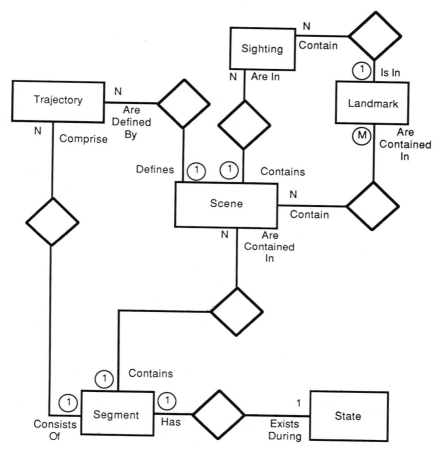

Figure 9-8   A preliminary database design.

Can an autonomous vehicle control itself using menus? Another look at Figure 9-9 will show that the vehicle, once underway, has no interaction with the menu structure whatsoever. The menu interface is only for the operator to use to initialize the vehicle prior to a test run or demonstration. Once "Start" is selected from the menu, on-board software modules operate without guidance from the menu system unless the operator selects "Quit."

In fact, a software-only prototype of this system could be developed to demonstrate system functionality without the existence of an actual vehicle. A sequence of 4GL algorithms could be invoked from the "Start" command on the main menu. These could produce a sequence of 4GL reports or displays simulating the results of an actual test run. Such a simulation would be realistic if the prototype database were loaded with actual data recorded on a video camera taken on the test track from a truck or jeep. The data could be digitized in the lab and then loaded into the scene table for processing by the prototype.

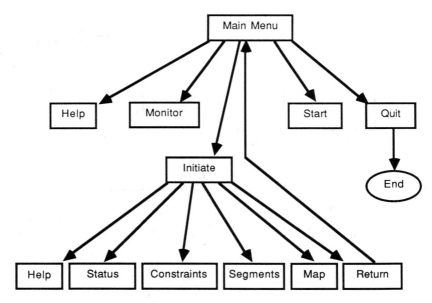

Figure 9-9 Menu-driven application control structure.

Using a rapid prototyping approach on this application would allow the complex details of the user interface to be worked out. A socketed framework with simple interfaces would be put into place as a structure for testing the goodness of various new algorithms. A low-cost means would exist for testing what-if scenarios involving different sets of parameters and constraints. Rapid prototyping would of course do little toward solving the traditionally much-worried-about problems regarding sufficient algorithm speed, hardware capabilities, and vehicle performance.

The management of this project believed that this system was typical of a class of real-time, embedded artificial intelligence applications using no human interface. The fact that an operator was needed to initialize experiments was viewed simply as an inconvenience rather than a feature or requirement of the system. Therefore, in the early months of the project, "prototyping" consisted of writing hundreds of thousands of lines of mostly third-generation language code on a VAX, rehosting the code to the on-board CPUs for field testing, and fiddling with the code until the vehicle would behave in some desirable way. Prototyping on this project simply meant it was acceptable to write code without a structured design and that deliverable specifications were not required by the customer.

An interesting result of this approach became evident in the project's second year. Initially, this quick and dirty approach to prototyping appeared to succeed. The first demonstration, a straight road run at three kilometers per hour, was a success. The second demonstration, which was to include negotiating curves and an increase in speed to 15 kilometers per hour, became much more problematic. Hundreds of thousands of undocumented lines of code were in place. The code had already been patched many times in many places and had by now grown unwieldy in terms of psychological complexity (way too many GO TO statements). Each new change became a little more difficult than the last.

There were separate teams writing each of the various software subsystems: vision, reasoning, communications, navigation, control, and utilities. Each team was most comfortable working in their own particular language and had their own particular target on-board CPU. There were modules in FORTRAN, Pascal, C, PLM, Assembler, LISP, and more. Almost as an afterthought, the utilities team wrote a low-level, interactive dialog program that would ask the operator to answer a series of questions and use the data thus obtained to initialize the vehicle.

The trouble was that all of these subsystems had interfaces, as shown in the dataflow diagram in Figure 9-7. Each team had various versions of their software, using different algorithms. Test conductors found it difficult to initialize the vehicle correctly. There was no operator's guide, the questions asked interactively during the initialization process were often difficult to understand, and error messages were cryptic. During the second year of testing, nine out of ten test runs failed before the thing to be tested was even exercised. Typically it was impossible to tell why the run had failed. Was the new vision module at fault, or was it a bug in the navigation subsystem that only surfaced with the introduction of the new vision module? When management became concerned about schedule slippage and set up investigative procedures to determine failure causes, it was discovered that nine out of ten test failures were caused by improper vehicle initialization on the part of the test conductor. This discovery caused project management to begin to wonder if a different view of the significance of the human interface should be adopted for this system.

Every software application has a human interface, and the human interface is the most significant part of any software application. After all, every software application is commissioned by humans, paid for by humans, developed by humans, and, in the final analysis, intended to be used by humans to accomplish some useful purpose. No software has ever been so deeply embedded that one could not determine whether it was serving its purpose or not. No matter how intelligent an AI application is, it was developed by humans to serve humans.

A philosophical issue brought to light by this case study is that of the importance of real-time system performance requirements and the feasibility of prototyping them using the approach recommended in this book. One school of thought says that, for real-time systems, performance requirements are always the most critical development problems and therefore should be addressed as early in the life cycle as possible. An example frequently used is a flight control system. Such a system must detect and make corrections for an upcoming mountain soon enough to prevent the airplane from crashing into the mountain.

We know of no feasible approach for prototyping the *performance* requirements of such a system, if prototyping means the development of a working model that uses actual application data and will be as easy to modify as a dataflow diagram. The tools to perform such prototyping do not exist today. We do not know how to host the RDMS on on-board processors (chips). We cannot obtain adequate performance from the 4GL report writer to prevent the airplane from crashing into the mountain. Therefore, if we are going to prototype, we must take the view that the functional requirements of the human interface are the critical problems to be solved through rapid prototyping at the beginning of the life cycle. We will solve performance problems during the tuning phase after the user has approved prototype functionality.

In the case of the flight control system, most such systems do two kinds of things: exert control over the airplane and provide information to the pilot. Most systems give the pilot a choice—if he or she does not like or does not trust the information being provided, manual control can be resumed. Therefore, it would seem that the quality, understandability, and obtainability of such information (the human interface) would be as critical to the success of such a system as the timing considerations.

Another philosophical issue relates to the evolvability of real-time applications prototyped using RDMS development environments. Obviously, in some cases, such a prototype will have to be completely replaced with flat file structures and low-level code to be embedded in hardware devices. It might still be worth the approximate ten percent additional cost to prototype the human interface to such systems in a throwaway mode to produce more useful and more usable real-time systems. There are a large number of real-time systems, however, where evolutionary rapid prototyping could be applied because there is a place to host the RDMS in the final production environment.

Returning to the case of the autonomous intelligent vehicle application, none of the rapid prototype could be installed in the actual physical vehicle, but much of the prototype software could be evolved into that portion of the system to be hosted at the remote experiment monitoring site. The RDMS could be hosted on the mainframe back at the lab. Functions at the experiment monitoring site have to duplicate on-board system functions anyway. It is no doubt true that the 4GL modules used in the early prototype to capture scene models, compute trajectories, and issue steering commands would all have to be replaced in the final product to meet performance requirements. It is also true, however, that probably none of the prototype modules used to provide the operator interface for vehicle initialization would need replacement to meet performance requirements because the vehicle is standing still at that time. Therefore we can visualize a final product which consists of some modules carried forward from the functionally approved prototype and other modules, developed during tuning, replacing modules developed during prototyping. Such a process equates to evolutionary prototyping.

Mainframe Prototyping

A large federal agency recently commissioned a study to investigate the feasibility of applying rapid prototyping to the development of a new agencywide information management and device control application. The application was to manage regulatory information at multiple locations across the United States. There was a current computerized system in place, but it did not provide information deemed useful by the users and therefore was not actually used.

Agency management believed that rapid prototyping was the answer to solving problems with the current system. An issue, however, was performance of the final product. The system would have to support thousands of users and many gigabytes of data. It would run on a large central mainframe in the Washington, D.C. area, and nationwide access would be through telecommunications. Some initial benchmarking of an RDMS caused management to believe that a quasi-relational network structured DBMS, designed specifically for use on the mainframe, would provide better results.

One thing leads to another, and so the decision to go with a quasi-relational product led to the need to perform extensive data modeling prior to prototyping. Six months and $175,000 were spent preparing a four-volume corporate data model. It identified over 100 subject databases; the average database schema contained over 100 attributes. The size is not too surprising since user interviewees feel safer in mentioning all known data rather than just the set of data they really need. The typical feeling is that if something is left out of the data model, it will never be obtainable from the resulting computer system. The way to minimize such a risk is to mention every data item imaginable.

The next step was to implement the data model. A request for proposal was issued with the four-volume data model included as an attachment. The winning bidder ended up with a three-year project worth $200 million. At the end of that three years, all that would be in place would be a monstrous database—an enormous electronic data warehouse—no programs, no application system, not even a prototype. An army of data entry clerks would have lifelong careers updating unnecessary and unused information.

There is no happy ending to this story. The contract was awarded, work on the database is currently underway. Only when this contract has been completed will the agency find out if all the work to get the schema right the first time will pay off by providing a solid foundation for prototyping applications. Without a large staff of database administrators, schema changes could consume 100 percent of all future effort and no application functionality will ever be forthcoming.

Do mainframe prototypers always have to make this difficult decision between adequate performance and adequate flexibility? Perhaps not, if a flexible development environment is chosen and an expert design job is done during the tuning phase of prototyping projects. With a flexible product, one opts not to worry too much about data redundancy. Electronic storage space is relatively inexpensive these days. A separate database for each application system is a perfectly acceptable design, even when it means some data attributes will be duplicated across many applications. This is particularly true when using a flexible RDMS that makes sharing information with other database systems easy. There is nothing about the relational model that causes poor performance by default. Poor performance is always caused by poor implementation of the relational model on the part of the RDMS vendor, or poor application design on the part of the developer, or both.

End User Rapid Prototyping in a Large Personal Computer Network

In one organization, a decision was made recently to put a personal computer on every white collar worker's desk in hopes of maximizing productivity. No one had to share a PC with anyone else and everyone could decide independently what type of PC would best meet their needs. There were no dictated standards. Some chose an IBM PC, some chose an Apple Macintosh, some chose a Zenith, and so forth. Software selection worked the same way—people selected what they felt they needed. Purchase limits were set by the budgets of individual work groups.

Although this environment might sound like total chaos, it actually worked very well. The net result was that an independent productivity audit, performed by a big eight accounting firm, indicated that a 28 percent productivity improvement was obtained. A small group of PC specialists made everything run smoothly despite the seeming anarchy. These specialists evaluated new hardware and software and made recommendations rather than dictating standards. Training courses were offered in the most highly recommended and widely used products. The specialists provided quick-response assistance when problems with networking and data integrity arose. One of the missions of the specialists was to make everything talk to everything else with no compatability problems. This turned out to be possible; it only took some motivation and effort to provide solutions. A network ultimately developed that resembled Figure 9-10.

There are some interesting aspects to end user rapid prototyping. First, the communication problems between developers and users are entirely eliminated. Second, given a minimum of training and some easy-to-use prototyping tools, users are capable of doing a fairly respectable job of developing software. Third, the term evolutionary prototyping takes on special meaning when there are hundreds of users involved in dozens of separate prototyping activities concurrently—the best efforts survive, the others are quickly recognized as junk—survival of the fittest, Darwin style.

The best user-developed prototypes naturally became candidates for multiuser applications. This is the point at which end user prototyping expertise tended to run thin. Data volumes of popular systems began to overflow the capacity of small PC hard disks. Re-hosts of the prototype were often necessary. With several users accessing significant amounts of data concurrently, response time sometimes became a problem. These and other problems were solved with help from the PC specialist team. The resulting solutions became multiuser software applications that were impossible to distinguish, in terms of either quality or efficiency, from professionally developed software on a mainframe. One such prototype was benchmarked by the productivity auditors to provide a 400:1 productivity improvement to users.

In two years of end user prototyping within this organization, there was not a single middle of the night maintenance crisis or major software development project debacle. Users had an option to request centrally developed software and not a single person took this option. Major software development projects did occur, but they always began as small single-user experiments. The success of this new approach to software development suggests that a new paradigm for development projects may replace the current user-developer model. In the future, given direct access to computing resources and easy-to-use development tools, users will tend to become increasingly involved in development activities. Software development professionals will assume more of a consulting role. There will continue to be a diminishing need for the skill of programming, as we currently know it.

Prototyping on a Strategic Defense Initiative Project

The Strategic Defense Initiative (SDI) is the collection of DoD-funded projects popularly known as "Star Wars." There are many misconceptions about these projects—many people believe SDI will be a proliferation of nuclear weapons in

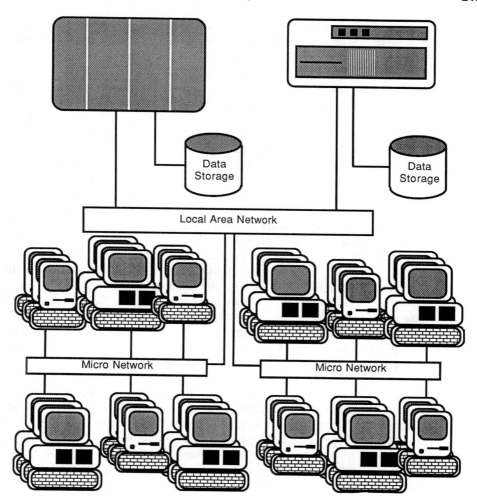

Figure 9-10 Personal computer network.

space. The real hope of SDI is to make nuclear weapons obsolete by making nuclear war impossible. The basic strategy for accomplishing this objective is to develop various antiweapon devices that will strike down enemy missiles before they can reach their targets. Such devices cannot possibly be used in an aggressive manner.

There is a heavy emphasis on computerized systems in general, and artificial intelligence specifically, throughout all of the SDI programs. Visualize an orbiting armada of smart autonomous weapons and you've got the basic concept. If enemy missiles try to lift off their launch pads, they will be automatically struck down from space. Such systems must have computerized acquisition and tracking systems and must be demonstrably smart enough to be able to discriminate between a peaceful space mission and a nuclear missile attack. Until well into the next century, such systems will exist mainly on the drawing boards of various defense contractors. Rather than build a lot of experimental hardware, many current contracts are pursuing computerized simulations as a means of experimenting with various strategic options at a relatively low cost. Perhaps if World War III is simulated on the computer screen enough times, the real thing will never happen—if it does, it will be the most rehearsed war in the history of mankind.

One such simulation-oriented project has effectively used rapid prototyping. Project management originally asked for a global project database—one that would manage all of the technical and management information on the project. A particular need was felt to have the computer simulations accessing the same set of parameter definitions as the deliverable specifications. Specifications called out parameters such as, "The axial velocity of the interceptor shall be_____miles per second," and "The orbital distance of the weapon platform shall be_____kilometers." Simulations used various combinations of such parameters to derive an optimized set. Therefore the simulations could be viewed as validating the system specifications, but only if there was some way to insure that both were using the same set of parameters. This global parameter data dictionary, together with configuration management functions, was the primary purpose of the project database as shown in Figure 9-11.

An active application system was needed, not a passive database. Since no one seemed to have a clear idea of what the functional requirements for this application should be, rapid prototyping seemed a natural approach. No one on this project knew what rapid prototyping was—an ideal opportunity to do things the right way with minimal management interference. Beginning with the preparation of a project plan that specified the textbook approach to prototyping, all of the techniques described in this book were applied exactly as described.

Management and users paid little attention to what was going on during project planning and rapid analysis, but were absolutely fascinated by the crystallization of requirements through dynamic example during early prototype iterations. One manager exclaimed, "Never before have I had such a clear sense that something productive was actually happening so early in the project." Users were riding the critical edge of prototyping the correct way. On the one hand, users were afraid the prototype would be implemented too soon, because they were fully aware it was only a model. On the other hand, they were delighted to see useful functionality developing so rapidly.

Because everything was going so well and because neither managers nor users had preconceptions about how rapid prototyping should be approached, the database-prototyping team was allowed to proceed as they saw fit. Specifications evolved concurrently with the prototype. Neither system requirements review nor a design review was held until after final user approval of prototype functionality was obtained. Stress testing and tuning was extensive. The percentage of the prototype leveraged into production was maximized: No prototype modules were replaced by conventional programs.

There were other interesting aspects to this project. Initial prototyping was performed on a parallel processor. After the first prototype demonstration, the developers decided to do part of the prototype using a multiuser RDMS hosted on a networked personal computer architecture. Concurrent processing offered speed, but the PC-based RDMS provided a more user-friendly front end. It seemed relatively easy to make the two parts of the prototype appear to be one system using concepts

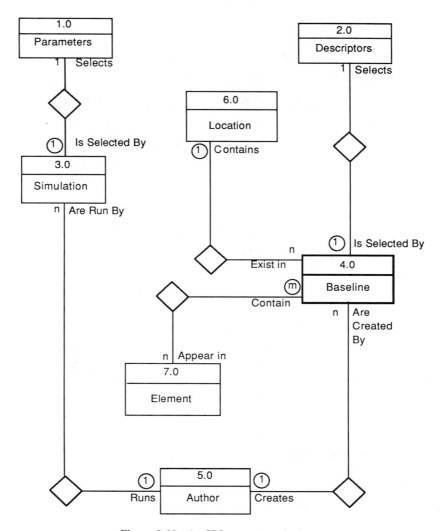

Figure 9-11   An SDI parameters database.

such as local area networking, file serving, and telecommunications. Figure 9-12 shows the original architecture plan. A curious thing happened. The PC-based RDMS completely overwhelmed the mainframe product in terms of both development speed and user-friendliness; to the point that users ceased to care about gaining fractions of a second in response time. The PC-based prototype stress tested at adequate performance levels, and the mainframe prototype was abandoned.

Another interesting phenomenon was that project management was sufficiently impressed with the rapid prototyping approach that they decided to sell the concept to the customer (United States Air Force) as the way all software on the project would be developed in the future (despite technical arguments raging at the worker level). Conventional programmers argued that this particular approach to prototyping was

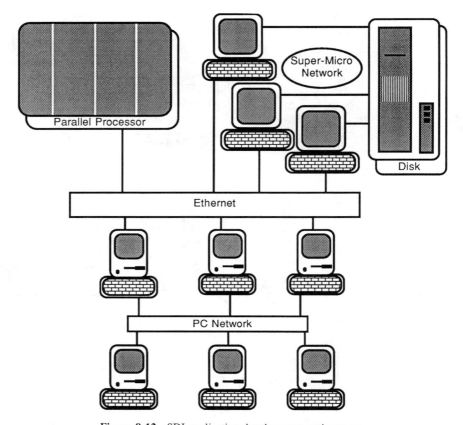

Figure 9-12   SDI application development environment.

all right for data-oriented applications such as the project database but not appropriate for real-time applications such as an SDI simulation. Others were saying that an SDI simulation is just as data oriented as anything else—the output produced by a simulation is totally dependent on the data it is fed. GIGO (garbage in, garbage out) appears to be an inescapable concept.

It has already been determined that simulations are extremely valuable on such projects and this SDI project is proving that simulations can be effectively prototyped. Although the jury is still out, because the project is far from finished in 1988, we even go so far as to believe that much of such a prototype can be evolved into the final product—prototypes in space!

REFERENCES

1. Stephen M. McMenamin and John F. Palmer, *Essential Systems Analysis* (New York: Yourdon Press, 1984).

2. F. Brooks, "No Silver Bullet—Essence and Accidents of Software Engineering," *Information Processing 86*, ed. H. J. Kugler (North-Holland: Elsevier Science Publishers, 1986).

10

Do-It-Yourself Rapid Prototyping

As with automobile maintenance and home remodeling, there is a do-it-yourself movement in the software development field. Frustrated and angered by long backlogs for requested new applications and communication problems with software professionals, many users have learned to do their own software development and taken on the job of developing their own applications by themselves. This chapter explores the implications of rapid prototyping for this user movement.

MANAGING EXPECTATIONS

If rapid prototyping is such a simple and straightforward way to conduct system development and if the supporting tools are now so easily available, then why don't users just do it themselves? In fact, sometimes they do. Other times the job is too big, or the skills needed for prototyping are not resident in the user community. In all but the most trivial kinds of systems, easier-to-use software and hardware tools must become available before software professionals can be completely removed from the software development loop. A few years ago, the information center approach was a very popular new method for getting users involved in automated system life cycles and promised huge productivity gains. While certainly an important phase in the search for solutions to the application backlog problem and to the user-developer miscommunication problem, it has yet to prove to be the final answer. As application development tools get easier to use, applications seem to get more difficult to understand and develop.

Users are developing their own prototypes more frequently every day. A paradigm for software development of the future is developing whereby users might prototype their desired application and then software professionals might be requested to evolve (tune and document) the prototype into a final product. From the software developer's point of view, this would drop iteration to user approval of prototype functionality from the process, producing the process model shown in Figure 10-1. The motivation for this approach exists when only the users have the professional knowledge needed for even a basic understanding of software application functional requirements.

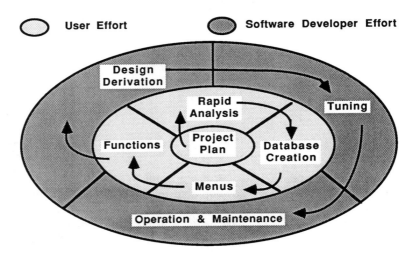

Figure 10-1   An emerging process model.

THE UNLEARNING CURVE

On the positive side, users tend to make better prototypers, given adequate training, than programmers. This is in part because they have less to unlearn. Programmers, trained in the art of software engineering, often feel they are violating a sacrosanct law if they do not write conventional programs for the sake of efficiency or if they do not complete detailed specifications before beginning to develop a working system. We were all told by our secondary school English teachers to write an outline before we start to write a theme paper or anything else. As hurried adults, we frequently tend to compose our writings from the hip, but more often than not we do so with a twinge of guilt. Programmers feel the same way—anyone who has been in the business for more than a couple of years feels uncomfortable without the crutch of detailed specifications. Some even feel the need for a flowchart or the semblance thereof, even though they do not enjoy preparing that kind of detailed specification and are fully aware that the final system will almost never match it.

A recurring theme in this book is that the basic tenets of software engineering remain as integral parts of rapid prototyping. They are not thrown away, since they exist for historically sound reasons. Analysis, design, and programming must continue to adhere to the structured approach because it has served us better than any other. What is very different about rapid prototyping is that the structured techniques are applied in a new order—this is the concept that programmers (but not users) have trouble accepting. Detailed analysis, design, and program specifications are not produced before users are able to exercise the system. Users, unencumbered with those ideas in the first place, can quite easily accept that it is "OK" to analyze a little, design a little, then test to see how we are doing.

PROTOTYPING ON THE PERSONAL COMPUTER

As of 1987, there is a better than 100 to 1 ratio of personal computers to mainframes in the United States. In 1983, at the beginning of the big boom, 1.85 million PCs were shipped. The total base of installed PCs exceeded 20 million by the end of 1987.[1] As Figure 10-2 shows, the number of computer users is also growing, but not as rapidly as the number of computers. By 1990 there will be one computer for every two knowledge workers. More than 100,000 individual types of commercial software application packages are available to support these PCs. There are word processors, graphics packages, database management, spreadsheets, project management, and telecommunications, to name just a few. In addition, there are tools specific to a prototyping environment, for which we have provided a partial list in Table 11-1 in the next chapter. The list includes computer-aided software engineering (CASE) tools to create models such as the dataflow diagrams, entity-relationship diagrams,

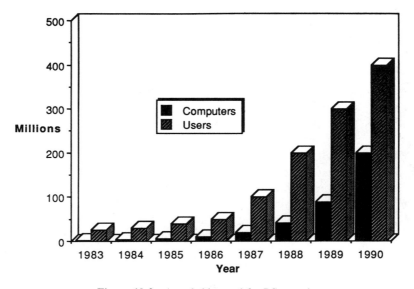

Figure 10-2   A probable trend for PC growth.

and control flow graphs recommended in this book. It also includes tools not created specifically for prototyping, but perceived by some as useful in augmenting the process, such as code generators.

Most personal computers have gone to knowledge workers who use the devices to do what is now referred to as *end user computing*. The advantages of end user computing on PCs are so obvious, it seems inappropriate to talk about stemming the tide (although some data processing departments still do). The real question is how can this totally unmanaged trend avoid the disasters that usually attend any area of such topsy-turvy growth.

As a quick review, Dr. Couger of the University of Colorado has cited the following advantages of end user computing:

1. Simplified tools for individuals to build their own applications and models
2. Improved access to databases
    a. For information retrieval
    b. For data as input to models
3. Increased productivity of users
    a. Able to eliminate time required to translate their requirement to software professionals for development of systems by the software department
    b. Able to reduce implementation time by prototyping their own systems
    c. Able to build applications tailored to their individual needs[1]

End user computing is not without its problems. They are beginning to be documented along with the advantages.

- PCs have added to the number of remote data entry sources; with the distribution of data entry comes the lack of a central, controlling, responsible organizational entity; quality cannot be controlled in the same way as with a centralized system
- Security issues are posed by the intrusion opportunities naturally present in PC networks
- The proliferation of decentralized data storage devices (floppy disks, hard disk file servers) leads to personal file management systems, most without version control
- Software written by users is a boon to the "application backlog dilemma" until it becomes critical to business operations; then, like the software in a traditional information systems department, it must be maintained; at that point, it can become a maintenance nightmare because it was probably not developed using any of the software engineering practices believed to reduce such problems
- Interfaces between and among tools are often difficult for the user to learn and problematic even when used correctly
- Data proliferation problems are increased

The data proliferation problem is perhaps the most insidious and costly. Database security procedures prevent users access to the on-line databases, except in retrieval-only mode so they cannot alter the data. Users who want to manipulate data to perform analyses must be provided copies of a database. The resultant problem is inconsistency of reports when persons are using databases not as up-to-date as the reports produced by the transaction processing applications. The solution that has been used is to give everyone current data. In this mode a "shadow" database copy is provided daily from the corporate mainframes. While the currency problem is resolved, a significant increase in database cost occurs.[2]

CASE STUDIES IN END USER RAPID PROTOTYPING

The following are some examples of cases in which we have actually seen end user prototyping successfully applied. Some of these cases follow the approach advocated in this book, others are quite divergent. Our observation is that end user prototyping is always more likely to lead to project success, regardless of the specific prototyping approach, than any conventional software development approach. Perhaps one reason for this is that the users "buy in" to the project sooner when they are more directly involved. The battle cry against end user prototyping has always been, "I don't do computers, I do engineering (accounting, manufacturing, whatever)." As the tools for software development get increasingly easy to use, this attitude will be increasingly embarrassing to espouse—it will be like saying, "I don't do writing," or "I don't do thinking."

A Team Approach Applied to End User Prototyping

In one laboratory of over 7,000 employees, the department responsible for the budget realized that standing in line at the computer systems services window was a losing proposition. The budget department (BD) had a great deal of respect for the computer department (CD), but simply could not afford the length of time, caused by the classic backlog, for their computing needs to be considered, addressed, met, and modified. Even when BD needs rose to the top of the priority queue over in computing, there was the old problem of technically competent computer professionals who were not trained in the language of the budget area.

The following scenario qualifies quite well as end user prototyping. First, a team was formed to be managed by BD. This team consisted of members of both the budget and computing departments. The BD people were armed with some specialized software tools and some minimal training in the use of those tools. The CD people, called system specialists, had MBAs with concentrations in information systems. They had been trained in programming languages, operating systems, database management systems, and local analysis-design-programming standards.

The CD system specialists knew the terminology and general concepts of budgeting, but had no opportunity to know the laboratory's specific data. They became trained by the budget department, in just those specifics, including what the data looked like for the company, what the sources of data were, and what modeling techniques were useful. In turn, the budget analysts were trained by the system specialists to know the basics of personal computers, both hardware and software. Together, the team investigated new software running on personal computers that might be directly applicable to BD application prototyping. A characteristic that all team members were required to have in common with all of the others is "people skills." Thus, the adversarial relationship that so often develops between the user and the developer did not develop amongst those chosen for the prototyping team.

There were a couple of minor problems that could occur with the team, primarily from the computer department's point of view. One concern was that it was sometimes difficult to find, train, and furnish qualified team members to the budget department. The range of skills must be broad and not just everyone in data processing possessed the people skills necessary for successful team dynamics. The system specialists also needed to have a project-oriented personality. It really was not practical to leave them on the team forever, where their computer specialties could deteriorate. Rather, they were better off if they returned to the computer department after a minimum amount of time (about one year) to keep up with the latest developments in computing and retain an interaction with their peers in that profession. Some computer professionals were too conservative to appreciate what might be called this "lack of stability" and preferred to remain with larger, ongoing projects or with the maintenance of existing systems in CD.

Once the team was formed, they realized that gross budget data were available in the company's central data bank, yet there was scarce opportunity to manipulate that data in a meaningful way. It was largely accounting department information (after the fact instead of forecasts), and so the meaningful portion needed to be extracted for budget's particular needs. ASCII report files were downloaded from the mainframe into budget's PCs. Once the information was there, it was formatted by an inexpensive PC package that can, for example, extract data by columns appearing on a report and place that data into a file of fixed formats and lengths. From there, it was an easy step to load the formatted data directly into a spreadsheet package that could be used for linear programming and graphics, among other things.

The budget department was now producing models, downloaded from the mainframe with extraneous information removed, in a matter of hours—not the days or weeks it would have taken just to attempt to communicate the idea to the computer department. In addition, BD was able to iterate the models, playing the "what-if" games that are so crucial to budget and forecasting activities, without the additional baggage of having to placate CD, which often viewed change requests as error corrections. While not exactly paranoid, the CD needed to justify each and every change to protect themselves, and this often led to finding "fault." In responding to a change request, the CD had to either accept blame for a job incorrectly done, or place blame on customers for not being able to make up their minds. In either case, flexibility was lost and the rapid iteration of what-if scenarios became almost impossible.

Another advantage the BD saw in doing it themselves was that they would be able to load their walkthru teams with budget analysts. This was an advantage because if the work had been done in the CD, the walkthru teams would have consisted of analysts schooled in the art and craft of computer programming and system design, not in the subtleties of budgeting for large organizations. The budget application development "experts" were the experts in the functionality of the end product, not in the use of the tools to create the end product. The budget analysts found that when they prototyped their own systems, they could better control the requirements that were important to them, such as user-friendliness and built-in checks for simple things like data entry, without worrying about how elegant the underlying code might be.

The methodology used by this budget department to prototype systems is not formally documented, yet any team member can describe its basic components. It sounds a great deal like the methodology presented earlier in this book, but the team members had not read the book at the time the technique was adopted. They developed it from a common sense approach to the quickest way to get their work done.

First, the problem to be worked with an automated solution is described. The initial format is narrative, but it is very lean and bears a distinct resemblance to the evolutionary rapid prototyping project plan as described in Chapters 3 and 4. It is not a lengthy systems requirements document. No cost-benefit analysis is performed; the assumption is that if a knowledgeable budget analyst requests the work to be performed, then it will be done and for a good reason. The project plan describes data sources, the data, and a plan of attack. Dataflow diagrams are rarely used by the team. The schedule is firm only for the first phase of the work; that is, the first two or three weeks of the project are planned out. After that, the schedule is only a ball-park idea. It is not even remotely considered cast in concrete, as all team members and managers are well aware that deviations *will* occur, thereby accepting them as a fact of life. A review at the end of each short phase allows for go/no-go decisions, for a refined estimate of the remaining work, and for scheduling intervening work on other things.

Secondly, the project team roles are assigned. Budget analysts and system specialists come to a firm agreement on any adjustments to either roles or methodologies, or both, necessary to best accomplish the task at hand. They also discuss tools applicable to the project. There are no rules about mandatory tools. Any tool that appears to be useful and can be acquired is fair game. The system specialists, when trained by BD to be up to speed on the applications, usually regularly read 10 to 12 trade magazines to keep abreast of new software packages. Examples of four tools that proved useful are CELLMATE, which converts cell names into English, tells where they are used, tells the data validation requirements, and so on; PRE-DICT, which gives additional spreadsheet capability; DATAPREP, which formats files downloaded from the mainframe; and LOTUS SYMPHONY.

In the near future, the BD expects that life will continue pretty much as it is, now that the kinks have been worked out of the team process and a lot of work is getting done in the area of validating ideas by using this shortened version of the prototyping methodology. However, at least two future scenarios loom on the not-too-distant horizon. First, greater computing power will almost certainly be needed.

While the speed and capacity of personal computers is increasing with enormous rapidity, it probably is not fast enough to handle what the BD prototyping team is almost ready to do with huge amounts of data. A mid-size computer (say, VAX-8xxx class) is really necessary to process more data faster. The functionality of models currently being built is quite adequate—the quest is not for increased functionality at all, but for more processing power.

Budget envisions that the acquisition of a more powerful computer would also mean new tools and a better way to evolve the PC models into final systems. In some cases, the prototyping itself would take place directly on the mid-range computer where third-generation language modules would replace some of the prototype functions for efficiency. The plan would then be for budget analysts to direct the system specialists in writing the efficient code which would then be maintained by the computer department. In that environment, budget will acquire CASE tools compatible with those over in computing and will probably also acquire a documentation specialist or two.

The second future scenario of this case study involves that ever popular buzzword, expert systems. Because knowledge of the data is of utmost importance for BD, the analysts are carefully trained in being able to spot "goodness" of data as well as knowing what to model and what metadata (data about data) is important. Clearly, when only a certain small set of human beings is able to validate answers, the door is open for transferring those mental thought processes and rules to expert systems. Budget does not believe that the acquisition of expert system software will reduce the current prototyping atmosphere—only the tools will change.

The person responsible for implementing this prototyping approach within the budget department has never completed a course in prototyping, nor does he have time to perform a constant literature search in all computer trade and academic journals on the subject of prototyping. Rather, he developed the idea from a common sense approach to getting his job done. He simply knows from experience that it is cheaper to smooth out algorithms and do iterations on a virtually free PC than it is to write code, even 4GL, on a mainframe where time is purchased. He says it does not make sense to "build the assembly line before it is known what the product will be."[3]

To summarize how this financial organization uses prototyping to reduce uncertainty and confusion, they insist on the following factors:

- In-depth knowlege of the data and of the application is a must for budget analysts

- The communication gap that normally occurs between user and developer is bridged by a system specialist

- A learning process takes place whereby budget analysts train system specialists in the generalities of the application and system specialists train budget analysts in the use of prototyping tools

- The building of prototype models need not follow the traditional life cycle development of systems

- A hardware-software environment that allows quick turnaround for iterations is provided

- Live data are always used, thereby disallowing any executable code to be built to pass known test data

When the budget area was called upon to examine the amount and application of overhead rates for the laboratory, they prototyped several phases. First, they did a gross feasibility study on the PC, based on a simple spreadsheet model. This study only took about two hours, but the conclusions led to the decision to draw up some report formats that could be used by the laboratory directors in decision support. Figuring out how those reports should be formatted and what data they should contain took about one week using screen generators and packaged report formatters. The modeled reports led to a go-ahead decision from the directors to prototype a full-blown proposal using a full fiscal year's past data. The prototype, also to be done on the PC, will take about six weeks and will demonstrate all of the functionality of the target system. It will be used as a requirements specification for the computer department which will take an estimated six months to one year to turn the approved model into a production system.

Hardware Engineers Prototype Space Station Information Systems

A major aerospace firm recently staffed a large Space Station design project with aerospace hardware engineers who had, for the most part, no previous computer experience, and gave each of them a personal computer and, within reason, software of their choice. A small team of six computer professionals was assigned to the project to provide training and consulting to the engineers. Many of these hardware engineers quickly began to use tools such as spreadsheets with macro languages and relational database management systems with 4GLs to develop their own information systems. They did not think of what they did as prototyping—they simply considered it part of getting the job done. The following are some examples of prototypes developed by individual engineers.

One mechanical engineer was part of a team analyzing Space Station payload components for physical properties such as weight and power requirements. The team found the job to be almost impossibly complex, with thousands of components and interrelated trade-offs—for example, total weight and power requirements are fixed so the more allocated to one component, the less can be allocated to others. The mechanical engineer spent the better part of a month mastering the use of the macro programming language of Excel, a very powerful PC spreadsheet package, so he could effectively model the complex interrelationships involved in payload analysis. The result of his prototype was that the team could study the merits of several configurations in a single day. Configurations having particular merit could be automatically graphed for quickly prepared presentations in response to the NASA customer questions. On previous projects a single iteration of such an analysis would take months using hand-held calculators.

One prototype was begun by software professionals. This was an automated system to track and inventory Space Station requirements and provide traceability of project-generated requirements to customer-stated requirements. Top management of the Space Station Project dictated that engineers would use this automated system to write requirements for customer-deliverable specifications. A typical user revolt ensued when it became obvious that the software professionals were having a great deal of trouble understanding end user functional requirements for the system. Fortunately for them, the end users in this case had a choice—they had the tools available to prototype their own version of the application. When management caught them doing this, they were told to cease and desist—it was reiterated that there would only be one official project requirements database. This did not deter the engineers. They simply continued work on their own system in secret and made it interface so transparently with the official system that it appeared to management that the latter was indeed being used. At the end of the project, a survey revealed that more engineers were using the unsanctioned user-developed requirements database than the official version by a ratio of 30 to one.

Over a two-year period, engineers used computer-aided drawing packages to generate thousands of drawings of Space Station design concepts. These drawings were used in presentations to the customer and in design documents delivered to the customer. Over 3,000 of the computer-generated drawing files were considered good enough to be archived for possible future reuse. At the end of the two-year period, a proposal had to be submitted to the customer to obtain additional funding. Naturally, it was desired to use the best of the computer-generated design concepts as artwork in the proposal. A conventional graphics support team was called in to support the proposal activity. Soon these conventional graphics artists were overcome by the high level of end user computing on the project. They found themselves prototyping a complex networked graphics storage and retrieval system. The benefit of this user-prototyped system was that engineers could have more intimate final say over the appearance of their artwork in the proposal and managers could demand and get many more revisions, working toward a higher quality proposal within a normal proposal budget.

One person on the project was responsible for tracking all customer-deliverable documentation. Over a 15-year period, there will be 81 million pages of documentation delivered to the customer, representing hundreds of individual specifications. Each document has a title, a due date, and a responsible engineer. The person responsible for tracking this information decided that an automated system (sort of an information information system) would provide a big assistance and decided to prototype one himself, using a relational database management system with an associated 4GL. This particular user ran into difficulty getting the 4GL to do what he wanted and asked for help from the software professionals after the first two weeks of prototyping. Enough of a prototype was in place, however, to give the software professionals a good idea of what the user wanted. Software professionals then took over prototype iteration and a successful system was produced shortly thereafter. The resulting system eventually became multiuser as all the responsible documentation authors expressed an interest in obtaining access to the information.

Artificial Intelligence Technology Applied to End User Prototyping

In one instance, a member of a machine shop attended a four-month intensive course in artificial intelligence approaches and tools to bring that education back to the machine shop and develop applications independently of the information systems department. The machine shop employee belonged to middle management and did not have a programming or software engineering background. When he returned from the AI course, he was able to offer a great deal more to his organization than if he had simply picked up a personal computer and begun to prototype.

The problem that was tackled, using AI approaches and tools, was the scheduling of tasks, personnel, and machines in an acceptable order. The first solution did not attempt to involve any real conflict resolution, but to create an intelligent advisor that would develop an initial schedule. The prototype resided on a LISP machine and used Intellicorp's KEE software development system.[4]

The following methodology was suggested in the class attended by the user:

1. Define the problem in a one- or two-sentence statement of the problem or task
2. Determine the type of reasoning to be used to solve the problem
3. Determine the type of representation to be used to describe the problem
4. Determine a testing method or procedure for model validation
5. Determine the appropriate explanation facility for interfacing with users

It was also suggested that while one could begin anywhere in the five-step process, moving to the areas of the process that cause the most anxiety is wise, and that the place to start is with the simplest problem case.

Armed with his recent AI training, the manager-turned-prototyper set out to develop a model that would "schedule a number of tasks, personnel and other resources in a job-shop type machine shop operation, while trying to meet the customer's required delivery date." Scheduling requirements really come into play when a task is larger than one person can do in the requested time frame or when critical machine tools or other resources are required and there are competing tasks. In this case, there were scheduling concerns such as priority of tasks, due dates of tasks, length of time to complete tasks and quite a few organizational factors (Where can additional resources be obtained? Is overtime allowed? Are multiple shifts allowed?). There were physical constraints such as machine availability, tooling availability, human resource availability, material availability, and so on. There were several potential scheduling priority methods such as first in first out, last in first out, random, shortest time tasks first, longest time tasks first, and others commonly defined by operations research.

Work began on the prototype by trying to identify those objects that would be involved in the scheduling activity. Some of the objects that came readily to mind were time or calendar, people, machines, tooling, materials, work orders, and maintenance activities. Initially, an active calendar module was created that would transform calendar days into manufacturing days. Next, the definition of the machine tool objects was refined. The object classes included location, manufacturer, and physical attributes. Subclasses included machine control and machine tools which, in turn, included subclasses of such objects as saws, lathes, shapers, planers, welders, drillers, and presses. Effort was then expended to identify as objects all other items such as work orders, tooling components, materials, and processes. When the object classes for the machine shop were graphed using the AI tool KEE, it became obvious that the prototype was too ambitious, that too large a chunk had been bitten off. Then, the simplest test case that seemed worth modeling was chosen.

The five-step methodology applied to a very simple model (model #1) looked something like the following:

1. Schedule a single person for two tasks with a selection of three types of machine tools, on a calendar with a small number of days
2. All decisions will use a separately constructed methods file
3. Object-oriented programming within the KEE environment will be used
4. The model will schedule a task and its resources so the task's requirements are met
5. Initial user interviews will be sufficient to begin the modeling process

When tested, model #1 was able to vary the capabilities and availability of an individual worker and when the requirements of the two tasks were changed, the model gave the expected results. Once this very simple model was conquered, it was time to move on to a slightly more complex model.

The methodology then changed slightly to become the following:

1. Schedule many persons with differing skills, for four tasks with a selection of five types of machine tools, on a calendar with a small number of days
2. All decisions will use a separately constructed methods file
3. Object-oriented programming within the KEE environment will be used
4. The model will schedule multiple tasks and associated resources so the task's requirements are met
5. Initial user interviews will be sufficient to begin the modeling process

When model #2 completed the testing phase, it was capable of meeting the scheduling goals when many persons and tasks were involved. Conditions were indicated when a task could not be scheduled. The prototyper felt confident enough to begin model #3 at this point, which was the result of model #2 after it had been shown to the user and additional capabilities in scheduling requirements were added.

Model #3 contained the capability to evaluate a potential schedule for a given task. The system evaluated the availability of all required resources and calendar time to see if the task could be scheduled according to requirements. If so, the potential schedule was produced, listing acceptable personnel and machine indicators. If not, the scheduling problem area was returned.

The next model, the final one, applied the methodology the following way:

1. Schedule many persons with differing titles and skills, with several tasks, multiple resource types including tooling and machines, a broad range of processes, on a calendar with a small number of days

2. Decisions will be made from a separate methods file or with the use of a separate rule system to be constructed

3. Object-oriented programming within the KEE environment will be used

4. The model will schedule all tasks and necessary resources in a way that meets the task's requirements or gives alternatives

5. The user will be consulted about additional capabilities in scheduling requirements, including a potential scheduling evaluation. KEE's graphical interface will be used as a communication tool

The real purpose of this prototype was to produce a proof of the concept that many of the factors that an individual performs in a machine shop scheduling process can be included in an intelligent scheduling system. Existing human expertise in developing acceptable schedules in a job-shop operation can be captured and included in an automated scheduling system. When the final model is asked to provide a potential schedule for a given task, the system responds with the available dates, a list of all potential personnel sorted in preferential order, and notes concerning the availability of machines and whether or not the potential schedule is driven by a required delivery date. When asked to schedule a task, the name(s) of the assigned individual(s) is returned. All scheduling information is contained in the knowledge base master schedule. If the task could not be scheduled, the actual reasons for the inability to schedule would be given on the screen to the user.

This is an example of a prototype performed independently of knowledge of the methods presented in this book. It is actually considered one of the most advanced—if not futuristic—approaches known to the industry. Upon scrutiny, it parallels the prototyping methodology presented in earlier chapters but uses different automated tools. To recap, here are some characteristics of the machine shop prototype:

- It was performed by an end user—someone who would normally (and actually had for years) been dependent upon the software department for all automation needs—who took the opportunity to train himself in one state-of-the-art methodology and learn some new tools

- The prototype model proved that tasks, tools, personnel and other resources could be scheduled in a job-shop machine shop

- The end user did not produce dangerous, unmaintainable, or overly complex code

- The equivalent of a condensed project plan was produced in the form of the five-step method statements

- Once the project was defined, it was segmented into a manageable chunk for the initial prototype (an intentionally incomplete working model)
- Rapid analysis was accomplished by virtue of some initial user interviews which could be minimized because the main developer was the same person as the main user
- The equivalent of an information model was produced by the identification of objects and subclasses of objects relating to the project
- The equivalent of prototype iteration took place when each of five models was successively refined until the user specification was met
- The prototype may evolve into the final system

This case differs from the evolutionary rapid prototyping methodology in the following respects:

- The project plan was not as thorough as the one suggested in this book, although it might be suggested that it need not be, since the project plan is the contract between the users and the developers and in this case, they are one and the same
- The rapid analysis phase did not include dataflow diagrams or control flow graphs, both of which might have helped the user-developer keep track of the big picture
- The database creation step was essentially skipped because the automated prototyping tool essentially took care of it once the objects were defined
- The final model was not thoroughly tested with existing historical data, probably because it was considered as a proof of concept model and the decision had not yet been made regarding whether or not it would become an evolvable model

This is a very important case study because it may well become one wave of the future. It is quite analogous to the problem of the research study group presented in earlier chapters. In both cases, a task involving employees, schedules, budgets and resources was to be tracked. In both cases, management and customer information was to be retrieved. In the abstract, resource-task scheduling and tracking are not very different between writing briefs for congressmen or making widgets. In both cases prototyping was used. In one, it was done by developers with software engineering analysis and design tools, relational databases, and 4GLs. In the other, it was done by an end user with artificial intelligence-expert system tools.

An important conclusion to be drawn from this case study is that, while evolutionary rapid prototyping has been touted as a communication tool between user and developer, it is really that and much more. When the machine shop end user developed a system, he also produced a prototype, and he had no need for communication with himself. He did need a way to define a complex problem through a series of iterative steps which successively refined the specifications. When the day comes to turn his prototype model into a functioning system with true conflict resolution, he *may* be able to do it using the prototype tools. On the other hand, he may need to turn it over to the information systems department to code in some very efficient programming language which will better support the size and complexity of the application. Then the tuning and testing phase should occur exactly as outlined in this book. The prototype will have served as a correct dynamic requirements specification, with the error-prone communication during analysis completely removed.

REFERENCES

1. Daniel J. Couger, "End-user Computing: A Grand Concept Running 'Amuck'," AFIPS Conference *Proceedings*, National Computer Conference, 56, 1987, 293–99.
2. Carma L. McClure, "Software Workbenches: The New Software Development Environment," AFIPS Conference *Proceedings*, National Computer Conference, 56, 1987, 459–66.
3. Glenn Lockhart and R.O. McMaster, with acknowledgments to Terry Gibbs, "Proposed Model to Study Modified Total Cost and 2-Pool Methods of Computing Burden," Los Alamos National Laboratory Memorandum, August 6, 1987.
4. Elbert W. Colston, with acknowledgments to John Kunz of Intellicorp, "A Simplified AI Approach to a Shop Scheduling Problem," Knowledge Systems Laboratory, Los Alamos National Laboratory, 1987.

11

Future Trends in Rapid Prototyping

Structured rapid prototyping *is* the future of software development because future hardware and software advances will make an already sensible approach into an irresistible approach. Just as current toolkits have made software rapid prototyping more feasible by removing the issue of flexibility, future toolkits will make evolutionary rapid prototyping more feasible by removing such issues as performance and portability. This chapter investigates future possibilities of what some of the hardware and software advances are likely to be.

ENHANCEMENTS OF THE TOOLS USED FOR PROTOTYPING

Specific prototyping environment packages, as described in previous chapters, will continue to appear, running on many classes of machines, from micro to supercomputer, and offered by many vendors. Distributed and networked database capabilities will continue to become more sophisticated. Further gains in RDMS performance efficiency will be forthcoming. Prototyping toolkits will become even easier to use, especially for those who are not computer professionals.

Compatibility between More Environments

And, as more time passes, vendors of powerful RDMS packages will tend to offer more in terms of interface features and portability. All of the more popular packages run on a variety of computers, interface with a larger number of programming languages, and share data more easily than they did in 1985. In the early part of the 1980s, the RDMS market was not crowded. Vendors eschewed the issue of compatibility—incompatibility was one way to lock users into a proprietary environment. Increasing competition, coupled with user demand, has brought on the development of products that attempt to run on all machines, interface with all programming languages, and import and export data to and from every external system.

User demand for universal compatibility and portability has come about as a result of the continued proliferation of diverse hardware and software environments. Often, such proliferation exists even within a single organization. Many organizations tried to dictate standardization during the early 1980s but the attempt met with little success when users found that it only discouraged technological advance. When technological advances occurred anyway, users insisted on acquiring the advanced products whether they complied with current internal standards or not. Funds were wasted writing justifications for nonstandard products and in attending standards compliance review board meetings, and nonstandard equipment was purchased in greater and greater quantities despite the institutionally dictated bureaucracy of the keepers of the standards.

By the mid 1980s, when organizations forged ahead and purchased hardware and software from different vendors, the inevitable compatibility problems resulted. Sometimes users were told that the data they needed could not possibly be transferred electronically from its central host environment to their distributed environments. More often they were told that their favorite software application would not run on the new hardware they wanted to acquire.

The difference between today and the early 1980s is that the onus of compatibility is on vendors rather than users, and fierce competition is forcing vendors to do something about the issue. As a result, no one company has a stranglehold on either the computer software or the computer hardware industry. As users continue to demand more innovation, standards will continue to exist, but they will be based on universal interface specifications rather than a particular vendor's product specifications.

Users are demanding and getting compatibility in three areas: data transfer, application availability, and application transfer. When all three become widely available, interfaces similar to the ones shown in Figure 11-1 will be possible in all environments. Data transfer between disparate environments has been available with many systems for quite some time. All that is required is the ability to import and export data in some universally agreed upon standard such as "ASCII flat files." Some systems go one step further and allow the data transferer to specify an alien system's proprietary format. Application availability—for example, an RDMS that runs on many brands of hardware under many different operating systems—is also becoming quite widespread. Unfortunately, availability does not always equate with transferability. Just because a customized application was developed with an RDMS in one environment and that same RDMS exists in a target re-host environment, does not mean that the re-host will be electronic, automatic, or effortless. Vendors are working in this direction, but at present the machine-independent RDMS is in the same category as the machine-independent programming language—computer science fiction.

The future of rapid prototyping environment compatibility is *not* one RDMS running on one brand of computer in all organizations. There can be no one best choice when individuals have different needs and different preferences. Often products have relatively equal features and price performance but differ radically in terms of user interface implementation. Users do not all want the same interface. Therefore, we will see individual organizations tending to use an increasing variety of software and hardware to develop and host customized applications. Vendors will create features making incompatibility increasingly less of an issue.

Performance Efficiency

During the 80s, the RDMS evolved from an academic toy to a serious development environment, suitable for creation of large complex applications. In the beginning, RDMS vendors often actively discouraged their customers from developing serious applications of any kind with their product. Over the years, competition has forced vendors to make vast improvements to the performance characteristics of their products. Every new release of a product (which, in the case of popular products, is about once every six months) will typically offer improved response time from 20 percent to 50 percent.

In the beginning, internal data storage formats for the typical RDMS consisted of sequential structures; that is, they looked like sequentially accessed flat files. Most internal data structures have now been converted to more efficient formats like inverted binary tree structures, vastly improving access time. When a prototyper writes 4GL, the typical RDMS generates 3GL as a result. The 3GL is then compiled into object code when the developer chooses to create an executable image of the application. In the beginning, vendors did not look closely at the efficiency of code generated in this fashion. Now optimizing routines are part of many packages.

These efficiency-improving techniques have a limit of effectiveness, of course, but the day is already at hand when we can say that the RDMS is not necessarily less efficient than any other data storage structure. C.J. Date, one of the fathers of relational theory, feels that he has a benchmarked proof that the relational model is just as fast as a hierarchical model.[1] The impact of such improvements in performance is that we as prototypers have less reason to consider throwing prototypes away and rewriting the system in a third-generation language.

As shown in Figure 11-1, we now have three levels of software compatibility among a three-tiered hardware architecture (micro, midrange, mainframe): files, tools, and applications. On the "lowest" level, and having existed for the longest time, is the ability to transfer files back and forth among the three hardware environments. More recently, another level of software compatibility exists whereby tools such as editors and compilers can be shared. Those two software levels plus the capabilities offered by data management vendors, such as applications created by forms and report writers, now allow prototypes to also be compatible among the three hardware environments. It is easy to develop a prototype in one hardware environment and port it to another, or even simultaneously develop a prototype in both places.

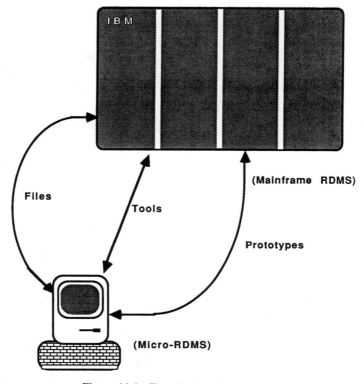

Figure 11-1 Three levels of compatibility.

Ease of Use

In the early days of prototyping, there was a barrier to entry represented by the difficulty of learning how to work with a 4GL and an RDMS. Vendors were of little help because their training programs were immature or nonexistent. The typical product was shipped with incomplete technical documentation only understandable to the programmer who wrote it. On-screen error messages were frequently ridiculously cryptic and often did not remain on the screen long enough to read. One example is a message that appeared from an early RDMS running on a Cray supercomputer which read something like: "You have caused error 1234. You better call (developer's name) at 800-555-1999". Such problems caused particularly acute difficulties when end users with little training attempted to develop their own prototypes, or when COBOL programmers attempted to maintain prototype-developed applications. A lot of money stood to be made from training and an RDMS-4GL high priesthood developed.

Things are very different now. Error messages are clear and meaningful, with complementary detailed explanations in the technical documentation. The trend is increasingly for technical documentation to be written by professional writers rather than programmers. There is a decreasing need to master even a simple 4GL syntax, as visual programming capabilities become ever more powerful. Reports that used to require a fairly complex report writer script can often be produced in modern systems by using visual programming techniques to create the report by example. Virtually every popular system now has interactive technical help which offers all the important highlights of the printed documentation.

In just a few short years the RDMS and the 4GL have evolved from somewhat difficult to learn and use to fairly easy to learn and use. It is safe to predict that in a few more years prototyping environments will be almost trivially easy to learn and use, eliminating altogether the need for the high priesthood.

HARDWARE ADVANCES

It is readily apparent when a working environment improves in terms of speed, storage capacity, and reliability. Prototyping is, admittedly, a process that is careless of machine resources in the early stages of a project. Even with the speedy RDMS systems just referred to, it is quite easy for the database developer to accidentally create structures that are extremely inefficient. Powerful hardware can therefore make a prototyping project a lot more fun. During the early stages of prototyping, we want to concentrate on functionality rather than performance. This does not mean that we can live with a two-hour response time to queries. Powerful hardware can use brute force to push its way through even the most convoluted of relational joins.

Distributed personal computer networks seem to be gradually taking over much of the work previously done by mainframes and minicomputers. Many people like personal computers better than mainframes because they are so accessible and, well—personal. Critics say, "Yes, but you can't do X on a personal computer." Complex weapon system simulations, parimutuel betting systems, and airline reservation systems are typical examples of "X."

Every year, some application that used to be a good example of "X" is developed and hosted on a personal computer network, as PC horsepower continues to increase. Measures such as addressable RAM, clock speed, and instructions per second have increased geometrically over the last ten years: from 64 bytes to over a gigabyte; from less than one mega-hertz to over 24 mega-hertz; from thousands of instructions per second to millions of instructions per second. PC power is increasing because of market pressures. Vendors supporting both PCs and mainframes often find that the PC market is more lucrative—profit is made by volume.

The logical conclusion of this trend may be one user, one computer. It makes sense from the vendor's point of view, and it makes sense from the user's point of view. Computers may well become like pencil sharpeners and staplers—a standard supplied item for all office workers. Computerphobia, a phenomenon that has been working against this trend, is disappearing as a new generation of computer literate workers emerges from our public and private schools.

Powerful personal computers have many advantages for prototyping. An important part of prototyping is to prototype the rules for a proposed new system's administration. On a mainframe or minicomputer this is difficult because system administration is typically not under control of the prototyper. On a personal computer, however, there are no rules except those set by the owner or custodian.

Prototype demonstrations can be distributed on a floppy disk for users to exercise. There is no need to worry about whether the user will try to do "real" work with the prototype—it is not the "real" database, anyway. Prototype demonstrations on floppies can be mailed to users in remote parts of the world. A portable PC can bring a live prototype demonstration to a remote user in a quick plane hop. A useful tactic in bringing reluctant new users into the fold on a prototyping project is to bring the prototype to them.

Evolutionary rapid prototyping on personal computers is today's reality rather than only a future possibility. Large complex prototypes can be developed on a personal computer and then evolved into multiuser application systems that will be hosted on a network of those same personal computers. There are a few problem areas—things to be aware of—but many advantages over mainframe prototyping.

PROTOTYPING LANGUAGE ADVANCES

People often ask if future prototyping will always require an RDMS and a fourth-generation language. Is there, or will there soon be, such a thing as fifth-generation languages and hardware architectures? What do such terms actually mean? How long will computer hardware and software keep developing? Can we envision the day when we will use a 99GL on a ninety-eighth-generation hardware architecture? No one really knows the answers to such questions, but some trends seem obvious and are described in the following paragraphs.

Object-oriented languages such as Flavors, Smalltalk, and even Ada have been discussed as fifth-generation prototyping environments. No doubt, as character-string, syntax-oriented, command-driven languages go, each of these languages has some unique capabilities. If being object-oriented is definitive of a 5GL, then this classification can even be granted. None of these languages is an effective stand-alone prototyping environment, however, and none of them even makes very good evolutionary function-building tools within a prototyping environment. Using such languages in a stand-alone mode, what do we do for application structure generation or data storage structure generation? The answer is that we must do very conventional things, similar to how we did software development 20 years ago—we must write job control routines and data declarations. To evaluate such languages as evolutionary prototyping environments one must ask how easy it will be to make many iterative modifications to a prototype developed in a language that allows the introduction of psychological complexity through the use of sophisticated control logic.

It would seem that if object-oriented languages are 5GL, then visual programming environments must be 6GL. The trend for generations of languages from first to fourth was always that fewer instructions were needed to create equivalent functionality. Thus a language that uses no written instructions whatsoever must be given the highest generation number possible. The generation issue is important to prototyping because the fewer statements needed to create a function, the faster it can be prototyped and the easier it can be modified.

There is a relatively new development in visual programming—the development of icon-based syntax to replace character-string syntax. Could this development result in a 7GL? In 1985, at the National Computer Conference in Chicago, a panel discussion was held to discuss visual programming. One speaker referred to SQL, an example of a 4GL, as an example of visual programming. Another speaker raised the possibility of icon-based languages, but this notion was dismissed by the panel for two reasons:

- Human language used to be based on hieroglyphics and other kinds of iconic symbols, but mankind has progressed to character-based languages
- Verbs are very difficult to represent in an icon-based language

Yet, not all peoples have abandoned the use of an icon-based language. The Chinese and Japanese languages have been evolving for many more centuries than our Western languages, and are still based on iconic representation of words. Many people believe that it is normal to think in pictures and then translate those pictures into words for the purpose of writing and speaking. If this is true, then a character-based language is an artificial imposition on the communication process. Western civilization drifted away from icons because of the difficulties posed in writing and later in printing. Handwritten icons require artistic abilities and having an individual icon for each word requires a large set of type elements for manual typesetting. The computer age, however, eliminates these problems. Modern computers with high-resolution graphics capabilities can store the most complex icons electronically, available to users at the click of a pointing device such as a mouse. Large numbers of icons can be made available in hierarchically decomposed sets, using high-level icons to represent collections of lower-level icons.

The following examples represent some current developments in icon-based languages: IBOL, Helix (Figure 11-2), and Authorware's Course of Action devel-

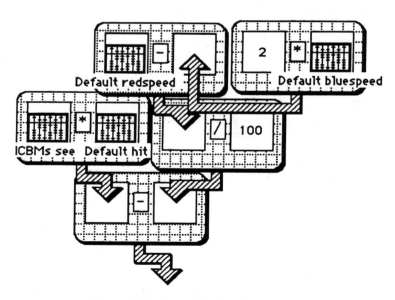

Figure 11-2 Helix 4GL algorithm.

opment environment (Figure 11-3). Of these languages, only Helix offers a generalized prototyping environment at present. IBOL (icon-based operating language) is a toy language used to program graphic screen-based representations of robots in an educational computer game called Chipwits. It is significant only in that it is, we believe, the very first instance of an icon-based computer programming language and demonstrates possibilities for representing verbs with icons very effectively. There are IBOL icons for Move, See, Eat, Zap, Touch, Turn, Smell, and Feel—all verbs. IBOL, however, cannot be used to prototype anything other than a game scenario in which your "programmed" robot tries to Eat Pie, Coffee, and Disks; negotiate mazes; Zap Bugs; and avoid getting blown up by Bombs.

Helix is significant for being the first RDMS-based prototyping environment to offer a 4GL based entirely on icons. Figure 11-2 is a sample printout of a Helix 4GL source code listing. Helix's 4GL is perhaps not quite as intuitive as IBOL, but easy enough to use once you master the icon set—perhaps a two-day process. With Helix, you also get visual programming features for application structure generation (menu-driven) and functionality by example. The fact that Helix also includes a fully relational data storage model makes it one of the more powerful rapid prototyping environments. The extent to which visual programming is carried in this product enables prototypers to compress iteration cycles by an order of magnitude over a character-based 4GL report writer approach. It is relatively easy to achieve several iterations per day on Helix prototyping projects.

Authorware's Course of Action software package offers what is certainly one of the most elegant icon-based programming languages in terms of both ease of use

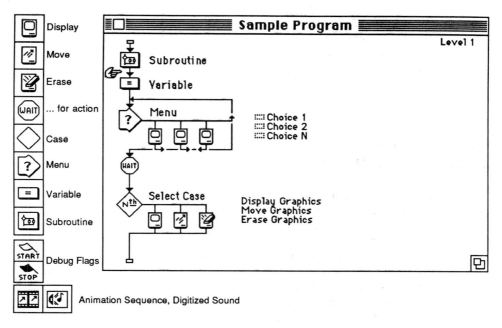

Figure 11-3 Sample Course of Action program with annotated "reserved icons."

and power. An example of Course of Action's set of "reserved words" is shown (annotated with the character-string equivalents) in Figure 11-3. It appears that the product will have one limitation in common with IBOL—it is intended primarily for the development of a single type of application. As the name implies, Course of Action is intended for use as a development environment in which to create computer-aided instruction (CAI) software. If what you want to create is a CAI program, Course of Action is a powerful rapid prototyping environment. If you want to create a general ledger system or a flight control system, this product may not work as well in a prototyping environment. The old saw about using the right tool for a job truly applies here.

Course of Action is another good example of how an elegant language used as a stand-alone prototyping tool can be powerful for the development of certain kinds of applications, but not universally applicable to the development of all types of applications. Although this package includes an icon to represent variables (a place to store data), that is a far cry from a flexible, easily generated storage structure, such as an RDMS, that allows for easy import of user-familiar data. Course of Action also is very limited in terms of how data may be transformed using algorithms. There are no icons for add, subtract, multiply, or divide.

One of the primary points of prototyping, in the broadest sense, is to experiment with user interfaces with the objective of providing the information and results most beneficial to the user. This objective is most easy to verify when actual user-familiar application data are used in the prototype. The information content and storage structure of an application are just as dynamically volatile as an application's functional requirements. Therefore, some type of ultimately flexible data storage structure such as the RDMS will always play a key role in a first-class prototyping environment. Certainly future programming languages will be in some ways more powerful than the languages that exist today. But languages alone do not make an evolutionary prototyping environment. The most successful vendors of future prototyping environments will find ways to tightly integrate the most powerful programming languages with the most powerful data-based information management systems.

AUTOMATED SOFTWARE DEVELOPMENT
PRODUCTIVITY ENHANCEMENT TOOLS

It has been said that rapid prototyping is not really as rapid as the term implies. Software developers have been searching for years for tools with magical properties that will compress development time by an order of magnitude. While the mainstream approach to rapid prototyping presented in this book will clearly not accomplish such an objective, it does not preclude the use of such tools should they be invented. Such tools are only future players in the rapid prototyping game because they do not exist today nor do they loom on the immediate horizon.

There is much computer science fiction revolving around buzzy phrases such as "computer-aided software engineering," "reusable code," "automated code generation," and "executable specifications." All of these catch phrases, like rapid prototyping, give the dangerous impression that you can get something for nothing. While there are automated tools available in each of these areas, no believable evidence has yet been produced that the use of these tools in any way reduces development time or effort. In some cases, use of such tools has been observed to increase development cost. Now that the reader's expectations are not set too high, it is fair to mention that there is reason to believe that the use of some of these new tools might greatly enhance productivity.

On the positive side, there is a history of better tools contributing directly to productivity, giving us much hope that the present and future tools will do the same. The results of a recent study showed that for 273 organizations, followed for ten years, productivity improved by 20 percent for those applying modern programming practices such as chief programmer teams, structured design, information hiding, and other aspects of modern software engineering.[2]

Computer-Aided Systems Engineering (CASE Tools)

As with most buzz phrases, there is much confusion over a definitive description of a CASE tool. Is an automated debugger a CASE tool? How about an automated flow chart checker? Since these two types of tools were invented before the term CASE came into common usage, they are not usually referred to as CASE tools. Thus, one possible description of a CASE tool is that it automates some portion of software development effort that was not automated in 1983. Examples are tools for computer-aided structured analysis, structured design, and information modeling. Such tools typically automate portions of a graphics-oriented development methodology by integrating computer-aided drawing features with linked textual specifications and consistency checking of violations of the methodology's guidelines.

At a 1987 CASE symposium, these tools were described as software development aids falling into these broad categories: diagramming and specification, design analysis, code generation, dictionary or encyclopedia maintenance, library maintenance, process modeling, and data modeling. CASE tools have also been described as automated support for applying software engineering methodologies, attempts to increase productivity by automating manual and tedious tasks, integrated textual and graphical approaches to software development, front end facilities that support the design and specification phases of the life cycle, techniques to automatically convert design specifications into code, and operational products implementing software engineering techniques. They are not concepts, principles, models, or methodologies. They are tools and environments which support the principles, models, and methodologies. There are no standards to which they must adhere, unless, of course, the tool is bound by other products it supports, such as Ada or SQL.

While only a very small percentage of software engineers currently use CASE tools, there is a strong sentiment in the software community that such tools will vastly increase in value and in popularity. The analogy to word processors and spreadsheets has been made. Ten years ago, they were crude and uncommon household products. Table 11.1 lists many (certainly not all) of CASE tools available in 1988. The purpose of the table is to point out that the software industry is taking productivity seriously. There are too many future systems of too great a complexity

TABLE 11.1

Product	Supplier	Environment	Type
AdaGraph	The Analytic Sciences Corp.	PC, Sun	Code generation for Ada
Ada Language System (ALS)	SofTech, Inc.	DEC VAX, MicroVax	Family of Ada development tools
Aims Plus	Aims Plus Inc.	Workstation	Application development system
Analyst/Designer Toolkit	Yourdon, Inc.	IBM PC, WANG, HP	Analysis, design, text formatting, standards customization
Rule Tool			Graphics customization for analyst-designer
Application Factory	Cortex Corp.	DEC VAX	Specification, code generation, maintenance
APS	Sage Software Inc.	IBM MF	COBOL application, generation
Ask Sam	Seaside Software	IBM PC	Free-form, text-oriented database management
Auto-Mate Plus	Learmonth Burchett Management Systems, Inc.	PC	Forms, reports, database design, normalization
Carleton Embedded Design Environment (CAEDE)	Carleton University	Sun	Design for Ada development
Complexity Analyzer Tool	McCabe & Associates		Complexity analysis, unit testing
Context	Context Corp.	Apollo	Documentation
CorVision	Cortex Corp.	DEC VAX	Application development system
Cullinet	Cullinet Software, Inc.	PC, MF	Entity-relationship, dataflow diagrams, normalization, logical data structures
DACOM	D. Appleton Company, Inc.		Planning, development
Dan Bricklin's Demo	Software Garden, Inc.	IBM PC	Screen painter
Database Design and Evaluation Workbench (DDEW)	Computer Corp. of America	Sun	Data modeling, normalization

TABLE 11.1 *(Continued)*

Product	Supplier	Environment	Type
Datatoolset (Sybase)	Sybase	Sun, DEC VAX, PC	Complex application tools, database management, dictionary,
Dataviews	Visual Intelligence Corp.		Interactive graphics
DB 2	IBM Corp.	IBM MF	Relational database management
dBase III	Ashton-Tate, Inc.	IBM PC Macintosh	Relational database management
DEFT/e	DISUS	Macintosh	Design, dictionary, forms data modeling
Design/1	Arthur Andersen & Co.	IBM PC	Planning, design, requirements, data modeling, process design
Design Aid and CASE 2000	Nastec	IBM PC, DEC VAX	Analysis, requirements, design, code generation, documentation, project management, dictionary
Design Machine	Ken Orr & Associates	IBM PC	Requirements, analysis
Developer Workstation	Asyst Technologies	IBM PC	Application development
Documentation Support Toolkit	Expertware	UNIX	Documentation
E-R Modeler Package	Chen & Associates	PC	Entity-relationship diagrams, database schema generation
Easyspec	EasySpec	IBM MF	Database modeling, normalization
EMERAUDE	Software Sciences, Ltd.	Sun & European workstations	Project support
Excelerator; Excelerator/Real Time Systems	Index Technologies Corporation	IBM PC, other PC's, VAX	Analysis, design, data modeling, documentation, code generation
Business Filevision	TELOS Software Products	Macintosh	Graphics-driven database
FOCUS	Information Builders	IBM MF, WANG PC, DEC VAX	Database management, code generation, spreadsheet

TABLE 11.1 *(Continued)*

Product	Supplier	Environment	Type
GENOS	GEC Software	HP-3000, Sun, Apollo, DEC VAX	Project management, definition, Ada development, and code generation
GRACE	EVB Software Engineering, Inc.		Reusable Ada components
HAPSE	Harris Corp.	Harris 1200	Family of Ada support tools, code and document generation
Double HELIX	Odesta Corp.	Macintosh	Data-based information management and decision support
IDMS-R	Cullinane	IBM MF	Relational database management
Info Model	INFOMODEL	IBM PC	Planning, application development, IRM
Information Engineering Facility	Texas Instruments, Inc.	Workstation, MF, PC	Planning, analysis, design, COBOL code generation, database generation
Information Engineering Workbench	KnowledgeWare, Arthur Young & Co.	PC AT	AI-based expert for system building; information engineering
Information Resource Management	Arthur D. Little, Inc.	IBM PC	Planning, data modeling, analysis
INFORMIX			Relational database management
INGRES	Relational Technology, Inc.	IBM MF VAX, IBM PC	Database management, forms application generation, report generation
Integral CASE Systems Solutions Aid (IRMA)	Tektronix, Inc.	Tektronix	Analysis, design (Yourdon, DeMarco) family of tools
Interactive Application Facility (ORACLE)	Oracle Corp.	IBM PC and MF, VAX	Database management, application generation, report generation, spreadsheet
KEEconnection &IntelliScope	IntelliCorp	Workstation	Connects knowledge-based systems to databases
Life Cycle Manager	Nastec Corp.	IBM PC	Project manager workbench and analysis tool kit

TABLE 11.1 *(Continued)*

Product	Supplier	Environment	Type
Life-Cycle Productivity	American Management Systems	IBM PC, IBM MF	Strategic planning, design, development, maintenance, project management
MANAGER	Manager Software Products	PC, IBM MF	Planning, analysis data modeling, data normalization, design, code generation, dictionary
META Systems	Meta Systems, Ltd.	MF, PC	Application development
Micro-CAPS	Software Research, Inc.	Convergent Technologies	COBOL development
Micro CICS	Unicorn Systems Co.	IBM PC/AT	Creates, tests CISS programs
Model-S	PC-Systems	IBM PC	Menu building, screen design, execution flow modeling
Multi/CAM	AGS Mgt. Systems, Inc.	Workstation	Application development
MultiPro	Cap Gemini Software	IBM PC/AT, XT	Development, project control, documentation
Natural	Software AG	IBM MF and PC AT, DEC VAX	4GL for Adabase dictionary
Netron/CAP	Netron, Inc.	IBM MF and PC, DEC VAX, WANG	Specifications, COBOL generation
Nomad 2	D & B Computing	IBM MF and PC AT	Database management
OMNIS 3	Blythe Software	Macintosh, IBM PC	Relational database management
Pacbase	CGI Systems, Inc.	MF, PC	Code generation from specs
PC/Hibol	Matterhorn Inc.	IBM MF, PC	Develops CICS programs; downloads data
POSE/PSR	Computer Systems Advisers Research	IBM PC	Data modeling, database design, data flow, dictionary, reporting
POWER	Expertware, Inc.	IBM PC	Knowledge-based Q/A
Progress Corp	Data Language	PC	Application development system w/4GL

TABLE 11.1 *(Continued)*

Product	Supplier	Environment	Type
ProKit Workbench	McDonnell Douglas	PC	Planning, analysis, design
ProMod	Promod Inc.	DEC VAX, IBM PC	Integrated software development tool
PVCS	Polytron Corp.	DEC VAX, IBM PC	Library maintenance of reusable code
Rand Development Center	Rand Systems, Inc.	IBM MF	Information tool management framework
Rapid/Use	Wasserman	DEC VAX, Sun	Application development, data flow, structure charts, entity-relationship, dictionary
Rational 1000	Rational Computer Co.	PC, MF	Knowledge-based, integrated development for Ada
Rbase System V	Micro-Rim	IBM PC	Relational database management
Rbase CLOUT	Micro-Rim	IBM PC	Interactive learner
REFINE	Reasoning	Symbolics, Sun	Knowledge-based programming environment
RIM	RIM Corp.	DEC VAX	Relational database management
Schemadesigner	Sun Microsystems	Sun	Database modeling
SPECIF-X	IGL Corporation, France	Apollo, SUN, VAX, SPS7	Analysis, data modeling, documentation (SADT)
Statemate1	AD CAD Corp.	MicroVAX	Analysis, design, management
Teamwork SA/SD/RT/IM	Cadre Technologies	Apollo, DEC, IBM, Sun	Structured analysis structured design, real-time, information modeling
Technology for the Automated Generation of Systems (TAGS)	Teledyne Brown Engineering	Apollo	Input-output requirements language for development, design, documentation
Telon	Pansophic Systems, Inc.	MF	Screen painting, documentation, COBOL and PL/1 code generation

TABLE 11.1 *(Continued)*

Product	Supplier	Environment	Type
THEMIS	Themis	DEC VAX	Natural language front end to relational database
TIP	Technology Information Products		Planning, requirements, specification, COBOL generation
Transform	Transform Logic Corporation	IBM MF	Application development in COBOL
USE.IT	Higher Order Software, Inc.	VAX and IBM MF, IBM PC	Specification, analysis, design code generation
Visible Analyst	Visible Systems Corp.	IBM PC	Graphics diagramming (Yourdon & Gane and Sarson)
VS-Designer	Visual Software Inc.	IBM PC	Family of tools

for any of us to treat *any possible* advance with a cavalier attitude. These are not prototyping tools *per se*, but just as the prototyping methodology draws upon the tenets of software engineering, it can also be supported by CASE tools. DFDs are not new as analysis/design tools, but they are used in a new way at different times in the prototyping life cycle. Soon, CASE products will no longer be new, there will be a larger, more affordable, and more accessible array from which to choose.

In Table 11.1, *PC* stands for any personal computer (IBM PCs are so designated), *MF* stands for mainframe, *SQL* stands for system query language, and *IRM* stands for information resource management. Strictly project management tools, compiler support tools, project cost estimation tools, local area networking tools, document control, or configuration management tools are not listed. Not all relational database management systems are listed, but the few that are known to have bundled CASE tools are. The intent of the list is to illustrate the functionality and availability of many products so software developers and end users can get a flavor of what direction productivity aids may be expected to take. Inconsistencies in descriptions of "type" of tool arise from inconsistencies in marketing terminology appearing in recent trade journals. Clearly, "Application development" leaves a lot to be desired as a description, but it may be the only one available from published advertisements or surveys. Suppliers are listed so the reader may contact them for more detailed information on the supplied product. The appearance of a product in Table 11.1 should not be interpreted as an endorsement or recommendation of that product by the publishers or the authors of this book.

While CASE tools are certainly helpful, they are *not* magic, and some even have conceptual or philosophical problems built into the design. Until such problems are resolved, CASE tools will not provide enormous productivy gains to software developers. To be more than simple computer-aided drawing tools, for instance, structured analysis and design tools must incorporate the guidelines of a particular methodology in order to perform automated consistency checking. Potential buyers of such programs are attracted to the idea of automated consistency checking—thinking that, if a compile with zero errors can be achieved, then the specification must be correct. Developers are attracted to these tools, thinking of the time that can be saved looking for inadvertent consistency errors. The problems with automated consistency checking are

- Checks are specific to one published version of a specific methodology
- Checks use some programmer's interpretation of a methodology
- Robust methodologies tend to evolve faster than the associated CASE product can be modified

The typical CASE product cannot be used effectively for even slight variations in a methodology. One must be much more specific than simply saying that support is desired for Yourdon structured techniques. Do you want a tool that automates DeMarco-style structured analysis, or Ward and Mellor's real-time structured analysis? Both of these methodology variations leave some consistency guidelines unspecified or only vaguely specified or give users options as to how to apply guidelines. Will you be satisfied with some junior programmer's attempt to fill in such voids? For some examples of voids,

- Should DFDs show offpage connectors to specify where net input and net output dataflows are coming from and going to?
- How should external system files be represented on a context diagram?
- What are the rules for annotating a physical DFD?

Just when you think such voids have all been filled by the latest and greatest published variation of the methodology, and you have acquired the latest and greatest CASE tool which faithfully embodies the correct interpretation of this methodology's guidelines, someone will publish a new version of the methodology that will be elegant enough to make your CASE tool obsolete. Some products allow a choice from among several known techniques, like choosing which language will be used for speaking and writing. Once locked in, translating from one to another becomes rather difficult.

Some consistency checks are worse than none at all when developers have to read through long printouts containing meaningless, uninteresting, and even incorrect information. Worse yet, some of these tools, due to specialized drawing requirements, must run on high-cost workstations that are not normally used by software developers to do other kinds of work. Thus we have a high-cost ineffective solution to a problem that only consumes a small percentage of developers' time.

Resulting productivity gains are rarely enough to pay for the required hardware and software.

CASE tools exist because of the market demand for them. Analysts and designers have long been saying that the problem with the structured modeling techniques is that they make draftsmen out of software developers and that checking the consistency of all the "gozintas equal the gozoutas" is boring drudgery. Is there an alternative solution to this problem, other than purchasing high-cost, low-return CASE tools? A long-range solution would be for vendors to develop methodology-generic tools with artificially intelligent expert system capabilities. Such tools would not incorporate the consistency checking guidelines until you told them interactively, and even then consistency rules could be modified at any time. Such software would probably be expensive, so it is imperative that it be executable on very low cost workstations that also support all other software development activities. An interim solution for developers is to run low-cost drawing programs on such workstations. Drawing programs can also be used to create viewgraphs for presentations and figures for reports. Structured walkthrus may be more effective in finding consistency errors than CASE tools for some time to come. On the bright side, IEF from TI is based on Information Engineering Methodology from James Martin Associates, Inc. The methodology and the tool are evaluated by both partners for upgrades. Users of that product, and a few others, can be confident that growth in one product will be mirrored by growth in the other.

Reusable Code

The theory of reusable code is that there are never any new computer applications under the sun, at least not down at the program module level. There are, and always will be, in future applications, sort routines, file reading routines, signal processing routines, error handling routines, screen refresh routines, add-change-delete routines, and so forth. A reusable code approach to prototyping is to have an electronic library full of such routines. Prototypers then would be able to mix and match modules to create any new desired application.

This subject area can be classified under automated productivity tools because its proponents see the key to its success lying in the right kind of library management system. A good reusable code library management system would be capable of intelligent version control, application subject matter classification, functional classification, domain classification, and performance benchmarking to name just a few desirable features. The notion of getting something for nothing surfaces again. Couldn't we just supply an intelligent library system with a paragraph or two of textual specification and have the system piece together a new application for us automatically?

One difficulty with reusable code is the personal nature of code. Very few programmers enjoy software maintenance assignments and have a real aversion to working with someone else's programs. Maintaining someone else's program is a bit like using someone else's toothbrush. Have you ever seen anyone else's code that you thought was wonderful? Programs are externalized manifestations of very internalized thought processes. A source listing is like a transcript of a daydream—

difficult to understand and devoid of interest to anyone but the dreamer. Developers usually get to escape doing maintenance work, but reusable code threatens this privilege by making someone else's code part of the proposed system at the beginning of the life cycle.

Another problem with reusable code is the number of features that must be optimized for a candidate module to be admitted into a reusable code library. Reusable code should be extremely fast, ultimately user-friendly, devoid of psychological complexity, meaningfully commented, and elegantly styled. It is hard to write a generic module to meet those criteria. Since such code is difficult to find, there are two alternate approaches to populating a code library:

- Take what you have and modify it to optimize the desirable features
- Take what you have and offer it on a "let the user beware" basis

No one ever has the resources to take the first approach, and the second approach tends to produce systems that have abominable maintenance characteristics.

Prototyping with suboptimal code libraries is particularly pernicious. Prototyping implies an approach that encourages changes based on discoveries made as a result of prototype demonstrations. Many ad hoc changes made to already poorly structured code will result in something that will resemble, but be somewhat less appetizing than, spaghetti. It would seem that the only way code libraries will ever be of any value is if they are filled with perfect code and changes to the code are not allowed.

Automated Code Generation

For years, skeptics doubted that code generators would ever work, while proponents spoke about them as though they were the Holy Grail of software engineering. Now that we have working code generators on the open market, we must remember that writing programs, in conventional software development, is only ten percent to 20 percent of total development effort and it is not the most difficult part of the process. On a prototyping project, writing programs will be even a smaller percentage of total effort, ideally approaching zero.

Nevertheless, code generators often come to mind in the context of prototyping. The seemingly logical link is that automatically generated code can be thought of as a free prototype or at least a free prototype module. It is much the same approach as reusable code: something for nothing—free code. Automatically generated code suffers from some of the same problems as reusable code, although prototyping approaches based on automatic code generation actually have some advantages over reusable code.

We have seen three approaches to automated code generation so far. The first is a DBMS approach which provides no functionality, but writes all data declarations for you. The second generates a throwaway prototype from structured analysis process specifications. The third generates code in a third-generation language, based on pseudocode provided in a structured design. The interesting part about all of these approaches is that they each have something in common with the approach recommended in this book, but none accomplishes nearly as much.

If your DBMS will automatically generate data declarations in your target application, then that is a worthwhile productivity enhancement, given that you will be undertaking conventional software development (writing programs). This capability does not have much to do with rapid prototyping, except it is interesting that a database is generally required in both cases. The danger with some DBMS products is that the buyer has a mistaken notion that functional code will be generated—all that has to be developed is the database structure; application functionality will be automatic. Sorry, there is no way to make that happen. There will never be such a tool because there would be no way for the tool to know what sort of functionality to generate.

Throwaway prototypes generated from structured analysis process specifications are not much advanced from the early 1980s when throwaway prototypes were generated from a 4GL such as MUMPS or FOCUS. In some ways the "mini-spec compilers" are less advanced than a stand-alone 4GL because they frequently do not have good data handling capabilities. Typically, this type of code generator constrains your process specifications to some reserved syntax set and compiles the specifications with accompanying error listings. For some perverse reason, many developers are enchanted with the idea of obtaining a "compile with zero errors" on their structured analysis specification. This is probably why the CASE tools previously referred to have become so popular.

Prototyping with a mini-spec compiler is not the ultimate in productivity because you will not get a prototype until you have written mini-specs. You do not write mini-specs until you have a complete requirements model, one that pretends to reflect an understanding of what the complete set of system requirements are. If the main purpose of prototyping is to discover requirements, why would you want to create a complete requirements model before your first prototype demonstration? Clearly, a lot of time would be wasted specifying things that are still in a state of high uncertainty. If the eventual prototype demonstration uncovers high-level errors in the specification, the entire model must be revised and new process specifications must be written.

On the one hand, design-based code generators avoid one of the problems of reusable code: the issue of maintainability. If you want to modify design-generated code, you can simply modify the design and regenerate the code. On the other hand, prototyping with a design-based code generator is even less productive than prototyping with a mini-spec compiler. Errors turned up by a prototype demonstration will now have an impact on, and force changes to, two specification levels: analysis and design. Consider design-based code generators as acceptably productive tools for use in conventional software development, not as prototyping tools. The changes will come too slowly and too far apart to be useful in rapid prototype iterations.

Executable Specifications

Suppose there is a need to develop and market an executable specification system. The first ground rule is that development must be done in LISP, PROLOG, or some other AI language to be perceived as credible. Executable specifications are considered to be an artificial intelligence application. Once again, the objective is code generation. At this time, there is at least one functional but experimental and proprietary system developed under contract for the Air Force.

Using such a system, the customer writes and submits a request for proposal (RFP) for a new application. The RFP is fed (manually input or optically scanned) to the executable specification system and, after some thrashing, out pops an executable system. In 1988, the code so generated is not deliverable—it is not well structured or optimized for performance. Data input and output are not handled well. The code is not structured very cleanly and thus does not lend itself readily to modification to become production code.

Despite the shortcomings of executable specification systems at present, they hold much promise for the future, particularly in the area of government software contracts. The RFP, often a barrier to effective software rapid prototyping, is necessary to obtain a government contract. The detail about system requirements present in an RFP constitutes a contractual agreement, even if some of the detail is erroneous. This may dissipate in the future somewhat as intelligent, well-read customers call more frequently in RFPs for a rapid prototyping approach and intelligent, well-read contractors specify what their approach to prototyping will be as opposed to specifying detailed contractual requirements in a proposal. But prototyping, as opposed to prespecifying, makes legal and financial professionals associated with government contracts very nervous. There will probably always be some desire to be as specific as possible in proposing a fixed price contract.

At present, such executable RFPs are usually rewritten. While expensive, this is better than being contractually bound to receive the wrong system. The fact that this is throwaway prototyping at present is not even important, given that it all happens before a contract is even started. Executable system specs in the form of RFPs amount to throwaway prototyping which for now is still an improvement over none at all and will probably mature in the near future. For this approach to become feasible for all government contractors, fidelity of the system must be rigorously checked (Does the prototype accurately model requested system functionality?) and it must become commercially available (currently it is a proprietary approach).

THE FUTURE ROLE OF ARTIFICIAL INTELLIGENCE TOOLS

In Chapter 3 we mentioned that some AI development environments are billed as rapid prototyping environments by their vendors. Unfortunately, some AI developers are "hackers"—a legacy of artificial intelligence dating back to the early days of AI research at MIT. Hackers are attracted to rapid prototyping because of the implication that nothing will be specified or documented (boring tasks at best). The truth is, a LISP compiler is not a rapid prototyping tool; a 19-inch, high-resolution color display monitor is not a rapid prototyping tool.

Despite the foregoing caveat, we are not saying that artificial intelligence does not have a very real role to play in the future of rapid prototyping and vice versa. There is already some evidence the two technologies are merging and indications are that the day will come when it will be impossible to distinguish the two fields. What we have now is a collection of prototyping tools, developed using AI techniques, that range from being readily available commercially to research-only proprietary packages; from useful and practical to esoteric and experimental. Specifically, we have natural language RDMS front ends, speech recognition, automatic prototype generation, and an RDMS written in an AI language.

The goal for a natural language front end is to replace "English-like" 4GL with plain everyday English for user database queries. Rigid syntax rules become unnecessary due to an AI technique known as iterative approximation. Using this technique, when the user types "Find worker number 53796," the system may come back with, "By 'worker', do you mean 'employee'?" When the user and the system have come to an agreement regarding all critical semantics, the retrieval will be processed. Vendors are also busily developing capability for such systems to learn the peculiar semantic idiosyncracies of specific users. Working examples of such systems today include THEMIS for INGRES and ORACLE; CLOUT for Rbase; and GURU, an interactive learner.

If natural language front ends make sense, then speech recognition is perhaps the next logical step—a system that would respond to everyday *spoken* English. The motivation for such systems comes from the fact that many users don't like typing as an interface to computers. To some executives, for instance, typing is thought of as a clerical task—"We have secretaries to do that." Experimental systems at this point use a microphone as one of the input devices and a speaker as one of the output devices. As these systems become more reliable, it is possible that voice input-output will someday replace the standard CRT-keyboard configuration of today.

The RDMS came out of university research environments and is thus typically written in Pascal or the C programming language. Such environments today are working on producing an RDMS written in an AI language such as LISP. While this might seem strange and perverse, it actually makes a certain amount of sense. The acronym, LISP, is short for LISt Processor. The language is optimized for processing lists of data. A relational database table is basically a list of data. Many AI applications are data-based in that they incorporate a knowledge and/or a rules database where information derived from experts or experience can be stored so the system can learn.

In the far distant future, computers may be effective members of prototyping teams. Such prototyping machines would be able to analyze data collected from external sources, such as sensor devices, and generate a functional prototype as a response to sensual stimulus. Such a system would have immense value in situations where system requirements can change in real time, such as is the case in Strategic Defense Initiative projects.

REFERENCES

1. C.J. Date, "De-bunking the Relational Myth," *Computerworld*, March 31, 1987.
2. Carma L. McClure, "Software Workbenches: The New Software Development Environment," AFIPS Conference *Proceedings*, National Computer Conference, vol. 56, 1987, 459–66.

12

Special Interest Topics in Rapid Prototyping

In addition to the "how-to's" of the structured approach to rapid prototyping presented in the previous chapters, we would like to present some other issues surrounding prototyping concepts. Those issues include alternative prototyping methodologies, data modeling, normalization of data, prototyping centers, the Ada™ programming language, and prototyping with limited software development tools.

ALTERNATIVE PROTOTYPING METHODOLOGIES

This book presents one approach to rapid prototyping. Yet many, somewhat divergent, approaches to prototyping are currently presented in the literature, discussed at professional conferences, and taught in seminars just as there are several competing philosophies about how to do structured analysis and design. Methodologies always tend to acquire "brand name" flavors. There is the Yourdon-DeMarco brand of structured analysis and design, the Ward-Mellor brand of real-time structured analysis and design, and now we have presented here our brand of structured rapid prototyping.

We hope we have presented our case in a manner that acknowledges the competition, presenting their approaches in as favorable a light as we can. There are a few we consider to be the giants in the field of rapid prototyping, and we encourage you to read their work as well. The rapid prototyping honor roll includes

- Fred Brooks
- Tom DeMarco
- Bruce Blum
- Bernard Boar
- Barry Boehm

256

Each of these brilliant software engineers contributed something very important to the concepts of prototyping. Today, some are offering alternative approaches to prototyping which are discussed in the following.

Fred Brooks and Tom DeMarco each had a profound effect on the concepts presented in this book. Brooks may have started everyone thinking about prototyping by introducing, in 1975, the notion that we should always plan to throw the first system away because experience shows that we always do so anyway. Unfortunately, as astute as that observation was in 1975, Brooks has not carried the idea into a proposal for a rapid prototyping approach. He continues with excellent critical observations about how far software engineering has come with solving the accidental tasks of systems development (the representation of abstract entities in programming languages and the mapping of them onto machine languages within space and speed constraints), how far it has yet to go with solving the essential tasks of systems development, and the importance of prototyping with the latter.[1] To our knowledge, he has not presented work in the area of formulating a specific technique for prototyping.

A master of technique formulation is, in our opinion, Tom DeMarco. To have developed a technique of structured analysis in the late 1970s that is still viable and widely practiced today is an amazing feat of software engineering, considering how fast things change in our field. The link between rapid prototyping and the DeMarco approach to structured analysis may not be an obvious one, but we feel it is a strong one.

Both structured analysis and rapid prototyping are requirements modeling approaches. One began as a static paper-based approach and the other is a dynamic machine-based approach, but they both have the same objective: to prevent software development project failure. Both techniques propose that an appropriate level of rigor applied to requirements definition will reduce the risk of producing a wrong system. DeMarco was also the first to propose that requirements should be modeled in as many dimensions as exist. He proposed a functional model, a data model, and a control model. It seems only natural to us to add a dynamic working model as the fourth dimension. We hope that DeMarco approves.

Bruce Blum appears to be the first one to actually do rapid prototyping and also write about it under that label. His early experiments with MUMPS (an old PDP-11 system: *M*assachusetts general hospital *U*sers *M*ulti-*P*rogramming *S*ystem) proved that new (at that time) tools made the development of a dynamic requirements model during the analysis phase of a project a practical approach. Blum demonstrated that a MUMPS prototype could be developed and modified as fast and easily as a structured specification. This made some structured advocates wonder whether it was still true that the development of an early working model always had the danger of locking developers into a premature technical solution. Blum showed that for only a small add-on cost—say ten percent—prototyping could provide a more accurate requirements definition than conventional paper specifications.

The Mainframe Approach

Bernard Boar was the first to market with a full-length book on prototyping. There is much conceptual sameness between Boar's approach and ours. We highly recommend his 1984 book to anyone who has a serious interest in the topic. Boar was writing about prototyping at a time when there was much skepticism about the approach. In 1983, many software engineers equated rapid prototyping with quick and dirty software development, or hacking. Boar helped legitimize prototyping by presenting a solid business case as justification and a somewhat formalized approach with preliminary guidelines that negated the hacker image.

We agree with many aspects of Boar's approach. We applaud the fact that it is data driven. We agree that a prototype based on actual application data is much more effective than mere "simulated screens." Boar also emphasizes the need for tools that provide fast and flexible application development, particularly a fourth-generation language. In addition, he recommends an integrated mix-and-match approach, where functions created with many kinds of development tools can be easily integrated into a modular application. The fact that Boar's approach is so similar to ours is coincidental and probably due to the simple fact that common sense is at the core of the ideas. Our articles and papers (previously cited) of the same era came to many of the same conclusions that Boar reached in his book.

The divergence between Boar's approach and ours is in two primary areas: the appropriate role of structured specification techniques, and the necessity of an RDMS. Boar believes that prototyping is the answer to the failure of the structured techniques to deliver on the promise of accurately defining requirements. He does not, however, advocate prototyping without any preliminary specification effort. Boar is an advocate of data modeling (discussed later in this chapter) as the critical specification technique for data-based prototyping, whereas we recommend data modeling as one of three (DFD, ERD, CFG) paper modeling techniques. Regarding the RDMS, Boar's pre-1984 application development experience showed then-current RDMS software to be inadequate for hosting mainframe applications with large numbers of users and huge volumes of data. Boar therefore advocated the use of a quasi-relational DBMS for mainframe prototyping—one with some of the rapid development features of an RDMS, but with apparently much better performance characteristics. Now we can fully endorse several performance-optimized RDMS's—even for mainframe environments.

The Programming Approach

We would like to think of Barry Boehm as the primary spokesman for what might be referred to as the programming approach to prototyping. Boehm is a relative latecomer to the prototyping arena, but his stature as a widely read author of excellent software engineering literature, particularly in the arena of "software engineering economics," guarantees him an audience when he writes about "Prototyping versus Specifying," or his "Spiral Model" of software development that includes the development of three prototype versions of a proposed system.

From his writings, it seems that Boehm thinks of prototyping as the writing of conventional programs with minimal preliminary specification in place. No doubt many organizations will try this approach under the banner of prototyping. An alternate prototyping methodology may arise around the programming approach, based on writing throwaway code as an early prototype, or based on a formalized incremental development methodology. This approach will have much appeal, particularly in government contracting environments; yet it may increase contract cost.

The specification requirements levied on government contractors by military standard guidelines make any prototyping approach that minimalizes specification effort extremely attractive. We are not talking about simple structured specifications here. We are talking about truckloads and warehouses full of specifications. The page estimates for large government contract specifications sometimes are in the millions. In such an environment, incremental development means you can actually deliver at least a portion of the software before it becomes obsolete.

The Homegrown Approach

There are many other approaches to prototyping, most of which have not been published or, when published, have not been adequately explained. We refer to these as homegrown approaches. Occasionally you will read about someone's successful experiences with prototyping in a computer magazine article or a professional journal. Most of these articles do not speak about what hardware and software were used for prototype development, nor do they adequately explain what are the steps in the prototyping process. This means they are assuming that reader and author have the same concepts in mind about what prototyping is—a dangerous assumption.

Such articles are certainly useful in spreading the word about prototyping, and case studies are the very best kind of advertisement. However, to accomplish more than entertainment or the sparking of interest, it is necessary to present the nuts and bolts how-to approach in a rigorous and robust manner. The latter type of treatment requires a book (like this one) because the periodical medium simply does not allow the room. A work that, in our opinion, successfully represents a how-to approach is a book titled *Rapid Systems Development* by Chris Gane. The book is oriented toward the use of Oracle™ as an RDMS and it covers the process of normalizing databases on a different level than we do, but in general, it does not conflict with the concepts presented here.[2]

THE ROLE OF NORMALIZATION IN PROTOTYPING

There is a strong feeling among the software engineering community that normalization has a role to play in data-based rapid prototyping. There is an even stronger feeling that normalization is central to the efficient design of an RDMS-based database schema. RDMS vendors often include tutorials on normalization in their training literature and technical manuals.

Normalization has not been described thoroughly in this book, not because we want to de-emphasize the process, but because it should not overshadow the process of prototyping. It is easy to get so caught up in data modeling and database design that the other dimensions of prototyping—functionality, control, and user interface—become slighted. Remember that one of the most important aspects of prototyping is to create a model quickly. Restructuring of the database can occur at any point in the process—easily if you are using an RDMS—and will only be finalized during the tuning phase.

The antithesis of normalization is one big database table containing all of the data elements belonging to an application. Remember the old days of program-managed sequential files when we often saw gargantuan file structures, such as the "Employee Information File," used to support many applications? Sometimes today we see attempts to recreate these good old days by using the RDMS as if it were nothing more than one big sequential file. Because an RDMS has powerful data manipulation capabilities built in and sequential file structures do not, such use of the RDMS is a terrible waste.

In the old sequential file days, there was much data redundancy and every time a record had to be updated with a new or changed field, or a new record had to be added, much unproductive work had to be done just to provide record completeness. Data entry work acquired the reputation of drudgery. Because the RDMS allows different types of application data to be stored in separate tables and then joined on output, much redundancy can be eliminated and the data entry load can be lightened. Information about the specific attributes of a worker can be stored in the Worker table, for instance, and information about the specific attributes of that worker's department can be stored in the Department table. Then, when a worker attribute such as telephone number changes, updates only need take place to the Worker table. When a department attribute such as building number changes, only the Department table need be updated. The same principle applies to the addition of new employees and new departments.

To further illustrate how data redundancy and database inconsistency can pose problems, consider the following example. Suppose a large organization has a file of records of employee raise histories as shown in Figure 12-1.

Employee	Department	Department Location	Dept. Manager	Amount of Raise	Date of Raise
Connell	IS	Building 23	Hall	$3,000	10/1/84
Connell	IS	Building 23	Hall	$5,000	10/1/86
Connell	IS	Building 23	Hall	$4,000	10/1/85
Shafer	ADP	Building 12	Tucker	$3,500	7/15/84

Figure 12-1 Raise history file.

This design allows for redundant data because Department, Department Location, and Department Manager are repeated for every employee record. Redundancy not only consumes more space than is necessary, it presents problems in keeping the data updated. Suppose Connell is transferred to another department, but only his first record, that of 10-1-84, is updated with the new department name, location, and manager. Then the database has become inconsistent because Connell's other two records still show him as being employed by the IS department. In addition, if the organization decides it needs to carry information about raises only from 1985 forward, and all records with an earlier raise date are deleted from the database, then important information is lost. Shafer's one record is deleted, leaving her with no representation as an employee in this database, the fact that Tucker manages ADP is lost, and Connell's new department information is lost. If the database were restructured to look like Figure 12-2, containing two tables where attributes are functionally dependent upon the keys, then department-related information is carried only once, and updating and changing of the Raise table will not affect the Department table.

This database design still is not optimal because the department to which an employee belongs is still repeated for each record in the Raise table. Data modeling, using entity-relationship charts or logical data structures prior to database creation, prob-

Employee	Department	Amount of Raise	Date of Raise
Connell	IS	$3,000	10/1/84
Connell	IS	$5,000	10/1/86
Connell	IS	$4,000	10/1/85
Shafer	ADP	$3,500	7/15/84

Department	Department Location	Dept. Manager
IS	Building 23	Hall
ADP	Building 12	Tucker

Figure 12-2 Employee raise and department tables.

ably would solve many of these problems. Data modeling was discussed in Chapter 3 and will be reviewed briefly in the next section. There are many excellent articles and textbooks on the subject of normalization following data modeling. The reader is encouraged to consult them for greater depth of presentation and for other examples.[3-12]

A nice mind-jogger to help remember the first three forms of normalization is, "The key (first), the whole key (second), and nothing but the key (third)." In first normal form, every table has at least one attribute or some concatenation of attributes (the key) whose value is unique in each row of that table. This value can then be specified in query retrieval commands to obtain desired rows. In second normal form, the values of the attributes of any particular row are dependent on the value of the whole key (whatever combination of attributes uniquely defines a row). In third normal form, attributes are dependent for their values only on the value of the key for that row—not on the value of any other attribute in that row.

In the example just referred to of the Employee Raise Table, we would typically expect each record to be identified by an employee identification number. Such a file would thus be in first normal form. We would also expect, however, that each record would contain data that had nothing specifically to do with an employee identification number. Therefore, such a file does not meet the criterion of second normal form—that the attributes of any particular record be dependent on the value of the key. We would also expect that some data in the Employee Raise Table be related to specific employees but also dependent on some other piece of information. Building number is an example of such data. If employees change departments, their building number may change. Knowing the employee identification is not sufficient to determine an employee's building number. This aspect of the Employee Raise Table therefore violates third normal form—attributes of a record must be dependent for their value only on the value of the key.

Thus, the normalization process consists of inspecting database table attribute lists to see if the guidelines of a normal form have been violated. If such violations are discovered, they may be removed by splitting the table into two or more new tables with common attributes for joining purposes where required. In principle, this process should continue until all redundancy and unproductive data entry effort have been removed from the database structure.

Software developers will benefit from training in normalization as it helps to prevent development of database structures that are difficult to maintain. There is also help in automated form (see Table 11.1). Yet, it is possible to go overboard on normalization and experienced prototypers will take a pragmatic view. They know that pushing for all database tables to be in third normal form might result in poor system performance characteristics caused by the many joining operations needed to put report retrievals together. The more normalized a database is, the more tables it will have, and the more joins will be needed to create required output. The joining of tables to produce needed output takes large amounts of I/O time and temporary storage space. Sometimes it is even best to "denormalize" for the sake of efficiency and better system performance.[12]

Clearly there is a trade-off between performance and normalization. What then is the optimum level of normalization? This is a good question to pose in a book about prototyping because it turns out that this question, like many other software engineering questions, can be answered most effectively by the act of prototyping. We use an RDMS because it is flexible. That means that you don't have to be in third normal form or optimum normal form to start prototype iteration. The experienced prototyper knows that whatever level of normalization is decided upon for the initial prototype will probably be the wrong level for the final system. Let the requirements for normalization be driven out, along with all the other requirements, by prototyping. The optimum compromise between fastest response time and lightest data entry load will be best determined by experimenting with the prototype.

This leads us to offer the following heuristic for normalization level of a prototype. We call this level "best normal form." Prototype-determined best normal form might be less normalized than second normal form or more normalized than third normal form, depending on user requirements for a specific application. A practical rule of thumb is to begin with a data structure that has some way of uniquely defining each table row, has no repeating groups, and contains seven, plus or minus two, attributes per table. Determine what attributes to include in each initial table as being those needed to create initial data entry screens for the preliminary prototype. This nonacademic heuristic is not elegant, but has the advantage of providing a fast-build approach that will not get the database architect into very much trouble.

THE ROLE OF DATA MODELING

Data modeling and normalization are somewhat related concepts. In fact, normalization is typically described as being a critical part of the data modeling process. The objective of data modeling is to use an analytical process that includes normalization to prespecify an optimal database schema. Like structured analysis, the process begins with user interviews. Users within various functional departments are interviewed concerning the information they need to do their job. An inventory of data requirements by job function is thus acquired. From this information a corporate data model is specified. The corporate data model contains subject databases for all major areas of related job functions such as finance, marketing, manufacturing, and so forth. Each subject database contains all the information specified by workers in that area as needed to do their job. The information is represented by data attributes, normalized into as many tables as needed to obtain third normal form.

A limited form of data modeling—with the goal of establishing "best normal form"—is useful and is a helpful technique during prototyping. If you are one of the many people in the computer field who define their job as the development of information management systems, then data-oriented analysis probably makes a lot of sense to you. Of course, the dataflow and entity-relationship diagrams of rapid analysis are examples of data-oriented analysis as well. As with all other forms of requirements analysis, it is good to keep a balanced perspective and not delude yourself into thinking that you will be able to prepare 100 percent accurate specifications before you have a working model with which to experiment. Another criterion for balance is to remember that a stored information model only represents one dimension of the proposed system. It is also important to model the functional and control flow dimensions of a system prior to prototyping.

One danger of data modeling is early intimidation of users. It might be easy for you to think of your users' jobs in terms of the information they manage, but is it really all that easy for them? How easy is it for you to recite all the information you need to do your job? Don't most people think of their job primarily as a set of procedures they must perform (I do this, then I do that, then I go home)? The smarter your user is, the less certain he or she will be about what information is needed to do their job. Uncertainty breeds intimidation and intimidation impedes progress. Some organizations make the intimidation factor worse by distributing an obviously computer-generated "Required Information Survey" to prospective users—everybody knows how hard it is to change something once it gets in the computer.

Another danger of data modeling is that it tends to create data structures that have expensive maintenance characteristics. When databases are created to support tasks, there is a tendency to create one database structure for each new application. Fanatical data modelers consider this approach terribly inefficient because of the inevitable data redundancy. On the other hand, subject databases which support multiple applications must be modified every time any one of the applications supported is modified with respect to data attributes. This means that every application that accesses the modified subject database must be carefully inspected for possible change impact. In most environments, increasing the maintenance effort will be more costly than increasing data redundancy.

A final danger is that, for relational databases, data modeling, using a conventional prespecification approach, can be deadly because it has the tendency to create large, elaborate data structures that will be populated by gigabytes of data. This spells poor response time for relational queries. There are several reasons for such expansiveness:

- The need to support many applications
- Many users supplying new data concurrently
- The conservative user's response to data modeling to specify all the data that can possibly be conceived of as ever being needed (all the data you can't prove I won't need someday)

The bottom line is that extensive data modeling makes sense only if the quasi-relational database (you know—the one with the inflexible internal data storage structure) you are using for performance reasons in a mainframe environment requires that you be fairly sure what the final schema will be before you load the database with data. Even then, you should be prepared to stipulate (or mandate) that organizational data requirements are not dynamic but are, in fact, rather static. Finally, extensive data modeling is not a logical substitute for multidimensional system modeling—there are more dimensions to a software application than merely data.

The alternative to data modeling is application modeling—what this book is all about. When you model an application, you begin with a context diagram, specifying the interfaces of your system with external systems. The promises made by the context diagram are contractual and must continue to be supported when future modifications to your system are undertaken. New systems coming on-line must develop and maintain their own interfaces with your system where needed but can do so safely by picking up output promised by your context diagram. Logically, if RDMS tools and the methodology outlined in this book are used to develop applications, there will be one database for each application. There will also be some data redundancy within organizations, but then data storage is getting cheaper all the time.

THE ROLE OF PROTOTYPING CENTERS AND INFORMATION CENTERS

Prototyping or information centers are also related to normalization and data modeling. Normalization is something one does when modeling data. Data modeling is something done in an information center. Subject databases are housed in an information center. There seem to be few distinctions between a prototyping center and an information center and therefore the two terms will be used interchangeably. A prototyping center could be something entirely different from an information center. It could be a place where prototypers have access to resources dedicated to prototyping, but this is not the common meaning of the jargon.

The information center was originally conceived as an alternative to the conventional data processing software support organization. This kind of information center was similar to a library. You could come to the center and check out many commercial software packages, but you could not request a new custom-built application. This concept was supposed to eliminate software maintenance. There were a few flies in this ointment. One problem was sharing data among applications. Another problem was lost opportunities for information management capabilities due to the generic nature of commercial packages.

Where organizations resisted solving the problems of the information center, users supplied their own solutions. Where there are computers there will always be computer programmers. Some user departments hired their own programmers, giving them different kinds of job titles if necessary. Some users became programmers. One way or another, custom-built applications continued to be developed. Ultimately, many information centers recognized the need to support custom applications and became prototyping centers. This meant, in many cases, that access to database tools was granted to end users and they were supposed to build their own customized input and output procedures. The data structures these users needed would already be there as a result of data modeling activities. In some cases, software professionals acted as consultants in such environments.

Information centers can be good things. It is nice to have a place to go to get advice about and fast access to commercial software packages. It has been proven effective to have users do their own prototyping, with consultation and assistance from software professionals. There is, however, nothing about the basic nature of rapid prototyping that depends on the existence of an information center. Protoyping can be just as effective outside the information center as it does not have to be centralized.

RAPID PROTOTYPING IN THE ADA-VHDL ENVIRONMENT

You probably have one of two likely reactions to the heading for this section. If you are a promoter of the Ada language, you might be wondering why Ada has been relegated to the backwaters of this book. Many Ada proponents feel that the language itself is one of the most powerful prototyping tools available. On the other hand, if you do not work for the U.S. government or a government contractor, you might be wondering why we are bothering at all with such a topic.

Ada is clearly here to stay. Too much has been invested in its development to expect that it will not be one of the pervasive programming languages of the future. The last time the U.S. government mandated a programming language, it was COBOL. COBOL eventually became the primary language in 90 percent of all programming environments. The defense budget represents about half the annual federal budget. Federal workers, federal contract workers, and suppliers of these two kinds of organizations represent about half the United States workforce.

Some Ada proponents refer to Ada as a prototyping environment mainly because of the ease with which the language facilitates callable packages. The reusable code concept was one of the primary motivators for the development of Ada. Researchers in this area write about libraries of reusable "black box modules" used to produce the preliminary prototype of any newly requested application. As we pointed out in Chapter 11, such concepts are not reality at present and may never be good ideas anyway. We do not recommend an Ada compiler, by itself, as an adequate rapid prototyping environment.

There are, however, some things we would like to be able to do while prototyping in this future, inescapable Ada environment. We would like to be able to write an Ada program that could access data stored in an RDMS. We would like to be able to invoke an Ada program from an RDMS-generated application menu structure. Some RDMS packages offer these features today, but quite a few popular systems do not.

There is also one area, having to do with new hardware technology, where Ada offers some advanced technological capabilities to prototypers. Recent advances in microchip technology have mostly been derived from a manufacturing process known as VHSIC (pronounced *vih-sik*), which stands for very high speed integrated circuits. This is a difficult technology because it has conflicting design goals: very small size and very fast performance. The problem is, the smaller chips are made, the slower they are able to perform, due to heat build-up.

The armed forces have contracted for and will mandate the use of a new hardware design language called VHDL—*VHSIC Hardware Description Language*. VHDL is, interestingly enough, a dialect of Ada. Actually, it is identical except for the fact that there are some additional reserved words in VHDL used to describe hardware components.

Why is this interesting? For one thing, it allows Ada-like programs to be written as a hardware design process. Silicon compilers are under development that will compile VHDL programs. The output will be an acetate mask that can be photographically reduced and then burned into silicon to produce the actual chip, if you can imagine writing programs to produce hardware. Also, since Ada and VHDL are actually dialects of the same language, translators between the two will be easy to develop and are, in fact, on the way.

When all this falls into place, rapid prototyping in the Ada-VHDL environment may resemble the process modeled by Figure 12-3. First, a model is developed using strictly RDMS-based tools. During tuning it may be decided that some of these prototype modules need to be replaced by Ada programs for performance reasons. Additionally, stringent performance requirements might entail actually burning a functional module into a VHSIC chip. Conventional development of such performance-critical systems always entails much agonizing over the allocation between hardware and software. Because of the long lead times inherent in the acquisition of components necessary to build hardware devices embodying new technology, mistakes in hardware-software allocation can spell total system failure. Using new tools, such as silicon compilers and Ada-VHDL translators, such agonizing is unneccessary. A process called "Change Mind," as shown in Figure 12-3, can be invoked at any time until the system goes into full-scale production.

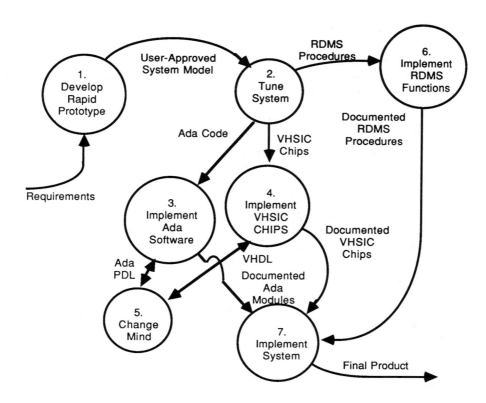

Figure 12-3 Ada-VHDL prototyping possibilities.

MODIFYING THE RAPID PROTOTYPING APPROACH
TO ALLOW FOR LIMITED TOOLS

Throughout this book, the availability of hardware and software tools suitable for structured evolutionary rapid prototyping has been assumed. The critical features and capabilities of such tools have been described in detail. The fact that rapid prototyping is a tool-dependent technique has been emphasized. Some readers may be discouraged because their organization does not own such tools and for various reasons may be resistant to the idea of acquiring them. Software organizations have all manner of politically based reasons for resisting technology from time to time.

If you work for such an organization and have to use tools with lesser capabilities than those described earlier in this book, here are three limited ways in which you can at least apply some of the ideas presented, thereby receiving at least some of the advantages of rapid prototyping within the confines of your restrictive environment. Each of the three limited approaches assumes a toolkit that is in certain respects less powerful than the ideal. Each builds a bit on the capabilities of the previously described approach. Pick the most powerful approach consistent with the capabilities of the tools at your disposal.

The Model Building Approach

This is the least powerful of the three limited approaches. It is called the model building approach because the result of prototype development using this approach will be something less than a working model incorporating actual application data—something akin to an architect's balsa wood model. In a way, such a model could be referred to as a simulation rather than a prototype. By definition, a prototype uses actual application data and performs verifiable functions.

Whether model building is real prototyping or not, it is a conceptually similar approach that you can use if you do not have an RDMS or even a 4GL to use. You can still create and iteratively modify the appearance of how the system will look to the user when it is finished. Such a model system can be built and modified quickly without writing programs, even if all you have to work with is a full-screen text editor. The high end of model building tools is specialized throwaway prototyping systems that allow you to build a model that actually performs functions interactively. Some CASE tools incorporate such prototyping tools as part of the package so you can generate a prototype automatically, derived from your structured specifications (see Table 11.1).

Using a model builder, the prototyping approach is to first create examples of all points of contact between the user and the proposed system—input screens, output displays, and reports. As with evolutionary rapid prototyping, since you are using tools which allow such examples to be easily modified, the preliminary model does not have to be complete or accurate. The preliminary model can then be iterated to user approval of system appearance. Note that *appearance* is different from user approval of system functionality. Functional correctness can only be verified using a model that incorporates real data. At user approval of system appearance, you have taken such a prototype as far as it can go and must now revert to conventional software development techniques. The prototype can be used as part of a detailed structured analysis and will be helpful in deriving a conventional detailed structured design. From then on, the conventional life cycle approach should be used, proceeding to conventional coding and testing of the actual system as shown in Figure 12-4.

There are some lost prototyping capabilities when using a model builder approach. Users will find it next to impossible to verify the accuracy of reports when actual user-familiar data are not present. Since model building is not a 100 percent definitive approach to requirements definition, prototype iteration cannot culminate with a system requirements review as it can with the evolutionary approach. Conventional structured analysis will have to be relied on to specify many of the functional, data, and control requirements. Models, by definition, cannot evolve into final software products, so the total development cost will be higher by the cost of developing and iterating the model. The delivered final product will also contain the same level of psychological complexity (be either just as hard or just as easy to maintain) as conventionally developed software.

Prototyping with model building tools is still worthwhile. Combined with conventional structured analysis and design tools, you will still be able to prepare a four-dimensional model of system requirements: a function model, a data model, a control model, and a user interface model. You will find it easier to communicate with users about requirements when such discussions take place with respect to actual examples of proposed key aspects of the system. Thus, you will increase the probability of building and delivering a system the customer will find useful and acceptable.

The Stand-Alone Function Building Approach

This is a more powerful, but still limited, approach to prototyping. We call it a stand-alone function building approach because the tools used lack the capabilities provided by a good application generator to prototype a modular, many-faceted, integrated system. That means no ability to generate a menu-driven application control structure using visual programming and a 4GL control language. This forces developers into

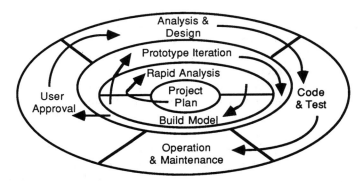

Figure 12-4   The model builder approach.

a totally different approach to prototyping—the one shown in Figure 12-5. Again, the result of prototype development using this approach will be something less than an integrated working model of a total system. The stand-alone function builder will allow you to incorporate actual application data and demonstrate working functions but you will be prototyping and demonstrating one function at a time rather than a total application.

The limited approach of prototyping stand-alone functions is still useful in helping to define system requirements. Returning once more to the custom-built automobile analogy, this approach is similar to bringing out one tire, all by itself, which the customer can kick; then bringing out a bucket seat, all by itself, in which the customer can sit. Results will not be as good as experimenting with a concept for a whole automobile, but demonstrating working models of real pieces of the automobile is an improvement over simply talking about ("the automobile shall have a bucket seat") and perhaps drawing some pictures of the proposed automobile.

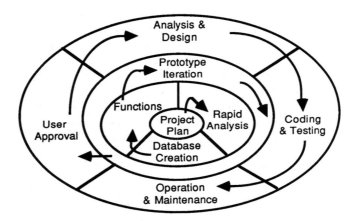

Figure 12-5   The stand-alone function building approach.

As this approach does not assist in defining the higher levels of system operation—for example, how functions are invoked by the user, or how successfully tightly coupled modules will integrate in the final product—the developer will be forced to revert to a very conventional approach to software development after user approval of the functionality of the prototyped functions has been obtained. Dataflow diagrams and structure charts can be used profitably in the conventional manner to specify a total integrated system architecture. However, having already prototyped and obtained user approval of some of the modules to be specified will help considerably in preparing analysis and design models that will be understandable to the customer.

The high end of stand-alone function building tools is relational database systems with a powerful 4GL and visual programming capabilities included. This means the applications data storage structure can be prototyped and default screens and reports may be created to work on with the visual programming tools. The low end of stand-alone function building tools is represented by stand-alone 4GLs (no integrated database management system). With a stand-alone 4GL you must begin from scratch to create each module—no default screens and no visual programming. In either case, what is always missing in this class of tool is an application structure generator that would allow you to easily combine all the prototyped pieces into one integrated application prototype.

As with a model builder, the prototyping approach with a stand-alone function builder is to first create examples of points of contact between the user and the proposed system such as input screens, output displays, and reports. At user approval of the functionality of these prototyped pieces, you must once again revert to conventional software development techniques. Some of the prototyped modules might find their way into the final product, if performance is found acceptable during testing, and thus provide this approach with some evolutionary aspects.

There are some distinct advantages here compared to the simple model builder approach. Users will be able to verify the accuracy of reports produced during prototype demonstrations because actual user-familiar data can be included. Developers will not have to rely totally on conventional structured analysis to discover all of the functional, data, and control requirements. More than just a model will be produced during prototyping and many user what-if questions can be answered conclusively. Since some of the prototyped modules may evolve into pieces of the final software product, there is a chance that total development cost will not be higher than the cost of conventional software development. The delivered final product may also contain a lower level of psychological complexity where prototyped modules are used.

The Integrated Nonevolutionary Approach

While still a limited approach, this is a still more powerful approach to prototyping than stand-alone function building. With this type of prototyping environment, you can create a total, menu-driven, integrated application system, but there is a very high risk that you will not be able to evolve the prototype into the final product. What you get with such products, missing in the previous two classes, is an application generator that allows prototype modules to be integrated easily using either a 4GL command language or visual programming, or both. What you don't get is the ability to escape temporarily from the prototyping environment to a more conventional software development environment and thereby include conventionally developed software modules in the final product. More specifically, you cannot call a conventional third-generation language program from the prototype menu structure and then have that program access data in the relational database.

Similar to a model prototype, a throwaway prototype does not evolve into a final software product, so the total development cost of this approach will also be higher by the cost of developing and iterating the prototype. The prototyping process, using a nonevolutionary approach, is shown in Figure 12-6. Since the entire prototype will be discarded after user approval of functionality, the delivered final product will contain the same level of psychological complexity as conventionally developed software.

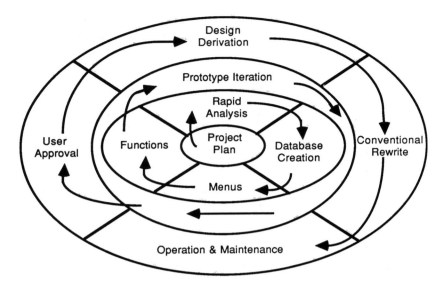

Figure 12-6   The integrated, nonevolutionary approach

It could reasonably be argued that the integrated but nonevoluntionary approach is less powerful than the stand-alone function prototyping approach, since at least some of the prototype stand-alone functions might be included in the final product. This is usually not the case—it is much more powerful to be able to demonstrate and iterate a total integrated working model of the entire application until user approval is reached. Using this approach, user approval of prototype functionality can be followed by a formal system requirements review at which time the system's functional requirements should be known. An accurate and feasible design can then be easily derived from the prototype in place. With software development, this is at least half the battle. Recoding the prototype to meet performance requirements often becomes nothing more than a minor nuisance.

EVALUATIONS OF SOME ACTUAL PRODUCTS

In Chapter 3, actual prototyping tools were not recommended, because we wanted to stress the fact that the reader should perform individual evaluations based on the critical features described and on individual environments. We will now offer as a special interest topic a few product evaluations based on our own experiences—but first some caveats. We must reiterate that any such published list of "worthy" products and their evaluations is guaranteed to be obsolete by the time it is published. By the time you read this chapter, there will be new products not on our list. Products on the list will have new features that will affect their evaluations. Finally, this is only a list of products actually used by the authors or by clients for whom we provided consulting services. There are, no doubt, a great number of other worthy products not on this list (see Table 11.1). Please do your own evaluations and use the following list only as a list of examples to give you an idea of the type of products we have been discussing and how tool features affect prototyping capabilities.

Figure 12-7 lists ten RDMS products and shows, on a one to five star basis for each of three categories, our evaluation of these products based on fairly extensive exposure. The three evaluation categories are those described as critical features for prototyping in Chapter 3. All of these products include a 4GL—we consider this a must for a prototyping tool. We do not rank the 4GLs specifically—they are all fairly equal. We include an evaluation of each product's capability to provide a procedure interface under the category, "Application Generator," since this is where procedures get interfaced. These products are available on a variety of makes and classes of computers from mainframes (MF), through minicomputers (MC), down to personal computers (PC). One of the differentiating characteristics of these products is their availability in a variety of environments.

If you are counting stars, you have already noted that we feel INGRES™, produced by Relational Technology Inc., is one of the most powerful prototyping environments available. The INGRES application generator, referred to by the vendor as Applications By Form (ABF), is perhaps its strongest feature—significantly superior to the application generators of other vendors. INGRES ABF allows for menu calls to more programming languages and utilities than any other package we know of. As far as we know, INGRES was the first RDMS to be fully compatible with the Ada programming language.

The only area in which INGRES falls somewhat short of ideal is in its visual programming capabilities. This is ironic, because INGRES was the product where we saw and used visual programming tools for the first time. They were and are, however, forms-based rather than icon-based tools and are today often somewhat archaically command-oriented. We prefer visual programming tools where there are

PRODUCT	Application Generator	Truly Relational	Visual Programming	Host
INGRES	☆☆☆☆☆	☆☆☆☆	☆☆☆	MF,MC,PC
ORACLE	☆☆☆☆	☆☆☆☆	☆☆☆	MF,MC,PC
IDMS-R	☆☆☆	☆☆☆	☆☆☆	MF,PC
DB2	☆☆	☆☆☆☆	☆☆	MF
Informix	☆☆☆	☆☆☆☆	☆☆☆	MC
Unify	☆☆	☆☆☆☆	☆☆	MC
Rbase System V	☆☆☆☆	☆☆☆☆	☆☆☆	PC
Double Helix II	☆☆☆	☆☆☆☆	☆☆☆☆	PC, MC
Dbase III +	☆☆	☆	☆☆	PC
HyperCard	☆☆☆☆☆	☆	☆☆☆☆☆	PC

Figure 12-7 Some worthy prototyping products.

absolutely no commands to memorize and where development is totally intuitive. These latter kinds of tools became available recently in personal computer environments while INGRES remained oriented primarily toward mainframe and minicomputer environments. Good visual programming is difficult to implement where the developer workstation is a dumb terminal—it almost requires a sophisticated pointing device, such as a mouse.

ORACLE is roughly equivalent to INGRES in all features. Not shown on the chart is the fact that, while both products run on mainframes, minicomputers, and personal computers, ORACLE runs on products made by a wider variety of hardware vendors than INGRES. Some feel this makes ORACLE-developed applications more portable. Others feel that slight differences in the various versions of ORACLE make conversion from one machine to another often less than trivial. This could also be said of INGRES. Some users also note performance differences between INGRES and ORACLE, but this is very difficult to benchmark scientifically and, in the final analysis, observed performance differences are probably mostly attributable to database design.

Both ORACLE and INGRES were originally developed for minicomputer (VAX) use. As the products grew in popularity and the vendors grew in financial resources, the products were ported to other machines: first to other minicomputers, after a few years to mainframes, and most recently to personal computers. The conversion to mainframes and PCs seemed an almost reluctant move on the part of the vendors, forced on them by an insistent marketplace. Both products appear to have a tendency to perform somewhat sluggishly on a mainframe compared to some products developed specifically for the mainframe. Both products seem to overburden the resources of a personal computer while at the same time providing less powerful features in a PC environment than they do in their larger versions.

IDMS-R™, produced by Cullinane, was developed specifically for the mainframe. It gets mediocre marks as a truly relational product because it is actually a quasi-relational DBMS. It represents an enhancement to an earlier Cullinane product, IDMS™. The enhancement consists of allowing for the creation of some relational-like operations on data sets, such as joins. The internal data structure, however, is still network style. There are chains, pointers, and master and slave data sets, and each data set is required to have an identified key field.

IDMS-R is not our favorite prototyping tool, but it is not our least favorite either. It does have a 4GL and integrated visual programming tools. In fact, it has a large number of integrated quick development tools that have some conceptual sameness to the class of tools we have been discussing in this book. While the lack of a truly relational data structure causes some problems during prototype iteration, this is partially compensated for by this product's fairly respectable performance characteristics when large numbers of users and volumes of data must be accommodated.

DB2™ is an IBM product. It is a truly relational database designed to run on IBM mainframes. It is difficult to know how many stars to give DB2. On the one hand, this is just a bare bones RDMS—no bundled application generation or visual programming tools. On the other hand, there are literally dozens of add-on products available which, when combined with DB2, provide a fairly powerful prototyping environment. One DB2 environment is not equivalent to another—it depends on how much money you spend on add-on tools. We tend to prefer bundled products because their pieces usually seem better integrated. IBM has an excellent reputation for upgrading to market demand. So, if you are an IBM mainframe shop, DB2 may be the RDMS of your choice. And given that, you will want to take a close look at IEF from TI, a possible prototyping tool based on DB2.

Informix and Unify have both grown from bare bones RDMS's to fairly full-featured prototyping environments. These are UNIX-based products and, while not the only database products for UNIX environments, are quite common. We have seen these products in use most frequently on UNIX supermicros such as those made by SUN Microsystems (minicomputers in very small packages). Informix gets better marks on application generation and visual programming because it does these things in a self-contained way using bundled tools. Unify, on the other hand, relies on add-on products to provide a full-featured development environment.

For the IBM PC and clones, we have Rbase: System V by Micro RIM. This is one of the more powerful prototyping tools available on any computer. It is truly relational, has powerful function development tools, and has an elegant application generator with the capability for including conventional programs in an Rbase-developed multiuser application. The only real weakness of Rbase is that at present it only runs on personal computers—there is no growth path or portability to minicomputers or mainframes. Also, the development environment for Rbase is integrated and all made by the same vendor, but it is not bundled. You pay one price for the database itself, then you pay extra for the application generator (Application Express) and pay again if you want the external procedure interface (Programmer's Interface).

The other prototyping tool contender for the MS-DOS PC market is Dbase III+ by Ashton-Tate. The vendor claims that this product is relational, but the way you have to design a database (with required keys) and the way joining operations are limited to access on key fields is a dead giveaway. This is use of the word "relational" as a buzz word only, with no substantial meaning. Dbase has been around since the introduction of the IBM PC, and its data structure is a somewhat dated hierarchical file-oriented affair.

The reason for including this product in our list is its omnipresence. It is certainly true that there are more Dbase users than there are users of any other DBMS in the world. In fact, you could probably add all the other DBMS users together and they would not equal the number of Dbase users. This creates a huge potential for after-market add-ons. Every time someone says, "You can't do X with Dbase," someone else can cite a third-party product that, when used with Dbase, allows you to do X. We have given Dbase low marks for the same reason we gave DB2 low marks—lack of an integrated, bundled, development environment. At the same time, we recognize that certain Dbase users will have put together a prototyping environment consisting of Dbase and a vast array of powerful third-party tools that will rival any other prototyping environment.

The Apple Macintosh PC has several RDMS products, two of which we have used enough that we feel competent to pass judgment: Double Helix II™ by Odesta and HyperCard™ by Apple Computer. Double Helix is, along with INGRES, one of our favorite prototyping tools these days. It is very flexibly relational. All fields are variable length. Helix never asks you to specify field length, which, along with a truly relational data structure, makes initial table creation and subsequent modification a breeze. Helix was referenced in Chapter 11 as being indicative of visual programming's future. There is no command language to memorize whatsoever. Everything is done with icons available from icon wells. We have found prototype development and modification with Helix to be an order of magnitude faster than with any other tool. Helix-developed multiuser applications are virtually indistinguishable, in terms of capabilities, from applications developed with much more expensive software on much larger computers.

Helix also does application generation in a faster, more intuitive manner than most of the other tools. You simply drag the names of functions you have created from a scrolling list to a menu that you have created by positioning the mouse cursor on the menu bar and typing the menu name. With Helix, there is no written 4GL, no command language, no lines of any kind of code—just application by example. Helix application generation would surpass all other products if it were not for the lack of an interface to externally developed procedures—a glaring weakness that a vendor spokesperson says will probably be corrected by the time you read this. At present, you cannot call a conventional program from a Helix menu, nor can a conventional program access data contained in a Helix database. Helix cannot be used for anything but small systems and throwaway prototypes. On the positive side, in terms of a growth path, it is possible to host Helix on some minicomputers.

HyperCard is an entirely different breed of prototyping tool. It is the only product on the list that the vendor does not at least claim is a relational database. Apple describes HyperCard as an application prototyping and information management authoring environment. While we mourn (a little) the fact that HyperCard has no inherent relational capabilities, you can see we give it the highest possible marks as an application generator and visual programming environment. HyperCard, which was called WildCard during its beta test period, is indeed the joker in the deck. Everything about this product is so different, that you must really see it to understand what it is and what it does. Some of the stranger differences include the following:

- It comes complete with painting tools which literally treat the screen as an electronic canvas
- Although a HyperCard application is interpreted at run time, it is very fast at some tasks such as information retrieval
- Records are stored as objects, using an index card as a data set metaphor
- A card has a background, a graphics layer, fields, buttons, and scripts
- A collection of HyperCard cards is referred to as a "stack"
- An application developed in HyperCard is referred to as "stackware"
- Backgrounds, cards, fields, buttons, and stacks can have their own scripts
- A script is a program module written in a new language called HyperTalk, an object-oriented derivative of Smalltalk

- The important HyperTalk objects are actual graphics objects that developer and user will see on the screen (paint them, then HyperTalk about them)
- The HyperTalk language is so English-like that it has almost no rigid syntax rules
- HyperTalk can make calls to most conventional programming languages
- Information managed by ⁻IyperCard can include graphics, digitized images, animation, and sound—providing a hypermedia environment
- A HyperCard application can invoke a foreign application and will resume control when the foreign application terminates

With all these strange and wonderful capabilities, we have found that HyperCard provides a nice application shell structure when interfaced with a relational database. There is almost nothing you can think of that cannot be done with HyperCard. Since HyperCard can easily put the Macintosh into terminal emulation mode, it will interface with any of the products shown on Figure 12-7, if you are willing to use the Macintosh as the application workstation.

Well, so much for the product evaluations. Did you see your favorite tool or the one you were planning to prototype with on the list? If not, remember the two golden rules of selecting a prototyping tool: The initial prototype must be as easy to modify as a set of dataflow diagrams; it must be nearly impossible to build psychological complexity into the prototype during iterations. These are the reasons for basing the approach on the use of a flexible RDMS data structure and an intuitive, compressed 4GL devoid of control logic syntax. If your intended prototyping environment meets these two criteria—go for it. Prototyping with Pascal (or any other conventional programming language) is simply not a smart (read cost-effective) idea.

REFERENCES

1. Frederick P. Brooks Jr., "No Silver Bullet—Essence and Accidents of Software Engineering," *Information Processing*, 1986, pp. 1069–76.

2. Chris Gane, *Rapid System Development: Using Structured Techniques and Relational Technology* (New York: Rapid System Development, Inc., 1987).

3. Philip A. Bernstein, "Synthesizing Third Normal Form Relations from Functional Dependencies," *ACM Transactions on Database Systems*, 1, no. 4, December, 1976, 277–298.

4. R. G. G. Cattell, *Design and Implementation of a Relationship-Entity-Datum Data Model*, Xerox PARC, CSL 83-4, May 1983.

5. John V. Carlis, *Logical Data Structures*, Computer Science Department, University of Minnesota, Minneapolis, MN, 1985.

6. C. J. Date, *An Introduction to Database Systems* (Reading, MA: Addison Wesley, 1986).

7. Matt Flavin, *Fundamental Concepts of Information Modeling* (New York: Yourdon Press, 1981).

8. J. Martin, *Computer Data-Base Organization* (Englewood Cliffs, NJ: Prentice Hall, 1977).

9. J. Martin, *An End-User's Guide to Data Base* (Englewood Cliffs, NJ: Prentice-Hall, 1977).

10. J. Martin and Carma McClure, *Software Maintenance: The Problem and Its Solutions* (Englewood Cliffs, NJ: Prentice Hall, 1983).

11. G. Sandberg, "A Primer on Relational Data Base Concepts," *IBM Systems Journal*, 20, no. 1, 1981, 23–40.

12. Betty Salzberg, "Third Normal Form Made Easy," *ACM SIGMOD Record*, 15, no. 4, December 1986, 2-18.

13

Making Prototyping Work in Your Environment

If you are one of the top executives of your company, then we hope you have come to the conclusion by now that rapid prototyping as a software development approach could make your company more competitive through the creation of more highly effective information management systems. If you are a software developer, then we hope you may have come to the conclusion that rapid prototyping could enhance your career by providing you with an approach that will lead to more successful software development projects. Are you a computer software user? Then we hope you have drawn the conclusion that rapid prototyping can provide you with more useful computer systems at a lower price. Within a particular organizational environment, the extent to which these expectations will be reliably realized will depend in large part on the manner in which prototyping is implemented as a mainstream approach to software development.

Chapter 7 described an approach to managing the rapid prototyping process on a project by project basis. If rapid prototyping is to become a mainstream approach rather than merely an experimental approach within your organization, it will be necessary to rethink your total software management approach. In the first half of the 1980s, software organizations found that a standardized approach to structured analysis and design was more effective than a project to project or person by person approach. In the 1990s, all software engineers within an organization will use the same methodology, supported by CASE-like tools—a fact that will affect the future success of the rapid prototyping approach presented in this book.

When an analyst in your organization states that the requirements specifications for a new project will be accurate, understandable, and unambiguous because a structured analysis approach is being used, do you have high confidence that you and the analyst mean the same thing when you say "structured analysis"? Have you ever worked in an environment where the "structured approach" was merely a nebulous ill-defined term? Similarly, when a software engineer says that some development is taking place on a project before the requirements specification has been published, but that's all right because "rapid prototyping" is being used, is the real meaning of the term well understood by all parties? Beware, you could be approving an approach that will lead to unacceptably high software maintenance costs.

How will embracing a rapid prototyping approach as the universal approach to software development affect your organization's standards, development environment, software maintenance, work requests, and development funding? The following material will serve to at least make you aware of what the issues and problems might be in moving from a conventional software development approach to evolutionary structured rapid prototyping.

RAPID PROTOTYPING WITHIN THE ORGANIZATIONAL ENVIRONMENT

Where will rapid prototyping take place within your environment? The choices are the following: in a centralized software development area or in distributed project areas in the users' locations. Who will perform rapid prototyping? The choices are the following: analysts, developers, or users. Will there be rules or at least guidelines to answer these questions, or will members of each project decide these issues autonomously? The answers to these questions must be provided uniquely by each organization. This is because the answers are critically dependent on factors unique to your domain.

Do you develop custom software under contract for specific external customers? If so, you may not have a central software department, but rather a number of projects, each staffed with software developers. Some writers, such as Boar,[1] have insisted on the importance of a prototyping center as an element critical to the success of the prototyping approach. Perhaps individual customers would indeed be better served by a centralized prototyping approach. This would allow the cost of prototyping resources such as computers, workstations, a relational database, and other software tools to be shared among all customers, thus lowering the cost of each contract and making bids more competitive. Within organizations that have software departments only for the purpose of developing and maintaining in-house applications, the same economic factors are at play—they are merely disguised somewhat when they are buried in the organization's overhead rate.

The trade-off with a centralized approach to prototyping is that it often tends to put some distance between the developers and the customers. The prototyping center is the developer's turf—it is full of computers, workstations, and other artifacts not part of the customer's everyday world. This may make users ill at ease and reluctant to spend a lot of time at the prototyping center. Distance between developers and users is antithetical and counterproductive to prototyping. This has led some organizations to take the approach that all prototyping shall take place at the user's workplace. Perhaps an ideal compromise between these two extremes would be to have a central hub for prototyping, with resources (people, computers, and software tools) that could be charged out to projects. This way, prototyping would be done at the user's site, but resources would be at least partially shareable between projects.

Now that we're at the prototyping site (wherever that is), who will do the prototyping? Many organizations tend to have strong lines of demarcation defining who does what kind of work. Often, these definitions are reduced to skills descriptions contained in a human resources database. Does your organization have a skill category for rapid prototyping? Who is qualified to do this work? One approach that some organizations will probably take is to establish such a skill category and then, since no one within the organization will have established a track record of rapid prototyping skills, undertake a hiring program to fill newly established "rapid prototyper" positions.

We have said that anyone with a certain minimal amount of training can do rapid prototyping. We have said that users as well as professional software developers are entirely capable of undertaking most rapid prototyping tasks. We have, however, noticed that rapid prototyping, while not a complex science, is definitely a creative art form. Techniques are involved which have little to do with formal computer science doctrine—for example, group dynamics, ego suppression, willingness to admit ignorance, empathy with other people's problems, creative laziness, passion for experimentation, and so forth. This means some people, users or developers, trained or untrained, will make better prototypers than others because they will have a natural talent for prototyping.

Do you have basic training in the use of the prototyping tools described in this book? Do you feel you possess the creative talents described in the preceding paragraph? Then, having read this book, you are a highly qualified rapid prototyper—regardless of your current education or job description. On every software project that you are involved with in the future you should be extremely active in performing rapid prototyping tasks. If not, your organization will experience the loss of the expert rapid prototyper, which is a potentially valuable resource.

If you are a manager responsible for training, you may be wondering who should receive specialized training in rapid prototyping techniques. You want the training dollars spent out of your budget to have a good return, so you want to train those who will have the highest probability of becoming outstanding prototypers. In our experience, those who have demonstrated excellence at system requirements analysis almost always make excellent prototypers. This is understandable because they have already demonstrated the ability to work effectively with users—the talent for understanding and providing effective solutions to other people's problems.

If you are or will be managing rapid prototyping projects, you may be wondering what the mix of job descriptions should be within your prototyping team—how many analysts, how many programmers, how many users? Using today's tools and techniques for prototyping, we feel the ideal mix, at the beginning of a prototyping project, is 50 percent professional software developers and 50 percent users. For large projects, the staff can be effectively broken up into small prototyping teams of one or two developers working with one or two users. At the beginning of a project, developers will need skills in the tools and techniques of structured specification, prototype development, and prototype iteration. If users are to participate in prototype development, they will need these same skills. The combination of two facts—that small teams are most effective and that there is a requirement for many different skills at the beginning of a prototyping project—means that you will be looking for very senior experienced people. Facility with structured analysis and design, 4GL, RDMS, and strong interpersonal skills all need to be embodied in one person. Almost every prototyping team will need at least one such member.

EXCLUSIVE TOOLS FOR PROTOTYPERS

What hardware and software will be used for prototyping? Will internal standards dictate specifics or merely provide evaluation criteria? Will prototyping resources be shared with production applications, or will there be exclusive development resources? Again, shared resources mean reduced expense and standards will result in greater compatibility between applications in environments where that is important. We have discussed the fact at length in previous chapters that prototyping intentionally focuses on functionality rather than performance during the early stages of a project. This means that sharing prototyping resources with production applications puts those applications at a great risk of experiencing performance problems and therefore the project manager risks experiencing user dissatisfaction.

The foregoing factors have led many organizations to the implementation of a prototyping center, furnished with exclusive resources for prototypers. Using this approach, all applications will be developed within this environment and then re-hosted in the user's environment. This means there will be no issues of compatibility or performance. Users will use the hardware and software brands found in the prototyping center, or they will not have applications developed for them. Users' applications are never hosted on prototyping center computers.

There have proven to be a few problems with this very centralized, somewhat autocratic approach. When an empire is established, it has borders that must be protected. Users are not part of the empire. Who sets the standards—prototyping center managers, users, or committees? How long does it take for good new technology to become accepted as a new standard? There is a tendency for standards to enforce mediocrity. If you are part of such a centralized empire, you may feel resentful about these words yet perhaps you should be aware that the rest of the organization may find more freedom to be both rewarding and productive.

Fortunately, there is an alternative to the overly centralized approach that will not result in total anarchy. This is the distributed hub-based approach recently alluded to briefly. The staff of such a prototyping hub would be experts in making all types of hardware and software compatible on at least an information exchange basis. The staff would be encouraged to continually seek out and acquire more powerful new technology. Prototyping hub computer resources would be mostly on the small end, at least in terms of actual physical size, for the purpose of portability. This way computing power could be carried to the customer's site for prototype development, demonstration, and iteration. This approach is counter to the previously established procedure of centralized mainframe prototyping. The typical corporate mainframe may gradually diminish in importance as the host for all user applications and become merely a big hard disk and file server for some of the distributed applications.

A METHODOLOGY FOR EVOLUTIONARY RAPID PROTOTYPING

Rapid prototyping projects of today often get into trouble because the rapid prototyping approach is somehow at odds with the formal software methodology dictated by either the organization's management or the auditors, or both. Should we advocate that new internal guidelines need to be developed that specify the required critical tasks, milestones, and deliverables of a *standard* rapid prototyping project, and thus run the risk of getting future projects into trouble because software engineers of the future will find legitimate reasons for violating such standards? If you have embraced the philosophy of the project plan presented in this book, then you understand that the basis of all effective internal software development standards should be a methodology for tailoring methodologies.

There will never be a methodology that will accurately be able to specify the critical tasks, milestones, and deliverables for quality software development for every future project. It is probable that there will never be a methodology that will be able to make such a specification even for all current projects. This does not mean it is not good to have a foundation to start from in developing the project plan. Chapter 4 pointed out that rapid prototyping is really not that incompatible with existing methodologies. Each new project can begin with a project plan template that has proven to be an approach that

- Allows the rapid prototyping process described in this book to take place
- Will be generally acceptable to managers, developers, users, and auditors
- Does not allow for unacceptable shortcuts on the path to delivery of a quality software product

Such a template would reference internal standards and restate a tenet of those internal standards—that each project may be tailored to deviate from the guidelines by a project plan approved by a walkthru team of experienced prototypers. Let's be brave and offer some suggestions as to what some of the referenced internal standards elements might contain.

We would certainly recommend the development and delivery of analysis and design specifications. We would also recommend that these specifications be developed using structured analysis and design techniques (we find Yourdon to be quite adequate). Internal standards should dictate that every project must have a project plan and that the plan must be approved by a walkthru team before the project is allowed to proceed. Guidelines would state that an evaluation committee must certify that approved prototyping tools are powerful enough to create working models of applications that will be no more difficult to modify than a set of dataflow diagrams. Significant specification of prototyping project milestones in internal standards would include

- *Preliminary Requirements Review*—when a blueprint for prototype development has been approved by a walkthru team comprised of prototypers
- *First Prototype Demonstration*—when prototypers have a working model, which they feel faithfully implements the preliminary requirements blueprint, ready for demonstration
- *Intermediate Prototype Demonstrations*—when prototypers feel that they have implemented the changes requested at the previous prototype demonstration
- *Final Prototype Demonstration*—when the chief user agrees that the current version of the prototype incorporates all required functionality
- *Final Requirements Review*—when a published specification of system functional requirements has been approved by a walkthru team
- *Preliminary Design Review*—when a published specification of an as-prototyped design has been approved by a walkthru team
- *Stress Test Plan Review*—when a performance stress testing and tuning plan has been approved by a walkthru team
- *System Performance Acceptance*—when the chief user agrees that the current version of the system meets performance requirements
- *Final Design Review*—when a published specification of the as-tuned detailed design has been approved by a walkthru team comprised of proposed system maintenance staff
- *System Acceptance*—when a checklist has been signed and published certifying that all activities and deliverables called for in the project plan have been accomplished and produced

RAPID MAINTENANCE

Despite the tendency of the rapid prototyping approach to reduce maintenance costs for systems developed this way, it may always be true that organizations spend the biggest share of their computer operations budget on software maintenance. This is because people will always look to present systems for desired new functionality before they will consider requesting new application development. Notice that the majority of software change requests in your organization are probably for enhancements to current programs rather than requests to fix problems or adapt to required changes. The typical feeling is that a small inexpensive modification to a current application might provide the required functionality at a fraction of the expense of a new development project. While this is certainly often true, the quick economic analysis involved frequently overlooks the expense of continuing to maintain programs that become increasingly more complex with each new change. At some point it usually becomes cheaper to throw the old system out and replace it with software that will be easier to maintain.

It is difficult to convince managers and users to rewrite old software that is working and getting the job done, even when it can be proven that this would be economically beneficial. The difficulty arises from the fact that replacing something in current use usually requires freezing all changes until the rewrite is done. This freeze can be impossible to enforce when the software must be modified to adapt to environmental, legal, or organizational changes. This political difficulty has caused a software maintenance dilemma—software is never rewritten, becomes increasingly difficult to maintain, and software maintenance tends to eventually consume 100 percent of all available resources.

Fortunately, it is possible that adopting rapid prototyping as the mainstream approach to software development may provide a future solution to this dilemma. Imagine that an enhancement request is received for a system that has been developed using the approach described in this book. New functionality is desired, but it is to use data from the current application and is to be invokable from the current application control structure. Further, imagine that the system in place has been evolved to the extent that 75 percent of the functionally approved prototype was leveraged into production. In other words, only 25 percent of the prototype had to be replaced with conventional programs during system tuning. Furthermore, 100 percent of the application control structure still consists of the RDMS-based menu-driven architecture. You can imagine how easy it will be then to prototype the new functionality using either 4GL or visual programming techniques, or both.

For each system developed using rapid prototyping then, future maintenance work can be similar to a continuation of prototype iteration—just as easy, just as productive, and resulting in just as little added software complexity. If the application still uses an RDMS, new data requirements will be easy to incorporate and new interfaces to other systems will be easy to build. If the enhancement requires modifications to conventional programs that were written during system tuning, these changes could first be prototyped using either 4GL or visual programming techniques, or both. Proposed enhancement changes to existing systems could be prototyped to see if the change is really what the requester needs. The maintenance staff will acquire a startling new reputation for quick responsiveness to user requests.

A miniature version of the prototyping process described in this book could be used to perform maintenance tasks on software developed using the rapid prototyping approach. First, existing structured analysis and design specifications would be analyzed to determine where to make the changes and what the impact of the changes would be. Then a rapid paper model of the architecture of the new function(s) would be prepared. A prototype of the new functions would then be developed and a mechanism for invoking the new functions would be incorporated into a test copy of the current application's menu structure. Prototype demonstrations and iterations would then proceed just as if this were a new development project, until the users indicate satisfaction with the new functionality.

Maintenance may always consume a high percentage of the software budget, but with a rapid maintenance prototyping approach, a lot more can be accomplished with the same amount of money. Certainly the long backlog of current maintenance requests can be significantly reduced. Users can obtain what they want and need from computer systems in a more responsive and timely manner.

NEEDED MODIFICATIONS TO SERVICE REQUEST
AND PROPOSAL PROCEDURES

Speaking of users and requests, do you think rapid prototyping will change the way service request responses or, for very large projects, proposals are written? Perhaps even the basic format for such documents will change. Reproduced from *The Professional User's Guide to Acquiring Software*,[2] Figure 13-1 shows a typical software service request form. Which elements of such a form do you think are not appropriate for a prototyping project—either maintenance or new development?

We think it is obvious that most service request procedures (and most requests for proposals) assume that requesters know what their requirements are. Likewise,

Software Service Request

1. **Requester:** _____   2. **Date Required:** _____

3. **Departmental Approval:** _____

4. **Request Title:** _____

5. **Requirements:**

6. **Date Received:** _____   7. **Service Request ID:** _____

8. **Person Responsible:** _____   9. **System ID:** _____

10. **Type:** ____   11. **Software Department Approval:** _____

12. **Proposed Solution:**

13. **Estimated Hours:** ____   14. **Estimated Completion:** ____

Completion

15. **Actual Hours:** ____   16. **Actual Date:** _____

17. **Documentation Complete:** _____

18. **Acceptance:**

Software Department:	Date:
Requester:	Date:

Figure 13-1   Software service request form.

most service request responses (and formal project proposals) assume that developers know what the ideal solution is to the requester's stated requirements. The central thesis of rapid prototyping is that none of these assumptions has ever been true and that proceeding to operate under such assumptions will always produce software of very low quality and value. But, can you imagine a contractor being awarded a major software development contract on the basis of stating in their proposal that they had no idea what the customer's requirements were and neither did the customer? This kind of confession is indeed what is called for by both developers and users, for prototyping projects to be successful.

Perhaps Figure 13-1 should be amended to indicate an appropriate amount of uncertainty. For instance, field five, *Requirements*, could be replaced by *Functions Thought to Be Desirable* or *Suggested Existing Applications to Investigate*. Field 12, *Proposed Solution*, could be replaced with *Proposed Experiment* or *Existing System to Be Investigated*. Prototyping frees developers and users from the necessity to be contractually bound by ignorant, incorrect, and incomplete statements of prespecified requirements. Service requests and requests for proposals need to ask for rapid prototyping rather than demanding specific requirements as if they were well known and understood. Request responses and proposals need to promise prototyping rather than promising to fulfill all the requirements stated in the request and only those requirements. We need to stop playing this game of pretending that users know what their requirements are and that developers know how to satisfy those requirements.

FUNDING RAPID PROTOTYPING DEVELOPMENT CENTERS AND PROJECTS

We feel that it is an appropriate ending to the entire book to discuss funding for prototyping because, as far as we are aware, no one else has addressed this issue in the literature and money is, after all, the bottom line. Is the silence on this issue because it is not important, or is it because no one has any good answers? The basic issues are

- Who should pay for rapid prototyping projects and how should the charges be calculated?
- Are rechargeable prototyping projects more effective than those paid for out of central overhead—if so, why?
- Should the new requirement for additional user time be charged—if so, to whom?

Let's consider these questions in reverse order. The question of whether or not to charge a prototyping project for user time is very interesting. By convention, software project measured effort has never included user time—the time users normally spend being interviewed about their requirements, going to reviews, and so forth. From the user's point of view, this time is insignificant compared to developer effort. The question of interest to the user has always been, "How much are you going to charge me for this project?" Even when projects are paid for out of central overhead, the user as a loyal employee is interested to know how much developer effort it will take to satisfy their requirements.

Almost everyone who writes about prototyping is sure to issue the disclaimer that prototyping is not magic. In place of what sometimes seems like magic, there are some interesting phenomena, and there are illusions based on controlled perceptions. For many, there is apparent magic in rapid prototyping, but this appearance is based on perceptions contrasted with preconceptions. The preconceptions usually involve the notion that computers really don't do that much that is truly useful. The perception of magic is that prototyping delivers a product that is the exception to this rule at a lower cost than a conventional software development project—something for nothing. This perception is really an illusion.

We firmly believe in the principle of the conservation of matter and energy—you can't get something for nothing. The value added to a prototype-produced product is really mostly the result of increased user effort. All prototyping really does is provide much more opportunity for users to contribute much more effective effort to a software development project. In our society, effort costs money, whether it is accounted for or not. If you are the CEO or the comptroller for your company, and you want to know how much your software prototyping projects are costing, of course you should count user salary dollars. Don't be surprised if this accounting reveals that software development is now costing you more. If you are a software developer, on the other hand, your users will still mainly be interested in how much you will charge them for your part. From our experience the typical user is delighted to have the opportunity, at last, to be directly involved in a development effort that he or she knows will have a dramatic impact on their career. Users rarely object to the additional cost resulting from their increased involvement in the project.

So, if your organization uses the concept of charge numbers for projects, it would seem that users should be given charge numbers as well as developers. On a prototyping project, users are actually first-class members of the development team. One of the authors was recently involved in a prototyping project where users did charge directly to the project. The actual mix of project staff was four developers and six user representatives, all charging to the project. The users were delighted to charge their time to the project—viewing it as an opportunity rather than a penalty. Interestingly enough, management felt that the amount of money spent on this project produced at least twice as much useful software functionality as a conventional developer-dominated project would have produced with the same money. We can only hypothesize that this may have been due to the increased motivation for the users provided by the accountability that goes along with a charge number.

A charge number implies that someone—a customer, a department, or organizational overhead—is paying for the work to be done. Who should pay for prototyping projects? If user time is to be charged, it will be difficult to charge the using department for the project. This concept has an impact on large government software contracts as well. Should the SDI budget be debited from the salaries of Department of Defense user representatives on an SDI prototyping project? If so, shouldn't fixed price proposals for such contracts include an estimate of the cost of user time?

For large government contracts, the answer is that ultimately the taxpayer pays, but the using agency will have its budget used up by the cost of the project, including user time. For in-house software development in the commercial sector, the answer is that the company always pays for the development out of profits, but departments may also have their budgets reduced by the amount of the cost of the project. The fact that such budget reductions have not, in the past, included user time, has probably never been appropriate. Therefore, if someone wants to suggest that prototyping projects should be charged for user time, we certainly have no objections.

It is our experience that prototyping projects are more productive when funded directly out of the using department's budget, rather than out of some overhead slush fund. The direct recharge approach has the advantage of making the entire team more aware that they are working to provide a product for the using department. The using department has, in fact, contracted the prototyping team to provide a product, and should therefore have direct management control over the team—should ultimately be able to dismiss the team if they fail to perform adequately. The direct recharge approach also has the advantage of solidifying a team composed of both users and professional software developers—they are both now being paid out of the same budget and report to the same boss. This makes users and developers acutely aware that they are on the same team and are not expected to assume the conventional adversarial roles.

Nothing but project funding for prototyping, however, leaves much to be desired. Small projects will be resource-poor and even large projects will suffer from the syndrome of having to reinvent the wheel and reacquire basic resources at the start of each project. It is appropriate to have a prototyping hub, supported by central overhead funds, where prototyping experts between projects are waiting for their next assignment with hub-provided computing resources. Projects could be asked to pay a use charge for hub-provided computing resources, but the capital acquisition funds would be provided out of central overhead.

REFERENCES

1. B. Boar, *Application Prototyping: A Requirements Definition Strategy for the 80s* (New York: John Wiley & Sons, 1983).
2. John L. Connell and Linda Shafer, *The Professional User's Guide to Acquiring Software* (New York: Van Nostrand Reinhold, 1987).

Index

Index

TEAR OUT THIS PAGE TO ORDER THESE OTHER HIGH-QUALITY YOURDON PRESS COMPUTING SERIES TITLES

Quantity	Title/Author	ISBN	Price	Total $
_____	Agents of Change; Bouldin	013-018508-6	$32.00	_____
_____	Building Controls into Structured Systems; Brill	013-086059-X	$37.00	_____
_____	C Notes: Guide to C Programming; Zahn	013-109778-4	$21.95	_____
_____	Classics in Software Engineering; Yourdon	013-135179-6	$41.00	_____
_____	Concepts of Information Modeling; Flavin	013-335589-6	$29.00	_____
_____	Concise Notes on Software Engineering; DeMarco	013-167073-3	$22.00	_____
_____	Controlling Software Projects; DeMarco	013-171711-1	$41.00	_____
_____	Creating Effective Software; King	013-189242-8	$35.00	_____
_____	Crunch Mode; Boddie	013-194960-8	$31.00	_____
_____	Current Practices in Software Development; King	013-195678-7	$36.00	_____
_____	Data Factory; Roeske	013-196759-2	$26.00	_____
_____	Developing Structured Systems; Dickinson	013-205147-8	$36.00	_____
_____	Design of On-Line Computer Systems; Yourdon	013-201301-0	$50.00	_____
_____	Disaster Recovery Planning; Toigo	013-214941-9	$45.00	_____
_____	Essential Systems Analysis; McMenamin/Palmer	013-287905-0	$37.00	_____
_____	Expert System Technology; Keller	013-295577-6	$31.95	_____
_____	Game Plan for System Development; Frantzen/McEvoy	013-346156-4	$33.00	_____
_____	Intuition to Implementation; MacDonald	013-502196-0	$27.00	_____
_____	Managing Structured Techniques, 3/e; Yourdon	013-551680-3	$35.00	_____ \
_____	Modern Structured Analysis; Yourdon	013-598624-9	$34.00	_____
_____	Object Oriented Systems Analysis; Shlaer/Mellor	013-629023-X	$31.00	_____
_____	People & Project Management; Thomsett	013-655747-3	$24.00	_____
_____	Politics of Projects; Block	013-685553-9	$25.00	_____
_____	Practical Guide to Structured Systems 2/e; Page-Jones	013-690769-5	$37.00	_____
_____	Practice of Structured Analysis; Keller	013-693987-2	$29.00	_____
_____	Program It Right; Benton/Weekes	013-729005-5	$27.00	_____
_____	Software Design; Methods & Techniques; Peters	013-821828-5	$35.00	_____
_____	Structured Analysis; Weinberg	013-854414-X	$46.00	_____
_____	Structured Analysis & System Specifications; DeMarco	013-854380-1	$46.00	_____
_____	Structured Approach to Building Programs: BASIC; Wells	013-854076-4	$29.00	_____
_____	Structured Approach to Building Programs: COBOL; Wells	013-854084-5	$29.00	_____
_____	Structured Approach to Building Programs: Pascal; Wells	013-851536-0	$29.00	_____
_____	Structured Design; Yourdon/Constantine	013-854471-9	$51.00	_____
_____	Structured Development Real-Time Systems, Combined; Ward/Mellor	013-854654-1	$79.00	_____
_____	Structured Development Real-Time Systems, Vol. 1; Ward/Mellor	013-854787-4	$35.00	_____
_____	Structured Development Real-Time Systems, Vol. II; Ward/Mellor	013-854795-5	$35.00	_____
_____	Structured Development Real-Time Systems, Vol. III; Ward/Mellor	013-854803-X	$35.00	_____
_____	Structured Systems Development; Orr	013-855149-9	$35.00	_____
_____	Structured Walkthroughs, 4/e; Yourdon	013-855289-4	$28.00	_____
_____	System Development Without Pain; Ward	013-881392-2	$35.00	_____
_____	Teams in Information System Development; Semprivivo	013-896721-0	$31.00	_____
_____	Techniques of EDP Project Management; Brill	013-900358-4	$35.00	_____
_____	Techniques of Program Structure & Design; Yourdon	013-901702-X	$46.00	_____
_____	Up and Running; Hanson	013-937558-9	$34.00	_____
_____	Using the Structured Techniques; Weaver	013-940263-2	$28.00	_____
_____	Writing of the Revolution; Yourdon	013-970708-5	$40.00	_____

Total $	_____
Discount (if appropriate)	_____
New Total $	_____

AND TAKE ADVANTAGE OF THESE SPECIAL OFFERS!

a.) When ordering 3 or 4 copies (of the same or different titles), take 10% off the total list price (excluding sales tax, where applicable).

b.) When ordering 5 to 20 copies (of the same or different titles), take 15% off the total list price (excluding sales tax, where applicable).

c.) To receive a greater discount when ordering 20 or more copies, call or write:

Special Sales Department
College Marketing
Prentice Hall
Englewood Cliffs, NJ 07632
201-592-2498

SAVE!

If payment accompanies order, plus your state's sales tax where applicable, Prentice Hall pays postage and handling charges. Same return privilege refund guaranteed. Please do not mail in cash.

☐ **PAYMENT ENCLOSED**—shipping and handling to be paid by publisher (please include your state's tax where applicable).

☐ **SEND BOOKS ON 15-DAY TRIAL BASIS** & bill me (with small charge for shipping and handling).

Name _____

Address _____

City _____ State _____ Zip _____

I prefer to charge my ☐ Visa ☐ MasterCard

Card Number _____ Expiration Date _____

Signature _____

All prices listed are subject to change without notice

Mail your order to: Prentice Hall, Book Distribution Center, Route 59 at
Brook Hill Drive, West Nyack, NY 10995

Dept. 1   D-OFYP-FW(1)